Crime Scene
Management

Crime Scene Management

Scene Specific Methods

Editors

Raul Sutton

Department of Forensic Science, University of Wolverhampton

and

Keith Trueman

West Midlands Police Service (retired)

WILEY-BLACKWELL

A John Wiley & Sons, Ltd., Publication

Library of Congress Cataloguing-in-Publication Data

Crime scene management : scene specific methods / editors, Raul Sutton and Keith Trueman.
    p. ; cm.
  Includes bibliographical references and index.
  ISBN 978-0-470-01678-7 (cloth)
  1. Crime scene searches. 2. Forensic sciences. I. Sutton, Raul. II. Trueman, Keith.
  [DNLM: 1. Forensic Medicine—methods. 2. Crime W 700 C929 2009]
  HV8073.C6928 2009
  363.25′2—dc22

                                                 2008055971

A catalogue record for this book is available from the British Library.

ISBN: 978-0-470-01678-7 (HB)
ISBN: 978-0-470-01679-4 (PB)

Set in 10.5/13 pt Minion by Integra Software Services Pvt. Ltd. Pondicherry, India
Printed and bound in Great Britain by TJ International Ltd., Padstow, Cornwall

First impression 2009

Contents

Introduction and Use of This Text

This book is designed to provide a UK perspective on procedures and practices that are relevant to the processing of crime scenes. The identification and gathering of physical items of intelligence to police investigations at crime scenes that will subsequently become evidence in a court of law, in a manner that will stand the scrutiny of cross examination, requires the bringing together of several strands of knowledge. We are conscious of the relationship between the gathering of evidence and its subsequent scientific analysis in the context of the UK legal system. Without an understanding of the way in which the item may be subsequently analyzed, many of the methods of packaging items carry no significance. Only when the correct procedure is understood in the context of its protection from damage for subsequent analysis, will the rationale for a particular packaging procedure be apparent. Thus, in this book there are chapters devoted to different types of physical evidence, where the link between the evidence item and its subsequent analysis is made clear. The other aspect of evidence gathering is to ensure the continuity of the items so that the location and subsequent analysis of each item can be verified during its passage from the crime scene to the courtroom.

The first edition of this book is intended as an introductory text on common procedures for the identification and processing of evidence at scenes of crime. The course is largely based on operating practices that exist within management of crime scenes in the United Kingdom. The text is primarily aimed at people who are studying crime scenes as part of a study programme, but we think that the work will prove useful to a wider range of readers including:

- undergraduate students studying courses in the criminal justice sector, such as forensic science, criminalistics and policing;

- people employed in the criminal justice sector such as police officers, crime support teams, legal personnel and forensic science services, all of whom may need an introduction to crime scenes;

- members of the general public who want to know more about how crime scenes are processed.

Students who are using this text as a learning vehicle will be expected to study some crime scene work during their course and will need to understand selected fundamental principles, gain a knowledge of processes and the reasoning for operating procedures in order to underpin their subject. Thus, we have aimed to include only those aspects of crime scene processing that would be relevant as an introduction to such. Thus, each chapter begins with an introduction that explains the relevance of the contents. The significance of the material is given importance by the choice of examples, wherever possible. The text expects little in the way of prior knowledge and introduces concepts at a basic level. This keeps each chapter brief whilst covering most of the necessary material that you will require during your undergraduate course.

We realize that you may not feel confident in tackling concepts of which you have had little prior experience. Each chapter thus contains relevant questions that aim to assess your understanding of the materials presented, along with answers provided on the website that accompanies the book (www.wileyeurope.com/college/sutton).

The aim of the website is to provide high resolution images to support the text instead of including them in the book itself. In addition many photographs will lose quality when reproduced in a text such as this, and points that need illustrating may be better represented by images viewed on a PC.

The website contains many images including all the tables, photographs, drawings and many of the forms that are presented. These are in a downloadable format so that they can be adapted or integrated into a lecture series on the subject.

Some of the material covered in the chapters will require rote-learning and this is something that you will have to work towards. It would be impractical for you to remember such materials at the first attempt. Rote-learning can be made easier by breaking a subject down into small parts. The regular review of such material will also aid your memory. It is similar to other ideas that are introduced in the text. Concepts can sometimes seem difficult to grasp, but rereading material that you find difficult, slowly and carefully, will help you to gain a much clearer understanding of its meaning.

This text uses the term 'Scenes of Crime Officer (SOCO)' to denote the person responsible for the processing of crime scenes. In the United Kingdom, these personnel have different names, depending on the constabulary to which they are attached. In some areas, terms such as Crime Scene Examiner, Scientific Support Officer and Crime Scene Investigator are used instead. There is a different emphasis between a Crime Scene Investigator who can be seen as an active thinking investigator, and an examiner who can be viewed as a passive collector of evidence. A modern SOCO will need to be both of these.

The management of SOCOs varies between police forces. This can fall under the remit of a Scientific Support Department (that is sometimes called Scenes of Crime Department) but this is not always the case. Since the way in which SOCOs are managed does not impact materially on their day-to-day activities we shall refer to management structures using the term 'Scenes of Crime Department'.

Where possible, chapters include a list of suggested further reading where it is in the public domain. Much of the training materials given to SOCOs are restricted and not publically available. In some chapters there is also a reference list where it is felt that this may help the reader.

Raul Sutton and **Keith Trueman**

List of contributors

Terry Bartlett
School of Applied Sciences
University of Wolverhampton

David Charlton
Fingerprint Bureau
Sussex Police

Chris Crowe
West Midlands Police

Chris Perry
School of Applied Sciences
University of Wolverhampton

Raul Sutton
School of Applied Sciences
University of Wolverhampton

Keith Trueman
West Midlands Police (Retd.)

Craig Williams
School of Applied Sciences
University of Wolverhampton

PART I
Crime Scene Principles

1

The Crime Scene Context

Raul Sutton

1.1 Introduction

The management of the process of scene recording and evidence recovery is at a crossroads. The introduction of new technologies such as digital cameras, database storage systems for scene information management, automated three-dimensional scene reconstruction software, digital fingermark recovery systems, real-time methods for trace analysis amongst others will change the face of scene management. The development costs of introducing such equipment are expensive but the legal requirement of ensuring that continuity and integrity of items gathered at the scene mean that these methodologies are already being introduced for use in major crimes. However, after the recovery of development costs, the price of such equipment purchase will inevitably drop, making their introduction to the management of volume case work a realistic possibility.

In addition, there have been rapid changes to the way that Crime Scene Examiners are trained in the United Kingdom. There has been a growth in forensic science courses in Universities in the United Kingdom. A proportion of graduates are looking to gain employment within the area of crime scene examination. Such graduates, if properly educated, will inevitably add scientific rigour and graduate level of understanding to the crime scene aspect of forensic science. The Forensic Science Society has acknowledged this by incorporating crime scene investigation into the criteria for its accreditation process.

Crime Scene Management: Scene Specific Methods   Edited by Raul Sutton and Keith Trueman
© 2009 John Wiley & Sons, Ltd

There is also a need for other stakeholders who may have to attend scenes of crime to be aware of the role and remit of scene processing, understand the nature and types of evidence that can be found at scenes of crime and take appropriate measures to preserve and protect such evidence. These may include persons such as para-medical personnel, firefighters as well as serving police officers. Within the English legal system the increased role of forensic analysis in the successful prosecution of crimes has suggested that legal agencies need to be aware of the entire forensic process of which crime scene management forms a part.

1.2 What is a crime?

Crimes by their definition are those acts which are deemed contrary to the criminal law governing the country of concern. Nation States operate this in different ways, but they are underpinned by a philosophical framework. In European legislation the articles of the European Convention of Human Rights (1959) define the over-arching philosophy. In summary, this states the following:

- Article 1:   Protection of property.

- Article 2:   Right to life.

- Article 3:   Prohibition from torture, inhumane or degrading treatment.

- Article 5:   The right to liberty and security of person.

- Article 6:   The right to a fair hearing or trial.

- Article 8:   The right to respect for private and family life.

- Article 10: Freedom of expression.

These are embedded in various forms within the EU Member States, by acts in the partner countries and the legal framework within which law enforcement takes place must meet these obligations. The United Kingdom has embedded this convention by means of some Acts of Parliament, the latest of which is the Human Rights Act (1998). The national bodies responsible for implementing legislation have qualified some of these rights by virtue of the general well being of society, thus the rights may be curtailed if any of the following conditions are met:

- if the action is prohibited by law; *and*

- necessary actions within a democracy; *and*

- for any of the following reasons:

  - national security;
  - territorial integrity;
  - public safety;
  - preventing disorder or crime;
  - protecting health;
  - protecting morals;
  - protecting the rights of others.

Reasons of strategic handling of offences, that are deemed to be criminal acts within the United Kingdom, mean that crimes are normally categorized into two types: volume and major.

Crimes that are often categorized by Police Service/Force/Constabulary according to their seriousness include:

- murder (Common Law);

- manslaughter (Common Law);

- infanticide (Infanticide Act 1938);

- rape (Sexual Offences Act 2003);

- serious wounding (Offences Against the Person Act 1861);

- armed robbery (Theft Act 1968);

- aggravated burglary (Theft Act 1968);

- kidnapping (Common Law);

- terrorist offences (Terrorism Act 2000);

- any offence deemed 'major' by its significant impact on society (i.e. contamination of goods).

Many of these types of crime have a high media profile and so the treatment of the investigation of these assumes a priority and more time, effort and financial resources will go into investigating these.

Minor crimes make up the majority of Police Service/Force/Constabulary work and encompass anything not deemed to be a major crime. A small range of these criminal offences are called volume crime. The definition of these is:

- street robbery (Theft Act, 1968);

- burglary – dwelling (Theft Act, 1968);

- burglary, non-dwelling (Theft Act, 1968);

- theft (including shoplifting) (Theft Act, 1968);

- vehicle crime – theft of (Theft Act, 1968);

- vehicle crime – theft from (Theft Act, 1968);

- criminal damage (Criminal Damage Act, 1971);

- minor drugs offences that are linked with acquisitive crimes.

as defined by Association of Chief Police Officers (ACPO) (Garvin, 2002). The intensity with which minor and volume crimes are investigated will vary from force to force depending on available resources, initiatives etc. This situation, whilst not ideal, represents the best available use of resources within a Police Service/Force/Constabulary.

Self-assessed questions

1.1 (a) Describe what makes burglary a crime in the United Kingdom.
   (b) Which article(s) of the European Convention on Human Rights does burglary infringe?

1.2 Describe the major difference between volume and major crimes?

1.3 The nature of the UK legal system

The legal system in the United Kingdom is based upon common law and statute. Within the United Kingdom there are three separate, similar jurisdictions, England and Wales, Scotland and Northern Ireland. Whilst the laws are similar in each jurisdiction, they are not identical. The system is a balance between three interacting organs of the state, the executive (the government), the legislature (parliament) and the judiciary (the courts). In ideal circumstances these three organs of the state should be independent, but in the United Kingdom the functions overlap (particularly the executive). In Western-style democracies the role of the organs of the state is to maintain the rule of law. In many states these rules are underpinned by a series of articles, often called a constitution, which are seen to be the basis for the operation of a civilized society. The United States of America is an example of a Nation State with just such a constitution. The United Kingdom has no such underpinning articles of state and the rule of law is defined by the enacting of the wishes of the elected representatives of the people. Whilst there is no official constitution in the United Kingdom it can be argued that the precedent of Acts of Parliament, legislative assemblies such as exist in Northern Ireland, and judicial rulings have bestowed a pseudo – constitution in the United Kingdom.

Laws are put into practice that will affect the way society regards itself. Broadly these laws can be broken down into two types, civil or criminal. Individuals can choose to flout the given laws (by not paying bills, for example) and may face civil proceedings (in order to recover monies due etc.) or criminal prosecution (in the case of grievous bodily harm for example) as a consequence. The crime scene forms part of the criminal side of this process.

The Role of the European Union. The European Union (EU) plays an increasing part in forming UK legislation. This is because the UK legal system sits within EU rules, established by Maastricht and other relevant treaties, as well as legislation made by various European institutions, such as the Commission, under these treaties.

The fundamental principle at the centre of European legal order is that European law has priority over conflicting law in Member States. The national courts of each Member State must apply European law, but must not make any national law inconsistent with European Union rules. EU law is therefore an integral part of the law in the United Kingdom.

1.4 The legal system in England and Wales

1.4.1 Her Majesty's Courts Service

The operation of all the courts within England and Wales has been brought under one overarching organization, Her Majesty's Courts Service (HMCS), on 1 April 2005. This organization includes Magistrates' Courts Service Crown and County Court Service. The HMCS is the executive agency of the Department for Constitutional Affairs (DCA) and has the stated, 'Our purpose is to deliver justice effectively and efficiently to the public. We are responsible for the administration of the civil, family and criminal courts in England and Wales'.

1.4.2 The Crown Prosecution Service

The Crown Prosecution Service (CPS) is a government agency that decides whether criminal investigations, which have been started by the police, should progress to court. If a case is progressed, the CPS prepares and conducts prosecution court proceedings, provides prosecution solicitors and barristers and arranges for prosecution witnesses to attend court.

1.4.3 The Judiciary

The judiciary sits within a system that is the result of several centuries of development. There are a series of courts tiered to deal with offences against the rule of law. These range from low-level cases that are dealt with by a Magistrates' Court, through to rulings that may affect the laws of the nation that may be dealt with by parliament. A brief description of each tier will now be given:

The Magistrates' Court

The Magistrates' Courts are core to the UK criminal justice system – most criminal cases start in a Magistrates' Court with a large percentage completing there (95%). The Magistrates' Courts also undertake civil cases, such as family matters and liquor licensing and betting. Cases in the Magistrates' Courts are usually heard by panels of three magistrates (Justices of the Peace) supported by a clerk. The three magistrates are called a Bench and are assigned to a Local Area but have a national jurisdiction pursuant to the Courts Act, 2003. Magistrates are unpaid appointees of the Crown who are not usually legally qualified. Qualified clerks advise them on matters of law.

There are also about 130 District Judges, who sit alone in Magistrates' Courts. District Judges must have had seven years' experience as a barrister or solicitor and two years' experience as a Deputy District Judge. District Judges deal with more difficult cases such as extradition or serious fraud.

The range of cases that are tried in a Magistrates' Court fall into two categories:

- Summary offences – These are the least serious offences such as driving offences and common assault.

- Triable either way offences – These are the middle range of crimes including theft, assault causing actual bodily harm. These can be tried in either the Magistrates' Court or Crown Court.

Magistrates do not normally order prison sentences of more than six months or fines exceeding £5000. Such cases are normally committed by the magistrates to the Crown Court for sentencing.

The Crown Court

The Crown Court deals with cases transferred from the Magistrates' Courts. It also hears appeals against Magistrates' Courts' decisions, and deals with sentencing of some cases from Magistrates' Courts. In addition, the triable either way offences described above can be tried in the Crown Court. Generally speaking, Crown Courts deal with more serious criminal cases such as murder, rape or robbery. Trials are heard by a Judge and a 12-person jury. Members of the public are selected for jury service. Jurors must decide, based on the facts, whether a defendant is guilty or not guilty of the offences for which he or she is charged. In some cases, where specialist knowledge is required, such as complex fraud cases, it would be considered impossible for a jury to be knowledgeable enough to make a decision, and such cases may be tried in the absence of a jury.

Indictable Offences – These are the more serious crimes and include murder, manslaughter and rape. All indictable offences must be tried at the Crown Court, but the first hearing is dealt with at the Magistrates' Court. The magistrate will decide if the defendant should be given bail. The case is then transferred to the Crown Court.

1.5 Other courts

There are a large number of courts that primarily deal with civil issues. These include the County Court. The majority of County Courts' cases involve debts between individuals and/or business, claims as well as personal injury, property or disputes over contracts. They also deal with family issues, such as divorce and adoption. The High Court deals with the more complex civil cases as well as claims for libel. It also hears appeals against decisions made in the County Courts.

The right to appeal is one of the key principles of the justice system in England and Wales. The Court of Appeal hears appeals against decisions in the High Court and the Crown Court. Disputes not resolved there can be taken to the House of Lords.

There are a whole variety of civil courts with specialist applications, as well as military courts and tribunals that do not fall usually within the remit of the evidence gathering process for criminal processes.

Self-assessed questions

1.3 Does Her Majesty's Court Service solely look after criminal cases?

1.4 Describe the limitations on a Magistrates' Court in sentencing.

1.5 Can murder be tried at a Magistrates' Court?

1.6 Are all cases in Crown Courts tried before a jury?

1.7 What is the function of the jury in a Crown Court trial?

1.6 The judicial system in Northern Ireland

Northern Ireland's legal system is similar to that of England and Wales. Jury trials have the same place in the system. The major difference relates to offences involving acts of terrorism. In addition, cases go through stages in the courts. In offences specified under emergency legislation the case is tried in a Crown Court without a jury. Guilt must be proved beyond reasonable doubt with the defendant represented by a lawyer of their choice. The judge has to set out in a written statement the reasons for conviction with an automatic right of appeal, against conviction and/or sentence on points of fact as well as of law, at the Court of Appeal.

1.6.1 Courts in Northern Ireland

The Northern Irish courts consist of:

- superior courts comprising the Court of Appeal, the High Court and the Crown Court;
- inferior courts comprising County Courts and Magistrates' Courts.

Superior courts

All matters relating to the Court of Appeal, the High Court and the Crown Court are under the jurisdiction of the UK Parliament. Judges are appointed by the Crown. The Crown Court deals with all serious criminal cases.

The Court of Appeal has the power to review the civil law decisions of the High Court and the criminal law decisions of the Crown Court and may in certain cases review the decisions of County Courts and Magistrates' Courts. Subject to certain restrictions, an appeal from a judgment of the Court of Appeal can go to the House of Lords. The independent Criminal Cases Review Commission reviews alleged miscarriages of justice.

Inferior courts

The inferior courts are the County Courts and the Magistrates' Courts, both of which differ in a number of ways from their counterparts in England and Wales.

Magistrates' Courts carry out the day-to-day work of dealing with minor local criminal cases. These are presided over by a full-time, legally qualified, resident magistrate (RM). County Courts are primarily civil law courts presided over by

County Court judges; they also handle appeals from the Magistrates' Courts. Appeals from the County Courts are heard in the High Court.

Self-assessed questions

1.8 (a) What is the English equivalent of the Northern Ireland inferior courts?
(b) Who presides over the inferior court in Northern Ireland?

1.9 Name one type of case in Northern Ireland where a jury is not used.

1.7 The Scottish legal system

Scots' Law and the Scottish legal system's integrity and independence were acknowledged in the 1707 Act of Union along with the establishment of a UK Parliament at Westminster. Scots' law shares many statutory provisions with the law of England and Wales, but Scots' civil law remains substantially based on Scots' common law, rather than statute, sharing elements with Roman Dutch law rather than English common law traditions. In the criminal justice system, the role of the public prosecutor is critical.

The Crown Office and Procurator Fiscal Service, a Department of the Scottish Executive, provides Scotland's independent public prosecution and deaths investigation service. The position of the Lord Advocate is as head of criminal prosecution in Scotland, assisted by the Solicitor General for Scotland. They are the Scottish Law Officers and members of the Scottish Executive.

1.7.1 Criminal Courts in Scotland

Criminal justice procedure is divided into:

- Solemn – the most serious cases involving trial on indictment before a judge or sheriff sitting with a jury;

- Summary – less serious offences involving a trial before a sheriff, stipendiary magistrate or Justice of the Peace sitting alone.

The judiciary

The High Court of Justiciary is the country's supreme criminal court; handling the most serious crimes such as murder and rape. It is also the final court of appeal for criminal cases. It comprises the Lord Justice General, the Lord Justice Clerk and another 30 judges known formally as Lords Commissioners of Justiciary.

Judges take the title of Lord or Lady followed by their surname or territorial title and can preside over both criminal and civil courts. All criminal prosecutions are brought in the name of the Lord Advocate and prosecuted by his appointed Advocate Deputes.

The jury

The court presents evidence before a jury, which is required to reach a verdict on the case in question. A Scottish jury – for a criminal case – is made up of 15 people and a simple majority is sufficient to establish guilt or innocence. The jury is required to reach one of three verdicts: guilty, not guilty or not proven. A not proven verdict is the equivalent of not guilty in that it is an acquittal.

Sheriffs Courts

The Sheriff Courts, 49 of which are arranged into six Sheriffdoms organized geographically are overseen by a Sheriff Principal. Sheriffs have sentencing powers, which are limited to:

- up to three years' imprisonment and/or an unlimited fine in solemn cases;
- up to six months' imprisonment and/or £5000 fine for summary cases.

The court can remit a case to the High Court if a greater sentence is deemed necessary.

District Courts

District Courts are similar to Magistrates' Courts and sit in each local authority area. Each comprises one or more Justices of the Peace (lay magistrates) who sit alone or in threes with a qualified legal assessor as convener or clerk of court. They handle many cases of breach of the peace, drunkenness, minor assaults, petty theft and offences under the Civic Government (Scotland) Act 1982.

Self-assessed questions

1.10   What is the nearest English equivalent of the Sheriff Court in Scotland?

1.11   Describe the two important differences between the English and Scottish court systems.

1.8 Judicial processes that deal with causes of death

Deaths that need investigation are dealt with by the HM Coroner in England, Wales and Northern Ireland. The Coroner is one of the oldest secular appointments, established in 1194 as a form of medieval tax gatherer. This role has changed and now encompasses the investigation of sudden, violent or unnatural death. Coroner's activities are governed by the Coroner's Act 1988 and the Coroner's rules 1984. The Coroner, who is either a qualified lawyer or medical practitioner with at least five years of experience, will have many deaths reported as part of their duties. The Coroner may be satisfied, after due investigation, by the identity of the deceased and that the death was due to natural causes. In such cases the investigation can end at this stage and a death certificate can be issued.

In other cases the Coroner must call an inquest. The inquest, held in a Coroner's Court, has two major functions, categorization of the circumstances and cause of death and identification of the deceased persons. The remit of the inquest is determination of cause of death for the following reasons:

- a violent or unnatural death;

- a sudden death the cause of which is unknown;

- in prison;

- in such circumstances as to require an inquest under any other act.

A violent or unnatural death can occur for a variety of causes, such as:

- unlawful killing;

- suicide;

- accidental death;

- misadventure;

- industrial disease.

The Coroner will reach a decision as to which of the causes of death apply in the inquest. The Coroner remit does not include assigning liability. So, for example, a verdict of unlawful killing would not include a naming of persons liable for the death of deceased. In addition, there may not be enough evidence to determine a cause of death to the standard of proof required and the Coroner can also reach an open verdict. In most cases the standard of proof required to reach such a verdict is on the 'balance of probabilities', but in cases of unlawful killing and suicide it will normally be 'beyond all reasonable doubt'. In addition, the historical origins of the role of the Coroner means that he is responsible for issues relating to treasure trove.

The Court is inquisitorial, rather than adversarial, in nature. This means that there are significant differences from civil or criminal courts. Firstly, a jury is not necessarily required. When a jury is present, it will consist of an odd number of persons (between 5 and 11). Witnesses are required to attend and give evidence, as with criminal courts. However, persons are allowed to refuse to give evidence when it may incriminate them. In addition, witnesses can be questioned, not only by the Coroner, but by persons who are called 'properly interested parties'. Properly interested parties may include close relatives of the deceased, police services, insurers, employers and trade union officials or legal representatives of these parties.

Crime scene investigators may be called to present evidence in the Coroner's Court relating to the identification of the deceased as well as determination of the cause of death.

In Scotland all sudden, suspicious, accidental, unexpected and unexplained deaths and any death occurring in circumstances that give rise to serious public concern are dealt with by the Procurator Fiscal. The Procurator Fiscal does not hold an inquest but may ask for help via investigations from properly qualified persons, such as police forces and pathologists. After consideration of all the evidence, the Procurator Fiscal will reach a decision on the cause of death. In a few cases (for 2001–2002 only 62 out of 13 625 cases) the Procurator Fiscal will apply to the Sheriff for a public enquiry, called a Fatal Accident Inquiry into the cause of death.

A Fatal Accident Inquiry is similar to an inquest but carried out in the public interest. However, the rules of evidence and the standard of proof are the same as Scottish civil cases. The purpose is to determine where and when the death took place, the cause of the death, reasonable precautions whereby the death may have been avoided, any defects in any system of working that contributed to the death or any accident resulting in the death and any other facts relevant to the circumstances of the death. As with English Coroner's Courts, the purpose is not to apportion civil or criminal liability for the death. A mandatory Fatal Accident Inquiry will occur in relation to a death in custody or as a result of an accident in the course of employment.

Self-assessed questions

1.12 Name two differences between a Coroner and Crown Court proceeding.

1.13 What is the major difference in the investigation of suspicious death in Scotland compared to the rest of the United Kingdom?

1.9 What constitutes evidence?

Evidence is presented before any court of law in one of the following two ways:

- Oral testimony of a witness;
- Submission of a statement by a witness;

During testimony, a witness will introduce to the court information of fact that will include any physical items if evidential material. Under certain circumstances, instead of a witness appearing in person their evidence, including and material items, may be accepted from their written statement (details regarding this procedure may be found in Chapter 11).

Whichever the case the Scenes of Crime Officer (SOCO) will find that most of their work that ends up being presented in a Court of Law revolves around the recording of the crime scene by photography, drawing and documentation of the evidence gathering process and the recovery of physical evidence in a way that will render it suitable for subsequent analysis and presentation in court. This means that due care and attention must be paid to preserving the evidential value of items gathered at the scene. For example, there is no point in collecting DNA-rich evidence in such a way that the evidence may be contaminated or degraded so that the quality of that evidence becomes unusable in a court of law. Failure to present evidence may be as simple as a lack of appropriate control samples gathered at the scene, lack of attention in choosing appropriate packaging and storage, not being able to demonstrate that there was no opportunity for contamination to occur between evidence gathering, storage and analysis, and timeliness in delivery of samples to analysts. These issues are part of the 'continuity and integrity' of the evidential materials. Most of such evidence that is gathered by SOCO for subsequent scientific analysis comes into the category of contact or trace evidence (see Chapter 3).

The evidence that is presented by the SOCO may be the first step in providing material that can be used in court and as such needs a rigour that will withstand the scrutiny of hostile cross-examination. The processes needed to achieve this require a high level of expertise. The evidence that then is presented in the court falls under the remit of expert witness statements and should be presented accordingly (see Chapter 3 and 11).

Self-assessed questions

1.14 Name two classes of evidence that a SOCO may provide for court.

1.10 The chain of events in evidence gathering

The recording and gathering of items at the scene of crime are the first steps in the provision of evidence in a court of law. The requirement to present such evidence for this purpose means that specific issues are raised both in the identification of suitable items, but also their subsequent handling. One of the major considerations revolves around tracking of an item recovered from a scene of crime from the time it is identified to the time that it is presented in evidence in a court of law. A failure to provide documented evidence of the item's:

- whereabouts from the time of discovery at the scene to its presentation in court;

- security in terms of alteration by having evidence added to it either surreptitiously or otherwise.

may render the evidence that relates to the item as unsuitable.

Continuity is the term used to describe the handling of the item at all stages subsequent to identification. *Integrity* is the term used to describe the method used to describe the protection of the evidence from damage or alteration. These issues are central to the evidence gathering process and their importance will be emphasized throughout the text.

The steps in evidence gathering involve:

- identify the scene and make an assessment;

- recording and documentation of the scene;

- identification of items that may have evidential value;

- record and gathering the items for subsequent analysis from a Forensic Science Provider (FSP).

Each of these will be briefly described below. The recording and documentation of the scene is described in detail and a discussion of gathering items that have a likelihood of being of evidential value is in Chapter 3. The type of analysis that could be performed with the evidence is provided in Chapters 5–8.

1.10.1 Crime perpetration and evidence transfer

One of the important considerations is the way in which evidence is left at the scene, given that both the perpetrator and the area that the crime took place in are classed as scenes. Material will be transferred between the perpetrator and the scene of crime. The type and amount of material will depend on a number of factors that include:

- The nature of the recipient surfaces and the trace material. Rough surfaces will retain more material for longer than smooth surfaces.

- The degree of contact. This can vary both in pressure and time of contact and increasing both will increase the probability of material transfer.

- The nature of the transferred material. The adherence properties of this will affect both its residence on the recipient surface and the time of retention.

These phenomena should mean that when contact is made at a scene there is a two-way transfer. This means that you may find evidence of the scene on the perpetrator and vice versa. This type of evidence is referred to as 'trace' or 'contact' evidence. It underpins one of the important principles of forensic science, called 'Locard's Principle of Exchange'. This states:

> When two objects come into contact, each will leave a trace of itself upon the other

which has often been abbreviated to 'every contact leaves a trace'.

1.10.2 Scene documentation and recording

This is the initial stage in crime scene work. Initially the scene is surveyed whilst the investigator tries to form a picture of the *modus operandi*. In this survey detailed notes are made of the scene that may aid further enquiries. Items of potential evidential value are noted and their location recorded. Photographic and/or video records, and sketch plans are made noting the precise location of evidence items. This process is crucial to crime scene reconstruction and evidence presentation in court.

1.10.3 Identification of evidential items

Initial examination of the crime scene will allow identification of items that may contribute to the evidence needed in a court of law. The identification of such items is a precursor to their removal from the scene and subsequent storage. The selection of items for evaluation of evidence depends to some extent on a variety of factors. These include:

- The nature of the possible offence. In this case, although not ideal, the extent of the examination will depend on whether the offence is a volume or major crime. A higher labour and monetary budget will normally be allocated to the crime if it is considered to be 'major'. Unfortunately, this reflects the limited budgets that police services have to work with.

- The evidential value of the item. Most scenes contain a plethora of objects that could provide evidence. However, in a majority of cases only some will provide information that could lead to the identification and apprehension of a suspect or their subsequent prosecution. So, for example, a fingerprint has a high evidential value as it is highly likely to be associated with an individual and placing them at the scene. On the contrary, a blue fibre from denim jeans is unlikely to be able to be linked to a particular suspect (as this is a common fabric) unless some aspect of the fibre can provide physical fit evidence to a suspect's clothing (see Chapter 8).

- The experience of the investigator. Experienced investigators will know from their evidence gathering which items will provide the best information and concentrate on gathering these. Although one can list the items that are likely to yield useful information to an investigation, it will vary between cases and the investigator must be objective.

1.10.4 Packaging and removal of items from the scene

The items identified have to be removed from the scene. The first step is to document and number each item of possible evidence by placing it onto a list. This will give each evidence item, whether a photograph, fingerprint lift or DNA swab a reference number. This number is then bar-coded in all further processes allowing tracking of the progress of sample analysis and avoiding confusion between samples. This process may seem trivial but it is a key part of tracking the continuity of the item recovered from the scene.

Care must be taken to ensure that items are packaged in the correct containers. The packaging of the container is important. The packaging must provide a secure environment for the item, in that:

- it must be evident as to whether the package has been opened. Such packaging is described as being 'tamper-evident'.

- it must be packaged in a container that will not damage the material that needs to be analyzed. For example wet biological material (see Chapter 6) must not be packaged in air-tight containers, that would encourage microbial spoilage to occur.

The item must also be properly labelled. Lack of care in labelling affect its continuity.

Self-assessed questions

1.15   Outline the four stages in evidence gathering.

1.16   Describe what is meant by continuity in evidence processing.

1.17   Explain the possible evidential value of the following items:
(a) blood stain;
(b) glass from a broken UPVC window.

1.18   Explain how the integrity of semen stained clothing may be affected if:
(a) it sealed in a plastic bag whilst still wet;
(b) it is repackaged in the same room as clothing was removed from the suspect.

1.11 The relationship between evidence gatherers and analysts

Items gathered at the scene will be transferred into a secure storage area within the local police station. Subsequently, such items may be sent for scientific analysis by an appropriate FSP. Police Services vary in the amount of scientific support that is provided 'in-house'. Most services contain a fingerprint development laboratory that enhances latent fingerprints, linked to a facility that analyzes the prints against a database of stored prints. Other services may contain footwear analysis laboratories and some contain another scientific provision.

Services in England and Wales will send the majority of their samples to an independent FSP for analysis. This includes DNA analysis, hair, fibres, firearms and documents. The separation of FSP from police services avoids accusations of conflicts of interest between FSPs and the services. The FSP can be seen to provide analyses unbiased by pressures from within police services that expect that the evidence will help secure a prosecution. The FSP includes a number of larger providers such as the Forensic Science Service (FSS) and LGC-Forensics (a merging of Forensic Alliance with the Laboratory of the Government Chemist) as well a growing number of other companies with a specialist remit.

Scottish laboratories have been linked to police forces directly, but this situation is changing with a move to a separate laboratory facility for major forms of analysis, such as DNA-rich evidence. In Northern Ireland the FSP is Forensic Science Northern Ireland, which operates a monopoly with the police service.

1.12 Health and safety considerations

The gathering of items of potential evidence at scenes of crime remains an important step in the forensic process. There is a duty by the employer to ensure that the health and well being of employees involved in this process do not come under any risk to their health. The crime scenes that are visited are extremely varied and it is impossible to have sets of procedures that deal with every eventuality. This text will cover some of the major occupational hazards that are associated with scenes of crime work. These can be briefly covered by:

- Physical environment. An example may be a scene that is the result of fire or arson investigation where the building may be unsafe or there is a danger of further conflagration. In these cases there should not be any attempt to enter the scene to gather evidence until all such places have been declared safe.

- Chemical hazards. These are varied but can include toxic or pharmacoactive compounds that are dangerous to health. Appropriate care should be taken when handling substances of unknown origin.

- Biological hazards. These can be carried in bodily fluids, such as blood, where the agents of transmissible diseases may be present or there may be infectious organisms present whether deliberately, as in cases of biological weapons manufacture or surreptitiously as in cases where pathogens are in the environment.

This means that thought must be given to assessing the risk involved in dealing with a scene and some communication may take place between scene examiners and senior staff if the scene poses a potential hazard. This may result in evidence being lost as a consequence, but the welfare of the investigator must come first.

A formal risk assessment process must be carried out by those charged with performing investigations and crime scene examination tasks before an investigation takes place. The assessment must be documented and submitted as part of the scene management process.

Suggested further reading

Her Majesty's Court Services (2005). *Managing Courts, Delivering Justice*, HMSO. This provides a brief introduction to the system and variety of courts in England and Wales.

House of Commons Science and Technology Committee (2005). *Forensic Science on Trial*, The Stationery Office Limited This is a review of the state of Forensic Science in the UK and contains useful information in all areas relating to forensic science.

Garvin, P. (2002). *ACPO Investigation of Volume Crime Manual*, Association of Chief Police Officers of England, Wales and Northern Ireland. A comprehensive review of the investigation of volume crimes.

2
First Officer Attending

Keith Trueman

2.1 Introduction

An investigation into most criminal offences, no matter how complex they may become, begins with a member of the public making an initial visit or telephone call to a police station. The response and actions made during the initial stages of dealing with the complaint or information can greatly impact upon the subsequent enquiry in general and upon any scientific examination of the crime scene in particular.

The initial response is often carried out under extremely difficult and challenging circumstances. Making the right decisions that support the correct actions to ensure all relevant evidence is secured and preserved takes experience and skill. This chapter seeks to explain the process by giving an insight into the police structure and the procedures following the 'initial call'.

The purpose of this chapter is to explain the roles and responsibilities of police officers, of various ranks and who, from different departments, may attend a crime scene following the discovery or allegation that a criminal offence has taken place. For the process to be fully appreciated the categories of some offences that may be dealt with as 'Major' and 'Volume' crimes will be referred to. (These crime categories are discussed in Chapter 1).

Crime Scene Management: Scene Specific Methods   Edited by Raul Sutton and Keith Trueman
© 2009 John Wiley & Sons, Ltd

2.2 Response to incident report

The police service in the United Kingdom is made up of 52 independent forces. These comprise 43 in England and Wales, 8 in Scotland and 1 in Northern Ireland. The officer in charge of a police force is a chief constable except in the City of London and Metropolitan Force areas where they are referred to as commissioners. Officers of this rank are members of the Association of Chief Police Officers, which is generally referred to as ACPO. Each force is divided into smaller manageable areas. These were historically referred to as divisions but are now more often called basic or operational command units (BOCU or OCU). These smaller units are managed by police officers who hold the rank of chief superintendent. These officers are supported by, in descending order, superintendents, chief inspectors, inspectors, sergeants, constables and police community support officers. (The badges of rank, as worn by provincial police officers in England and Wales, can be found in the Appendix). Police Community Support Officers (PCSO) also display their collar or identification number, surmounted by their title, on an epaulette). In addition, every force employs a relevant number of civilian staff who work in support roles in every department.

Every police force has a central communications department staffed 24 hours a day 365 days a year. This department may be variously described as the force 'control', 'communications' or 'operations' centre. Staff employed in such centres handle '999' emergency and other incoming calls from members of the public and, where necessary, dispatch an immediate response to deal with an incident or complaint. Depending on the size of the force the central control will be supported by other, smaller, communications centres based locally in divisions or basic command units. Every message, whether emergency or routine, received in either central or local control centres will be recorded on a computer generated incident log and given a unique incident number. Every action taken and resource allocated to the incident will be recorded on the log. The initial response will normally involve dispatching a police constable or community support officer to the incident to make an early assessment.

As will be explained later, for one officer to make all the considerations and carry out every procedure required at the scene of a major incident is virtually impossible. It is therefore essential that control centre officers are kept fully informed of the current and developing situation at any incident. It will be the control centres' responsibility to provide assistance and support to officer(s) attending the incident. This can, sometimes, prove difficult for a variety of reasons. For example, police forces that cover large rural areas may have difficulty in providing immediate assistance to officers. Additionally, in smaller urban forces resources may be fully deployed elsewhere, making an immediate response difficult. Personnel staffing police control centres are a combination of police officers and civilian support staff. Usually a police officer holding the rank of Inspector or Chief Inspector is in overall charge. This has the distinct advantage that, at any given time, a senior police officer capable of making tactical decisions is in direct contact with officers dealing with the incident.

2.3 Personnel involved in the investigative process

The mainstay of the police service in the United Kingdom are the groups of officers who carry out patrol duties in uniform. These officers work a shift pattern to carry out their duties covering a 24-hour period every day of the year. The most senior police officer on duty covering the 24-hour shift system is normally the 'Duty Inspector'. Sergeants and constables support this officer. The total number of officers engaged in shift work depends on the geography and topography of a particular area and varies between police services. This method of policing is called the 'Uniform Shift System' because it engages officers from the uniform branch of the service.

Although over the years the police service has changed and adapted the actual shift patterns, the system itself is recognized as being the most efficient to provide the public with an effective service. Due to this method of policing an area it will, under most circumstances, be a constable or PCSO in uniform who first attends the scene of any incident to make an initial assessment. A colleague of supervisory rank who is a sergeant or inspector will support this officer if the incident is deemed to be of a serious nature. It will be the supervisory officer who, in most cases, arranges the level of further immediate support.

The responsibility for ongoing crime investigations usually falls to officers from the Criminal Investigations Department (CID). A Senior Investigating Officer (SIO) will direct crimes that fall into the 'Major' category. Again, individual police forces differ and so the SIO can be a Detective Inspector, Chief Inspector or Superintendent.

Whatever the rank of the SIO, it is the responsibility of that officer to deploy staff from all relevant police departments and other agencies with the aim of detecting the crime and providing sufficient evidence to bring the perpetrators before a court. Where scientific methods of detection are employed in the first instance the SIO will call upon the services of a Crime Scene Manager. This officer will be an experienced member of the force's Scenes of Crime Department. For the duration of the scene examination the CSM acts as a liaison between SOCO at the scene, the SIO, scientists and other experts. The CSM should also attend all briefings and intelligence meetings. When this function is performed correctly it greatly assists in keeping the investigation team fully informed on any scientific developments impacting on the enquiry. When several serious crimes are linked by scientific means another tier of supervision may need to be considered. This particular duty is carried out by a senior and very experienced SOCO, who takes the role of the Crime Scene Coordinator (CSC). This officer acts as an additional advisor to the SIO, provides a link between all of the different scenes and their CSM and ensures all pertinent forensic evidence is dealt with efficiently and effectively.

Another important link in the chain of the whole investigation is the Exhibits Officer: a detective officer specifically trained to deal with all items of potential evidence performs this role. It is the responsibility of this officer to ensure and maintain the integrity and continuity of each item of evidence from the moment it is recovered throughout its life until it is presented before a court and serves no further evidential value to the case or to an appeal.

2.4 Recording and recovery of scientific evidence

In general terms the recording and recovery of scientific evidence at crime scenes is undertaken by officers specifically trained to carry out the task. Depending on where, in England and Wales, the alleged offence has taken place, these officers may be police officers or support staff. Again, depending in which police area they are employed, support staff officers may be variously described as Scenes of Crime Officers (SOCO), Crime Scene Examiners (CSE), Crime Scene Investigators (CSI) or Scientific Support Officers (SSO). A relatively new concept has been the intro-duction of officers who are limited to examining scenes involving burglary or motor vehicles. These officers are termed Volume Crime Scene Examiners (VCSE). By whatever title an officer might be referred to, the duties carried out are the same. Therefore in order to save confusion, throughout this book the term SOCO will be used to describe this type of personnel.

Although SOCO play an important part in the investigation process it is unlikely that they would be first in attendance at the crime scene. This responsibility falls mainly to uniformed police patrol officers. The full duties and responsibilities of a SOCO can be seen in detail in Chapter 3.

2.5 Initial considerations of the first officer attending (FOA)

In terms of crime scene preservation and the later evidence recovery, the importance of correct, immediate actions taken by the first police officer(s) to attend any crime scene should not be underestimated. Mistakes or oversights made during this crucial stage of an investigation can have a great impact on the final outcome of the case.

So how does the process work? Firstly the crime has to come to the attention of the police. This is normally done by either the aggrieved or Injured Party (IP), or by a member of the public who may have witnessed the incident. Alternatively the crime may be discovered by a patrolling police officer.

The initial actions taken by police officers attending the scene may depend on one or more of the following criteria:

- the category or serious nature of the offence;

- their own observations;

- the information provided by the Injured Party;

- the information provided by witnesses.

Although the serious nature of an incident or criminal offence has no bearing on whether evidential material will be deposited at the scene it will influence initial actions taken at the scene. The principles governing evidential material are dealt with in Chapter 3.

Criminal offences can be categorized into those that have been accepted as 'Serious' or 'Major' crimes and others identified as 'Volume' crimes. Briefly, offences categorized as being 'Major' will include murders, manslaughter and rape. Those categorized as being 'Volume' will include burglary, theft and minor criminal damage.

Following the initial complaint that an alleged offence has taken place a patrolling police officer will attend the scene and make an assessment of the situation. In 'Major' crime this initial assessment is likely to be carried out under the chaotic and confused circumstances that often occur in the early stages of such an enquiry. The immediate responsibilities of a police officer, when attending any incident, are the *preservation of life* and the *protection of property*. The next considerations will be the *maintenance of order and the apprehension of the offender(s)*. Dealing with these issues in stressful circumstances, while at the same time taking steps to prevent the destruction of scientific evidence, requires great skill and is, to say the least, challenging.

An initial assessment at a 'Volume' crime will be less demanding. However, individuals that have returned home to discover their house has been forcibly entered, its contents in disarray and treasured possessions stolen will, quite understandably, be upset and annoyed. Dealing with victims of this type of incident also requires a balanced level of compassion and professionalism in order to elicit every pertinent detail while, at the same time, controlling the crime scene and preserving evidence.

Having considered the initial actions of police officers in general terms we should now look at each element in greater detail.

2.6 Dealing with the victim

Victims could be suffering from a variety of conditions. Obviously the 'Preservation of Life' takes precedence over everything else. Rendering first aid and saving life can mean that the victim will be able, later, to provide essential information that may lead to the identity of the offender and an arrest. If, however, the victim is unfortunately beyond resuscitation a careful and structured scientific examination of the deceased may provide the vital material capable of identifying the offender.

Even when the circumstances of the incident do not require the consideration of first aid, the victim may still be traumatized and confused. This could arise from the effects of an assault, drink, drugs, mental illness, shock or just simply anger. Whatever the situation, the victim must be dealt with properly for them to provide important factual information.

Depending on the type of crime that has been committed it may be essential for certain samples to be taken from victims. Where that is the case, relevant procedures should be carried out as soon as possible. Again every consideration should be given to the dignity of the victim. Whatever the nature of the alleged offence, *intimate* samples can only be taken from a victim by a registered Forensic Medical Examiner (FME). Depending on the circumstances of the offence the sampling will be carried out either at a doctor's surgery, a hospital or at a medical suite specially designed for the purpose. A police officer, of the same sex as the victim, will be present to act as a chaperone and provide the FME with any specialist equipment required. In other cases where *non-intimate* samples or clothing are required this may be better carried out at the home of the victim.

In order to clarify the legal procedures as they apply to persons in police custody, definitions describing intimate and non-intimate samples can be found in Code D Paragraph 6 of the Police and Criminal Evidence Act of 1984 (PACE Act). However, the samples themselves, if not the circumstances in which they are taken, apply equally to a victim. The samples are defined as follows:

Intimate sample means:

- dental impressions;

- sample of blood;

- sample of semen;

- sample of any other tissue;

- sample of urine;

- sample of pubic hair;

- swab taken from a person's genitals;

- swab taken from any body orifice other than the mouth.

Such samples must be taken by a suitably qualified person, such as a medical practitioner or dental surgeon.

Non-intimate sample means:

- sample of hair, other than pubic hair, which includes hair plucked with the root;

- sample taken from the nail or from under the nail;

- swab taken from any part of the person's body other than a part from which a swab taken would be classed as an intimate sample;

- sample of saliva;

- skin impression, other than a fingerprint, which is a record, in any form and produced by any method, of the skin pattern and any other physical characteristics or features of the whole, or any part of, a person's foot or of any other part of their body.

2.7 Dealing with witnesses

Witnesses to the incident require to be dealt with in a similar fashion to the victim. They may be friends of the victim in which case they could also be suffering from the effects of alcohol, drugs or shock. Friends may also put an interpretation on the incident that may be biased towards the victim. Witnesses who turn out to be friends of the suspect may do the same. Essentially, independent witnesses need to be located. Their information is more likely to be impartial and therefore have a greater validity at any subsequent court hearing.

Witness handling needs tact and diplomacy to get the best cooperation. Some individuals having witnessed the incident would prefer to keep information to themselves. The reason for this could be that they are afraid of reprisals or, perhaps they have been involved as a witness in other incidents and did not like the experience. It may be that they are not public spirited. 'I don't want to get involved' is a typical attitude in today's society. Other people are willing to give brief information but will then be anxious to leave the scene. Whatever the situation, as much detail as possible regarding the circumstances of the incident needs to be obtained. The very minimum information obtained from a witness should be their name, address, with verification and if possible a telephone number, thus allowing later contact by the investigation team. People who have witnessed a serious incident often have to be interviewed several times before every detail is elicited from them.

2.8 Dealing with suspects

Officers who attend the scene of an incident to find both victim and suspect present face a particular dilemma. Under these circumstances the possibility that scientific samples could be *contaminated* is real and could lead to some or all of the forensic evidence being negated. The actions of the officers will need to be carefully scrutinized and reported to the scientist so that any results are fair and balanced. For example, the above situation could occur where blood is transferred from the victim to the officer when rendering first aid. The officer then arrests the suspect, and they have physical contact. It could be argued that any blood found on the suspect's clothing could be there as a result of the arrest and is 'contamination by secondary transfer'. Should this situation arise, and the transference of blood from the victim to the suspect becomes an important issue, it is vital that the full circumstances are explained to the forensic scientist tasked with making the examination. This will ensure that the distribution of the blood will also be taken into account by the scientist and reported upon accordingly. The issues of contamination are further explained, together with contact trace material and crime scene examination, in Chapter 3.

2.9 Dealing with the crime scene(s)

Having established that a crime has been committed and the initial situation has been calmed, the First Officer Attending(FOA) then needs to consider taking the necessary action to preserve the scene and any potential evidence. What then is a crime scene? In general terms this can be anywhere but perhaps it is useful to be more prescriptive to define a crime scene as follows:
    Whether a major or volume crime the scene may include a:

- person
- place or
- premises (including vehicles, boats and aircraft).

where some physical action has occurred, and, there is a likelihood that transference of evidential material has taken place.
    It can be appreciated that officers faced with deciding the initial perimeters of any crime scene have a difficult task to perform. In 'Major Crime' urgent consideration

needs to be given to placing adequate inner and outer cordons using police barrier tape. Cordons are aimed at keeping all unauthorized persons out of, and all items of potential evidence in, the scene. In the early stages of the investigation the larger the outer cordon the better. The importance of having an adequate outer cordon cannot be overstated, although achieving this in operational circumstances can be difficult.

The outer cordon allows a thorough search to be made ensuring that no relevant contact trace evidence is overlooked.

Figures showing the location of inner and outer cordons in a typical, although fictional, scenario are shown in Figures 2.1 and 2.2. Study the figures and then consider the following situation. At 18.36 hours on a Saturday evening in August the Ambulance Service receive a '999' call to the effect that a man has been injured in Wood Street. Paramedics attend the scene to find a deceased male lying on a path outside 8 Wood Street. The man has suffered what appear to be stab wounds to the chest and neck. Police are informed and at 18.48 hours two uniformed police officers, who were on mobile patrol, attend the scene. Witnesses tell them that the deceased man, John SMITH, lived alone at no. 8. Apparently he had been involved in an argument with Tony GREEN who resides at no. 16 Wood Street. It was believed that GREEN was responsible for the assault and, after running back to his house, had, a short time later, driven off in his car. The officers still check no. 16 to find that the house does in fact appear unoccupied. The situation is reported back to the control centre with a request for the attendance of other officers to assist with setting out adequate cordons.

Some of the problems faced by officers placing cordons can be seen in Figures 2.1 and 2.2. Illustrated are the possible positions of outer and inner cordons in the above-described fictional situation. The figure attempts to detail a typically urban area. Well populated with a mix of houses, maisonettes, a college and open park land, all adjacent to main thoroughfares with a bus route. Even though details of a suspect have been provided, at this early stage nothing can be presumed. Until all the facts are known an adequate outer cordon still has to be set up. This is not only to control the movement of people into and out of the wider area, but also to ensure that places where weapons, clothing or any other item of evidential value could be deposited are not overlooked. Such places will include domestic dustbins, other rubbish bins, skips, storm water drains or any other close and convenient place. Although the home of the suspect would attract special attention the figure shows that there could be numerous places, within the outer cordon, that are more vulnerable to the elements or the general public and would require being searched as soon as possible.

Figure 2.1 shows an enlarged version of the inner cordon. This is protecting the deceased, his home address, the home address of the suspect and the area in the immediate vicinity. Because of the circumstances of the offence, these areas are likely to yield a high level of evidential material. The deceased is lying in the open

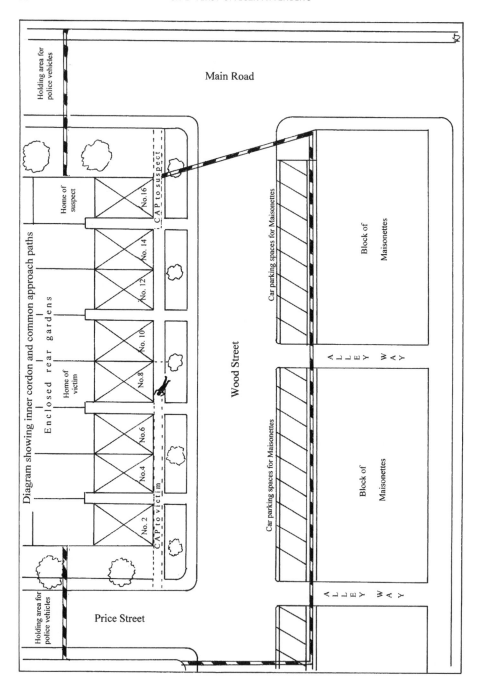

Figure 2.1   Diagram showing the cordoning of a crime scene.

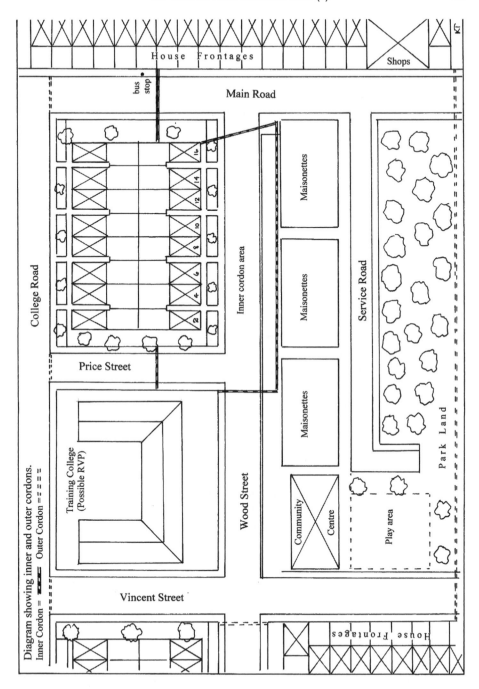

Figure 2.2 Appropriate inner and outer cordoning of a crime scene.

during the early evening and could easily be viewed by people in the nearby maisonettes and houses; urgent steps would be taken to provide tented cover and portable lighting. Also marked on the figure are common approach paths (CAP) that lead independently to the deceased and the suspect's house. The importance and purpose of a common approach path is described later.

The responsibility of searching areas within the outer cordon is usually given to a team of police officers belonging to units specially trained in search techniques and equipped to deal with most eventualities. These officers are managed and briefed by a Police Search Advisor (POLSA). In incidents that cover an extensive area and require the attendance of large numbers of staff, consideration should be given to identifying a point, if possible outside the outer cordon where officers may assemble to be briefed and tasked. This area is known as the 'Rendezvous Point' (RVP). Ideally such areas should be in buildings that will allow proper briefing facilities with refreshment and rest capabilities.

Depending on the circumstances of the incident there may be a need for one or more inner cordons to be put into place. These smaller inner cordons are easier to control and also serve the purpose of protecting evidential areas within the main scene or specific items that are some distance apart and in danger of being over-looked. The biggest problem with placing adequate cordons at a crime scene is in providing a sufficient number of officers to effectively control them. As can be seen in Figure 2.2 officers would be needed at each of the six access roads, plus at least another two patrolling the 'Park Land' cordon. Apart from keeping unauthorized members of the public out of the scene, the entry of authorized personnel must be fully recorded. This information is recorded by a police officer or PCSO given the specific task of completing a 'Crime Scene Attendance Log'. The 'Log' is intended to ensure that the date, time, name, department or organization and reasons for entering and the time of leaving the scene are accurately recorded. This is effective in keeping the number of officers or personnel entering the cordon or scene to an absolute minimum. It also serves the purpose of identifying personnel attending the scene in the event of an emergency or health and safety danger and provides details for the later elimination process. This means that any contact trace evidence recovered from the scene may be checked and eliminated to persons having legit-imate access to the scene. Thus ensuring, as far as possible, that only evidence that can be attributed to the offender will be entered onto the various databases. The elimination process can be vitally important to the final outcome of a case.

At the time cordons are put in place consideration should be given to providing a clearly marked route into the scene, allowing access from the outer cordon to a specific area, or areas, of interest. This is the CAP and again serves to ensure the preservation of potential evidence. Figure 2.1 shows the two distinctly separate CAP. It is also worth noting here, that two entirely different SOCO teams would be needed, one to deal with the deceased and the general scene, while the other deals with the suspect and his house. Overall responsibility for the crime scenes may rest with a CSM.

Wherever possible the common approach path should, for obvious reasons, follow an alternative route to that taken by the offender. However, in some situations, such as premises with only one entrance and exit, it is not possible to mark out a secondary route. In such an event there are two courses of action that may be considered. The CAP can either be thoroughly searched so that any evidence between the outer cordon, access point and the area of main consideration is recorded and recovered. Alternatively specialist equipment termed 'Stepping Plates' may be used. Stepping plates are usually made of pressed steel, for strength, and constructed to cover items of evidential value thus protecting them. Utilizing this equipment allows free passage and work to be carried out in the main evidence area, without compromising other evidence along the route. Health and safety assessments and risk assessment must be carried out before stepping plates can be used because, depending on the surfaces involved, this equipment is known to present the danger of slipping. High visibility warning signs must also be placed outside the scene informing all in attendance of the possible hazard.

Although 'Volume Crime' scenes do not attract such extensive methods and resources to protect the scene and preserve evidence the principles are exactly the same. Officers attending the scene of a burglary will arrange with the complainant to keep clear of areas where the offender is known to have been. This is, in effect, setting up an unmarked cordon, preserving evidence and allowing the SOCO to carry out relevant work unhindered. The complainant will know the people having access to the premises and so the process of elimination can be undertaken. Many parallels can be drawn between how volume and major crime scenes are managed in order to maximize evidence preservation.

Failure to adhere to the simple, yet effective, principles governing the position and supervision of cordons will undoubtedly have an adverse effect on a crime scene. Conversely, correct scene preservation will:

- prevent the movement of evidence;
- prevent the destruction of evidence;
- prevent the contamination of evidence;
- prevent the loss of evidence.

2.10 Documentation

It is vital that the prosecution prove that all issues regarding the integrity and continuity of evidence have been complied with in any criminal proceedings that take place subsequent to an investigation. The compliance to this requirement can easily be seen if all relevant documentation is expediently and accurately maintained.

All police officers are issued with official pocket notebooks. This document is used to record evidence and other information pertinent to an investigation. Circumstances at live active scenes have a potential to change. The scene confronting an SOCO may be very different to the original scenario. It is extremely important that notes and sketch plans recording the original circumstances are made to assist in a thorough and accurate examination. There are strict rules governing the use of pocket notebooks. When giving evidence in a court of law, before a police officer can relate to information contained in their notebook they must first prove that any notes taken, relating to the evidence, were contemporaneous (made at the time), or as soon as practicable after, the incident took place. If this cannot be proved then the evidence may not be accepted when presented in a court of law. Officers first in attendance at a crime scene will record pertinent information in their pocket notebooks. However to continue to use a notebook in serious or complicated enquiries would not be very practical or efficient. Therefore, other documents, more suitable for the purpose, have been designed for use once an investigation is under way. A good example of this is the previously described 'Crime Scene Attendance Log'. Ongoing enquiries may require a scene to be controlled for an extended period. Records of persons attending a scene may be kept, initially, in an officer's pocket notebook. However, during a protracted scene examination, officers controlling the cordon will change many times. Consequently, because the information is vital for subsequent elimination purposes, it would be impractical to rely on such diverse records. Therefore a log has been specially designed to serve as a permanent record. The log is recognized as an official document that must be accurately maintained by officers controlling cordons until such time that they are relieved of that duty. The handing over of the log to another officer requires that the issue of continuity be addressed. The information required to prove continuity is incorporated into the document.

2.11 Dealing with violent crime

Crime scenes that involve offences of a violent nature are worthy of special note for two reasons. Such crime scenes very often involve the distribution of blood and body tissue. For this reason they can provide excellent contact trace material and potential evidence. Not only can an accurate interpretation of blood spatter provide the chronology of events, blood that is dispersed in and around a scene in the shape of a fingerprint or footwear impression may provide a direct link to the offender(s). Similarly, weapons that have been used to inflict injuries may provide conclusive fingerprint or DNA evidence and it may be possible to match the weapon to the injury or projectile (see Chapter 8). Scenes that reveal information or evidence of this nature must be dealt with extremely carefully from the outset. Another consideration that must be given to a scene where blood or body tissue appears to be present is that of Health and Safety. At the time an offence is reported nothing will be known regarding the health of either the victim or suspect. Again if blood or body tissue is involved all personnel attending the scene, either immediately or subsequently, should take great care to eliminate the spread of any infectious disease such as Hepatitis or TB. Personal protective equipment (PPE), such as gloves and respiratory masks, should always be considered and worn at any scene where blood or body tissue is believed to be present.

The injuries that can be inflicted during a violent assault are often harrowing to view. It is accepted by police officers and support staff that this is all part of their expected duty. However, officers exposed to this type of crime on a regular basis need to be aware that help to deal with the build up of trauma is always available, by way of professional counselling.

2.12 Summary and conclusion

It can be seen that the investigation of any major crime scene can be quite complex. For a crime involving scientific evidence to be successfully dealt with it needs to be controlled carefully from the outset. All officers, of whatever rank or position, involved in the investigation work as a team, dedicated to bringing a case to the right conclusion before a criminal court.

Self-assessed questions

2.1 What is the badge of rank for a Chief Inspector?

2.2 What rank is the FOA at an incident likely to be?

2.3 Who directs the FOA to an incident?

2.4 What are the two main categories of crime?

2.5 How many police forces are there in England and Wales?

2.6 What do the acronyms RVP and CAP stand for?

2.7 Why are cordons essential to the investigation?

2.8 What four things can be achieved by good crime scene preservation?

2.9 What is the purpose of a 'Crime Scene Attendance Log'?

2.10 (a) What does the acronym PPE stand for?
(b) Name two types of commonly used PPE.

3

The Role of the Scenes of Crime Officer

Keith Trueman

3.1 Introduction

The previous chapter explained the actions and procedures that, when taken by police officers first in attendance at a crime scene, would contribute greatly to any subsequent scientific investigation. Such actions are commonly referred to as 'Crime Scene and Evidence Preservation'. Once a scene has been effectively preserved, it becomes the domain of an officer specially trained in the techniques required to successfully recover what is known as contact trace material. Depending upon the circumstances of the offence, this material can be virtually anything that, when examined and interpreted correctly, may connect the offender to the scene or victim or provide evidence to support a particular sequence of events (establishing that a crime has taken place for example). Before contact trace material can be adduced as evidential material certain procedures and processes must be adhered to. The importance of this will be fully explained later in this chapter. It may be useful here to explain that in order to successfully examine a crime scene and ensure that all potential evidential material is recognized, recorded and recovered; an individual officer needs a number of attributes. These will include good oral and written communication skills, a keen pair of eyes, common sense, imagination, patience, methodical approach, enthusiasm, a sense of humour and, of

Crime Scene Management: Scene Specific Methods   Edited by Raul Sutton and Keith Trueman
© 2009 John Wiley & Sons, Ltd

course, the skill to be able to develop latent fingerprints and correctly recover all other types of evidential material.

Communication and observational skills come naturally to some people, but in any case can be improved upon once it is known what questions to ask, what to look for and where to look for it. However, by their very nature, the practical competencies for recovery and packaging of evidence must be taught and practised before a trainee officer can become proficient in all of the different techniques involved. This helps people to understand why officers who deal with the collection of such material need to be carefully selected and specially trained.

The organizational structure of a particular police service will define whether such specialist officers are drawn from police ranks or specifically employed for the task in a support role. Again, depending on their location in the country, their title may differ. 'Scenes of Crime Officer' (SOCO), as a designation, was first used by the Metropolitan Police Service in the early 1970s when the role began to devolve from police to support staff. Gradually, other provincial police services have followed suit, and now support staff, almost exclusively, carry out the work. As the area of responsibility has changed, so the title has evolved. In addition to SOCO these officers are also referred to as Crime Scene Examiners (CSE), Crime Scene Investigators (CSI) and Scientific Support Officers (SSO). Recently, in an effort to combat the high incidence of burglary and car theft, another tier of officer has been introduced. Their duties are restricted to offences falling into the volume categories, hence the title Volume Crime Scene Examiner (VCSE). For the purposes of this book the term SOCO will mainly be used.

3.2 Training the SOCO

Whatever their title may be there is a nationally agreed syllabus for training to ensure a level standard. This training is almost exclusively conducted at the training centre of the National Police Improvement Agency (NPIA), situated in Crook, County Durham.

Candidates who successfully apply to an individual police service to become a SOCO will, following some instruction in local procedures, attend the NPIA Training Centre and undergo an initial residential training programme lasting for nine weeks. Initial training provides instruction in photography, fingerprint development and the recognition and recovery of all types of scientific evidence. Upon returning to the individual police service, the SOCO will continue to improve their skills in operational situations. It is generally recognized that it takes a minimum of two years before an officer becomes fully competent and able to deal with most eventualities at crime scenes. During this two-year period SOCO are continually assessed as part of their personal development. This whole programme ends when officers, having proved themselves capable, return to the NPIA Training Centre and attend a two-week development course. It is at that stage that officers are considered to be fully operational. In addition to this, trainee officers may, if they so wish, apply for academic validation of their skills and work towards achieving a Foundation Degree in Crime Scene Examination.

The subsequent career of a SOCO will involve them in attending many other continuing professional development programmes all aimed at honing their skills and keeping abreast of changes in criminal activity and modern technology. Depending on the subject matter this training can be provided by the NPIA and several other organizations. Some of the extra skills that may be needed at the crime scene are described below. Natural career progression involves carrying out the duty of 'Crime Scene Manager' (CSM) or Crime Scene Coordinator (CSC). These roles become relevant at scenes of a serious nature when the designated Senior Investigating Officer (SIO) requires an experienced scene examiner to oversee the evidence recovery process. The role of the CSC is to act as liaison between the investigation team and the crime scene examination teams. This helps to ensure that not a single piece of evidence is overlooked. These roles carry with them a great deal of extra responsibility and usually only come when an individual officer feels competent and has secured the confidence of their supervisory officers.

More recently an organization called the 'Council for the Registration of Forensic Practitioners' (CRFP) has been introduced into this field of work. CRFP has set a nationally recognized standard to prove the competence of officers who are engaged in any field of work that involves presenting scientific evidence before court. Officers wishing to become registered have their work assessed by persons recognized as specialists in that particular field. Successful assessment is followed by initial registration, which is re-evaluated every four years.

3.3 The responsibilities of a SOCO

Having looked at the process and requirements to become a SOCO, we should now examine the many responsibilities that are involved in carrying out the actual role. It is very important to appreciate that evidential material identified and recovered from any category of crime scene (see Chapter 1 for general crime categories) has the potential to identify an offender and results in that person receiving a term of imprisonment. To deprive a person of their liberty is a grave responsibility, and it is therefore vital that every stage of the process is conducted with integrity, impartiality and professionalism. This will help to establish the truth of the matter, assist the investigation and support a criminal prosecution, ensuring that only the guilty are convicted.

The responsibilities of a SOCO are now described in brief, under the headings shown below (more comprehensive information is given later):

- *Confirm that a crime has been committed.* Most enquiries are straightforward. Occasionally when a crime is investigated suspicion may be aroused that the complaint is spurious. A thorough investigation of the scene could provide evidence that will prove or disprove this suspicion.

- *Preservation of the scene.* It will be shown later that a SOCO will spend time, initially assessing and then recording the scene, before any consideration is given to the recovery of evidential material. This phase, which by its nature will delay the examination proper, may require necessary steps to be taken that ensure no evidence is lost or destroyed. For example, in inclement weather footwear impressions outside in the open will need to be covered over to protect them from the elements.

- *Identify key evidence areas.* These areas normally relate to parts of the scene where offenders are known to have been. Particular attention is always given to the point of entry into and the point of exit from the scene. These two, or in some cases more, areas are where it can be certain that the offender has been in definite contact for a longer period of time.

- *Identify key evidence types.* Some evidence types, as will be shown later, can actually identify the offender(s) and therefore may be described as *key* evidence. However, each and every type of trace material has its own potential to place a suspect at the scene and so, at least in the initial stages of the examination, must be treated with equal value.

- *Record all evidence.* The different methods to carry out this task are many and will be described in full later in this chapter.

- *Recovery of all evidence.* As mentioned above, no piece of potential evidential material can be discounted during the examination and must be recovered. It is at this stage, however, that consideration should be given to establish (especially where fingerprints and DNA are concerned) whether there is a legitimate reason for it being there. This will start the process of *elimination*. Also, when recovering any potential evidential material, documentation must be completed that will prove the *integrity* and *continuity* of each item.

- *Packaging and storing evidence.* Items of evidential material recovered from a crime scene are taken with the intention that they will be examined by one of a variety of other experts at some future time. When an item is delivered to the expert, in addition to its *integrity and continuity* being proved the suitability of its packaging and the method of storage will also need to be evidenced. If these other two very important details are found to be wanting, then the possibility that the exhibit could be *contaminated* may be difficult to rule out.

- *Briefing the investigating officer.* The police officer tasked with conducting the investigation will need to know the potential of evidential material recovered from a crime scene. The relevant information can be transmitted to the investigating officer in either verbal, documented or electronic form as appropriate.

- *Prepare statements of evidence.* Each witness completes and signs a written statement before any evidence can be presented before a court. Statements compiled by SOCOs can be long and involved (see Chapter 4). For this, and other reasons described later, making comprehensive notes at the crime scene is very important.

- *Present evidence before a court.* The whole process has been developed to ensure that any evidence recovered from any crime scene is to a standard that will be accepted in any court proceedings.

To fully appreciate the work carried out by a SOCO it is important to understand some of the terminology and principles involved. For instance what is meant by the term *'forensic evidence'* and what actually constitutes a *crime scene*? Clear knowledge of these elements can put the whole process into perspective.

3.4 Forensic evidence

The term 'forensic evidence' in now accepted by most people to mean scientific evidence, although this is not a strict interpretation. The word 'forensic' is actually defined 'of or used in courts of law' (Oxford English Dictionary) and derives from the Latin Forum. Therefore professional occupations that are carried out predominantly to provide evidence before a court of law may be prefixed with 'forensic'. Thus pathologists, scientists, archaeologists and accountants carrying out their work for criminal trials become forensic pathologists and so on.

What is this potentially evidential material that police officers take steps to preserve and SOCO so ardently search for at crime scenes? To answer this question we need to look back to the early part of the twentieth century, about 1910, when the French Scientist, Edmond Locard, first reported his theory that may be roughly translated as:

When two objects come into contact, each will leave a trace of itself upon the other.

This forms the basis of what is commonly termed as 'contact trace material' and, when found and recovered from a crime scene, may provide intelligence for the investigation. Only following further analysis by a forensic scientist or comparison by a fingerprint expert will that trace material become 'trace evidence' and support a prosecution. To determine a one-way transfer of material can be extremely useful to an investigation. By ascertaining a two-way material transfer (from the scene to the suspect and the suspect to the scene) conclusive evidence of contact of the suspect at the scene can be adduced.

A century later this theory still stands as the basis for all crime scene assessments and examination processes. However, expectations that transference has taken place needs to be kept in perspective. Firstly, even though the potential is there, contact trace material is not found at every scene. The absence of material should not be construed to mean that a particular individual has not been there. This must be balanced with other factors. Secondly, it must be appreciated that the category or seriousness of the offence has no impact upon trace evidence being left at the scene, on the offender or upon other items of potential evidence.

Transfer is totally dependent on the three criteria:

- length of contact;

- strength of contact;

- surfaces involved are receptive to a transference.

If the above criteria are met and material is actually transferred, to make it useful as evidence, it must be *unique* to the individual scene or person. The more unique the sample is the greater the likelihood of it being accepted as conclusive evidence. Uniqueness of the trace material is an important consideration when deciding its evidential value. The way in which the material is *distributed* at a scene or upon a suspect can also be crucial. This is because the distribution of material at the crime scene will allow investigators to reconstruct the possible chain of events before, during and after the commission of the offence.

Another important consideration on the theory and practice of the subject area relates to what is termed as the *retention time*. Once transference of material has taken place the length of time it will remain on any given surface is totally arbitrary. Many things will impact on this phenomenon including gravity, wind and weather conditions, loss by further contacts, destruction by poor crime scene preservation and, of course, the offender taking steps to remove or destroy the evidence.

The circumstances of the crime will determine what trace evidence is left at the scene. This places an importance upon accurate crime scene assessment as described later in this chapter.

Contact trace evidence types are normally divided into the following four categories:

- fingerprints

- DNA

- footwear

- all other types.

Some control or reference samples are stored on databases that have the ability to be searched against questioned samples taken from the crime scene. It is because of these various databases that fingerprints, DNA and footwear are differentiated from all other types of trace evidence. Under terms of the Police and Criminal Evidence Act of 1984 (PACE Act) Code D, where a person has been arrested on suspicion of having committed a criminal offence, their fingerprints and DNA can be taken and stored on the National Automated Fingerprint Identification System (NAFIS) or the National DNA Database (NDNAD) respectively.

Similarly, under terms of the PACE Act Code D, as amended by the Serious and Organized Crimes Act of 2005 (SOCA), when individuals are arrested on suspicion of committing a criminal offence they may also have the sole pattern of their footwear reproduced and entered onto the Shoe Impression Comparison And Recognition (SICAR) system. Whichever system is relevant to the particular type of evidence, the sample recorded on the database acts as the control sample. If fingerprints, DNA or footwear marks are recovered from a crime scene, after the elimination process has taken place, they are submitted for a 'speculative check' to be made against the relevant database. Results provided by any of the computer databases are treated, in the first instance, as intelligence information by the investigating officer. The information is then, depending on its type, verified either by fingerprint experts or a forensic scientist. Once this has been done the information may be presented before a court as actual evidence. The verification in cases involving footwear impressions will involve the actual footwear of the suspect being seized as a control sample and checked, by a forensic scientist, against the questioned sample(s) from the crime scene. The result of this examination will be used as the actual evidence in any subsequent trial. A slight variation to this procedure happens when police officers provide the names of persons who are believed to be responsible for committing a specific crime. The crime scene material is then only compared with the details kept on record of those individuals. This is termed a '*suspect check*' and is generally quicker than a '*speculative check*'. Any result obtained as a consequence of this still has to go through the verification process before it can be presented as evidence.

The course of action taken when dealing with any other type of contact trace evidence is somewhat different. The process to deal with 'other evidential types' normally commences when a person is in custody, having been arrested on suspicion of committing a specific criminal offence and it is known that scientific evidence from that crime scene exists.

This principle will be illustrated by an example. A burglary has been committed where, in order to gain entry to premises, the offender has smashed a pane of glass in a kitchen window. A witness has described a suspect who is arrested a short time later and some distance from the crime scene.

At the police station, following the arrest, the arresting officer takes the relevant clothing from the suspect and requests that the crime scene is examined by a SOCO. An examination is conducted and the glass in the broken window provides the only type of contact trace evidence that could possibly link a suspect to the crime scene. In order to make this link the SOCO must take a control sample of the broken glass from the window frame. If more than one pane of glass has been broken then a control sample is taken from each area. A diagram will be drawn and a record made of the height(s), location(s) and the inside or outside surface of the broken pane(s). The control sample(s) will be correctly documented and packaged. The questioned sample, that is the clothing, will also be correctly documented and packaged, care being taken to ensure that neither questioned nor control samples are ever in contact. Other relevant details of the suspect, such as height and handedness, will be documented and then everything submitted to a forensic science laboratory.

The submission report will contain a request for clothing to be examined and any fragments of glass on or in it recovered. When carrying out the examination the scientist will also note how the glass, if there is any, is distributed on the various items of clothing. The fragments of glass will then be compared with the control sample(s). The comparison will involve ascertaining the *refractive index* of both the control and the questioned samples (the methodology for this is explained in detail in Chapter 8). The glass fragments from the clothing may match the control sample, the scientist will report upon the findings and this information can be adduced as evidence. Interpretation of how the glass was distributed on the clothing can also add to the strength of the evidence, indicating if the suspect was very close to the glass at the time of impact and fragmentation.

In such cases the different heights involved can be a deciding factor when submitting items to the forensic science provider for examination. This emphasizes the importance of how making detailed notes and diagrams, giving the correct information and submitting pertinent samples for scientific examination can affect the final outcome of the case. Items submitted in a case where the glass is broken at head height to the offender will normally include hair combings or a hat, together with top outer clothing, a jacket or a jumper for instance. These items can prove that the suspect has been showered in broken glass fragments and was present at the time the glass was broken. This will be different in a case where the offender kicked in a pane of glass at just above ground level. In that instance the shoes, socks and trousers of a suspect will provide better evidence of contact because the distribution of glass fragments will, possibly, be retained in the laces, lace holes and welts of the footwear, the socks and the lower part of the trousers. Again relevant distribution of glass fragments on these items could provide good evidence that the wearer of the clothing actually smashed the pane of glass. This example shows the importance of correctly interpreting what has taken place at the crime scene and selecting items of evidence that are pertinent to those circumstances. If the SOCO carry out their tasks diligently and provide all relevant information to fingerprint experts and scientists it is more likely that a positive result will be achieved.

3.5 Request for SOCO attendance at crime scenes

The request for a SOCO to attend a scene is called tasking and can be done in any one of several ways including:

- *Tasking via a computer generated list.* When members of the public report that they have become a victim of crime, or have witnessed a criminal offence, relevant information is entered onto a 'Command and Control' computer incident log. If the crime category is one that a SOCO would attend as a matter of routine then an entry will be made on the log and it will be automatically transferred to the SOCO computer terminal. The information will then be collected by a supervisory SOCO who allocates the work to individual officers.

- *Tasking via personal radio or mobile telephone.* Once a SOCO is engaged in making visits to crime scenes they remain in contact with their area controller/dispatcher using either a VHF personal radio or a mobile telephone. Any crime included in the volume category that is reported and requires the routine attendance of a SOCO will be passed over the airwaves and added to the list of jobs to be attended in due course. Should a major incident be reported in this fashion, it will take precedence over any volume crime and the SOCO will make an immediate response. This will inevitably delay the examination of volume crime scenes for some time.

- *Tasking via a personal request.* Occasionally a police officer will visit a crime scene and be unsure whether it is necessary for a SOCO to attend or not. On such occasions the police officer may visit the Scenes of Crime Department to discuss the case and seek advice. The SOCO can then decide from the information given, whether a visit to the scene is required. Similarly, a member of the public may inform a SOCO that a crime has been committed. This may occur when the officer, making a scheduled examination is informed that premises close by have also been forcibly entered.

Whichever method is adopted there will always be an entry made on the Command and Control Incident Log, which will be updated when the SOCO has completed the scene examination.

3.6 Actions when attending the crime scene

Each and every crime scene is different. The procedure to ensure thorough and successful examinations is, however, always the same. The process to ensure comprehensive scene examinations may be described under the following general headings:

- initial assessment;
- identification of key evidence areas;
- preservation of the scene;
- planning the recovery of evidence;
- record the evidence;
- recover the evidence.

The process has been given individual headings for the ease of explanation but in practice the first three stages are combined. This will be made clearer in the following explanation of the terms.

3.7 Initial scene assessment (including health and safety considerations)

It can be argued, as shown by the above example dealing with glass distribution, that one of the most important tasks at the scene is the *initial assessment*. If the assessment is carried out carefully then everything else will fall into place and all pertinent evidential material will be identified recorded and recovered. However, before any evidence is recovered the SOCO needs to ensure that they are not putting their, or anyone else's, health and safety in jeopardy. It may be appreciated that climbing onto the roof of premises to recover important evidential footwear impressions left by offenders at points of entry will always pose risks. Therefore, prior to any action being taken to recover the evidence it will be the responsibility of the individual officer to make a dynamic risk assessment. This should result in a safe method being devised for sample recovery, before any attempt is made to collect the evidential material. It cannot be over emphasized that it is an integral part of the initial assessment to identify any dangers and take the appropriate action to implement health and safety procedures. This is described as a *dynamic risk assessment*. Although SOCO are issued with various items of personal protective equipment (PPE) and clothing, depending on the circumstances of the crime there may be a need to seek advice from a range of experts and employ specialist safety equipment. For example, at scenes of suspected arson, where the burned out shell of a building is likely to collapse, the advice of senior fire fighters, building surveyors and any other appropriate person will be sought, before entry to the scene is attempted. In such circumstances the advice given by the specialists, regarding the risks and the correct equipment needed to deal with the situation, would be resourced on an individual basis. Necessary steps, to safeguard the health and safety of all staff, must be taken before the scene itself is entered and investigated. There may be some risks that are occupational hazards and which the SOCO must protect themselves against. Such a risk is the constant use of fingerprint powder that can, like any other form of fine dust, irritate the respiratory system of the user. Because of this officers engaged in this work should wear dust masks to prevent inhalation of the powder. Frequent dangers such as this have been identified and suitable equipment issued to officers together with advice on its use.

The assessment stage will vary in length and complexity from scene to scene. At routine volume crime scenes both evidential and health and safety assessments may take only seconds and are completed during the introductory stage, when communicating with the complainant. Major crime scenes require a much longer and involved assessment period and are very often carried out in distressing circumstances. At scenes where the enquiry involves sudden and violent death a Senior Investigating Officer (SIO) is appointed. This officer, together with a Crime Scene Manager (CSM) will also be involved with the SOCO in making the scene assessment. Part of that assessment at scenes of suspicious death must always involve a post mortem examination of the deceased person. For this reason a forensic pathologist and forensic scientists may also be in attendance at the scene to assist in establishing the chronological course of events and interpret the distribution of the various types of contact trace material. Health and safety precautions, when dealing with deceased persons, are well established.

Personal protective clothing is issued to every officer attending the scene to alleviate the risks posed by pathogens. It is also recognized that, to relieve any stress that may occur when witnessing or working in distressing situations, officers may need the help and advice of specialist counsellors. This service is always considered during de-briefing sessions but is available at any time during an investigation.

The tried and tested system of policing where a small team of police officers has the responsibility for a defined area has been proved to pay dividends. An officer so employed gains a tremendous amount of local knowledge that may be useful in many different ways. This can include knowing local criminals who are active in a particular area and the methods used by them when committing crime. The same analogy can be levelled at the SOCO. The initial tasking of the SOCO will immediately get the local knowledge thought processes started.

Experienced SOCO will ask themselves such questions as:

- Have I been to the same premises before?

- What were the circumstances on that occasion?

- Have I been to similar premises nearby?

- What is the general condition of premises in the vicinity?

- How have offenders accessed the site or area previously?

- Which criminals do I know to be active in the area?

This thought process is carried out when travelling to the scene, and is sometimes useful, but the actual *scene assessment* only begins on arrival at the scene itself. Before entering the scene it is good practice to spend a short time observing the general exterior lay out. This can sometimes provide an idea of approach and escape routes. Proper introductions with the injured party or complainant are also important at this stage. Even though it is common now for SOCO to be provided with uniform work wear, it is still essential that officers produce their identity cards for examination by the injured party. This is especially important when the victim is old or otherwise vulnerable.

Having made the introductions the injured party is then invited to outline the circumstances of the complaint. This will involve an initial look around the scene, identifying areas of interest that need to be revisited. These areas may be described as 'Key Evidence Areas'. It should also be appreciated that, in this early stage of the scene investigation, the complainant, under the stress of the situation, may be making assumptions that are later proved to be inconsequential or wrong. The SOCO should ask questions but avoid making too much comment. Prudence is best, so just listen and observe at this stage. The possibility of evidential material being damaged or destroyed by inclement weather or other outside interference is very real. For this reason the areas exposed to the elements or general public should be considered a priority and protected. So having listened carefully to the information provided by the complainant the SOCO will request permission to go outside and see, first hand, the point(s) of entry into and exit(s) from the scene. These specific areas, sometimes referred to as the '*ingress*' and '*egress*' points, are extremely useful to the SOCO, because they are, sometimes, the only places where it is certain that the offender has had definite contact. Such areas are worthy of special attention, especially if any physical force has been used, and will be one of the main areas to concentrate on during the later examination. During this stage of the assessment it may also be necessary to take steps to *preserve* items, thereby preventing potential evidence being damaged or destroyed. It will also form part of the *action plan* when deciding which item of evidence to recover first.

The extent of the external assessment will depend on a number of factors that relate to how the offender(s) approached and left the crime scene and the type of terrain involved.

Imagine two very different situations. In the first an offender forcibly enters an office via a window on the third floor of a multi-storey office block in a city centre. In the second an offender climbed over a garden fence, crossed the garden and then gained entry to a house through an unlocked door. Each scene will be entirely different in terms of the approach and type of contact trace evidence left or deposited. In the first scenario, rooftops and fire escapes would be the areas to consider and they could cover a vast area. This then poses the question, 'How far away from the actual scene could you rely on any contact trace being evidence of that particular crime and not simply left by someone having legitimate access?'. In this case it would be advisable to concentrate on the window at the point of entry and the area immediately outside. In the second scenario, the parameters of the scene are much more confined and therefore easier to establish physical contact by a perpetrator who has no legitimate access to the area. The fence and garden soil are more likely to provide evidence of a contact than the unlocked door.

Having ascertained the extent of the scene and taken steps to ensure any vulnerable evidence is not damaged or destroyed it is now appropriate to re-enter the scene and implement a recovery strategy. This makes certain that all potential evidence is considered and nothing is overlooked.

3.8 Planning evidence recovery

As with the assessment process, planning how the evidence is recorded and then recovered differs between volume and major crime scenes. Volume crime cases need hardly any planning, other than to simply carry out the required methods of evidence recovery that have been carried out hundreds of time before at very similar scenes. The normal process involves identifying which items of interest fall into the categories of 'scientific samples' and include footwear, fibres, glass and so on. Footwear impressions often go unnoticed to the untrained eye and are consequently very vulnerable to being trodden on and destroyed. For this reason the recovery of footwear evidence must always be considered as a priority. Some surfaces often make footwear impressions difficult to see without proper lighting techniques, rendering them open to destruction. The next consideration should be given to items that may provide DNA material such as blood, cigarette ends, chewing gum and so on. This is done to avoid DNA material being contaminated with fingerprint powder. Finally, but just as importantly, consideration is given to items that have surfaces suitable to retain fingerprints. These areas or items, fall into two different categories. Surfaces that are clean, dry, smooth and non-porous may be examined, for latent fingerprints, using any of the various types of powder. Other surfaces that are wet or porous will reveal fingerprint impressions better by using any of the various chemical treatments (full details of fingerprint development methods may be found in Chapter 5). Placing the different types of evidence in this order is not a hard and fast rule and may be changed, especially where adverse weather conditions are likely to cause damage. However, it has been recognized that if evidential items are taken in this sequence, all evidence types may be recovered without any adverse effect on the others. Occasionally more than one evidence type may be present in one place or on one item. A good example of this is where the offender, in breaking glass to gain entry to premises receives a cut to the hand so producing blood. A shard of glass removed from the window reveals a fingerprint that has been made in blood. In such instances equal importance should be placed both on the fingerprint and the blood for DNA. The correct recovery of all evidence must be undertaken and is described later.

Planning evidence recovery at major crime scenes will involve making exactly the same considerations but on a much larger scale and with the help and assistance from other specialists and experts. Major crime investigations have the advantage that they are conducted, from an early stage, by a team of officers directed by an experienced SIO who is given help and advice from a CSM and Forensic Scientists. This is in an effort to ensure that all forensic avenues are fully explored and exploited.

When considering this process, remember the old adage 'Failing to plan is planning to fail'.

3.9 Record the evidence

Making clear and concise records of evidential material can be as important as the evidence itself. Detailed records have three main purposes. Firstly, such records are used by SOCO when compiling factual statements of evidence. In most cases this will be some considerable time after the event and without contemporaneous scene notes, mistakes or omissions will be inevitable. Secondly, other members of the enquiry team can, in the absence of the author, use and act upon comprehensively maintained records without fear of misunderstanding or misinterpretation. This can be important if issues regarding the possible contamination of evidence are raised. Thirdly, and arguably the most important, accurately maintained records of the scene and evidential items recovered there serve to prove the *integrity* and *continuity* of each item (these terms are explained later in this chapter). Without such proof the court may not accept the evidence and this could lead to the case being dismissed.

There are a number of accepted methods that may be used to record a crime scene. Again there are slight differences between recording major and volume crime scenes. The various methods are listed below.

3.9.1 Video recording

This task is normally only carried out at major crime scenes. Once the scene has been identified and secured making a video recording of it becomes a priority. The main purpose of the video is to enable every member of the investigation team to see and appreciate the dynamics of the scene without having to enter the cordoned area. The video should give a general overview only. Suggesting that a particular item has been used for a specific purpose should be avoided at this early stage of the enquiry. Volume crime scenes are very rarely recorded by this medium except for practice purposes. The methods used to record a scene with a video camera can be found in Chapter 4.

3.9.2 Photography

At major crime investigations, immediately following the video recording, still photographs will be taken, again to record the scene. Photography at any scene is ongoing and items of evidential interest that are revealed, as the scene examination progresses, will be photographed before being recovered. This process will continue until every piece of potential evidence has been identified and recovered. If the crime scene involves a death, then during the subsequent post mortem examination photographs will be taken at the direction of the pathologist. The final product will be an album of photographs that will provide a visual aid to anyone having an interest in the investigation but who are unable to visit the actual scene. That will include most of the investigation team, solicitors employed by the Crown Prosecution Service (CPS), the defence team of solicitors and the judge and jury at any subsequent trial. The importance of accurately and comprehensively recording a scene photographically can be vital to the enquiry. However photographs alone do not depict a scene in its true perspective. For that reason an album of photographs should be accompanied by an index explaining the content, relevance and relationship of each photograph to the scene and, where necessary, a plan to allow the viewer to orientate the images.

Volume crime scenes do not require such comprehensive photographic records to be made. Unless a police officer makes a specific request, it is normally left to the discretion of the SOCO whether photographs will assist the case. This discretion comes from experience. Chapter 4 explains Crime Scene Photography in greater detail.

3.9.3 Plans

Plans drawn at crime scenes fall into two categories:

1. Properly drawn architectural or area plans that are drawn to a correct scale.

2. Sketch plans that are rough and not to any scale.

Both, however, serve a useful purpose in their own right. Architectural plans are drawn by properly qualified surveyors and will normally only be required in serious cases. Rough sketch plans are made in the early stages of an enquiry. They are used to assist in briefing other officers and indicating the extent of search boundaries and the location of possible evidence. In volume crime the SOCO will draw a thumbnail sketch plan to record the location of fingerprints and other evidential items. An officer uses a sketch plan drawn for this purpose more as an aide memoire to assist in writing a statement, than it being used as evidence in its own right. Chapter 11 provides more information regarding sketch plans and the legal process.

3.9.4 Major crime scene logs

Major crime scene logs, as the title suggests, only require to be completed in the event of a crime being designated as a major incident. Once it has been established that a major crime has been committed a Crime Scene Manager (CSM) or Crime Scene Coordinator (CSC) will be appointed to assist and advise the Senior Investigating Officer (SIO) in matters relating to the scientific examination of the scene. The log is specific to that role. All briefings that take place and any decisions that are made relevant to the enquiry must be recorded in this document. The log will also record details of all other scenes examined during the enquiry and the officers tasked to make each examination. This record can help to ensure the main issue of 'contamination' does not arise from an officer being in contact with a scene and a suspect.

3.9.5 Crime scene examination records

Each and every crime scene examined by a SOCO must be fully documented on a Crime Scene Examination Report. A typical scene examination report is shown in Figure 3.1. This information can either be hand written or recorded onto a computer database. Whichever system is used, however, the record must include:

- Classification of the offence or incident with the time and date it was committed.
- A crime or similar number that is specific to the offence.
- Time and date of the examination and details of the examiner(s).
- Address or location of the scene.
- In vehicle crime full details of the motor vehicle involved.
- Modus Operandi (MO or circumstances of the crime).
- Details regarding the elimination process.
- Details of fingerprints, photographs and other evidential items with reference numbers.
- Diagrams showing location of evidential items.[1]
- Current location of each item of evidence.[2]
- Results obtained from any submission of evidence.[2]

This is explained in more detail below.

3.9.6 Classification of the offence or incident

When an offence is reported, it will initially be recorded and classified from the information provided by the complainant. Thus, if a person reports that they have had property stolen it will be recorded, for classification purposes, as *theft*. Similarly, if a person reports that their premises have been forcibly entered it will be classified as an offence of *burglary* and so on. A relevant list of general crime classifications with Acts of Parliament and sections can be found in Chapter 1). However, what is reported is not always a criminal offence. For example the report of a suspicious

---

[1] This can only be recorded on hand written systems.
[2] This can only be recorded on computer-generated records.

CRIME SCENE EXAMINATION FORM

Offence/Incident	Time:	Date:	Crime No.
Examination commenced	Time:	Date:	Incident Log No.

Address/Location/Vehicle:

	Examined by:

Motor vehicle stolen from: **Recovered at:**

MO

Number of elimination fingerprints attached ☐   Elimination completed ☐   Forms returned ☐   Officer eliminating ☐

Reference Nos.	Location of Fingerprints

Reference Nos.	Photographs Taken Yes ☐ No ☐

Reference Nos.	Other Trace Material Recovered	Position

Reference Nos.	Item(s) Recovered for Chemical Treatment (Fingerprints)

Figure 3.1 Crime scene examination form.

death may, when investigated, prove to be a suicide. This, in itself, is not a criminal offence but because the scene still has to be examined by a SOCO it will be classified as an *incident*. It is necessary to record the time and date of the offence because this information is used when compiling the MO (see below).

3.9.7 Time and date examination undertaken and by whom

This field is self-explanatory but the information is extremely useful in providing comprehensive information that can be referred to later when reports or statements are required.

3.9.8 Crime or incident numbers

When a crime is reported to the police it is allocated a unique 'Crime Number'. The reason for this is threefold. It provides statistical information; it provides the complainant with proof that the crime has been recorded and it acts as an easy reference when adding information to the file.

Different police forces use slightly different numbering systems but they will all contain relevant information to identify the force, an area or division within the force, the consecutive number and the year. Thus a typical number might read: 48Q6/12345/09 this interprets to 48(force PNC No.)Q6 (area code)/12345(consecutive number)/09(year).

3.9.10 Details of motor vehicles

When the crime scene happens to involve a motor vehicle then full details including make, type, colour and vehicle identification numbers (VIN) should be recorded. In addition to this, and for the same reasons as shown in the above paragraph, the address or location that the examination is carried out should also be included.

3.9.11 Modus operandi

The modus operandi, commonly referred to in its abbreviated form as MO, is used to describe the method used by the offender to carry out the criminal act. Again, this information should be as detailed as possible so that intelligence analysts can use it to link series of crimes. It is a fact that once an individual finds a successful way to commit a particular crime, they will continue with that same method for some time, usually until their criminal activity is disrupted following arrest.

The information contained in an MO needs to be factual and to the point. They can be recorded in essay form or more often, with computerized systems, shown as entries against a prescribed list of common methods. Further information describing how to compose a meaningful MO can be found in Chapter 11.

3.10 The elimination process

During the examination of a crime scene, although concentrating on areas where it is known or believed that the offenders have been in contact, it is inevitable that, on occasions, fingerprints and DNA will be recovered that actually belong to someone who has visited the scene legitimately and is totally innocent of the crime. It is therefore an important task of the scene investigator to ascertain the likelihood of this. If it is likely then the relevant samples must be taken so that the elimination process can be undertaken. If this is not done the evidence will be searched on a computer system without any hope of a match being made to identify the actual offender, thus wasting valuable time and resources.

3.11 Details of evidence recovered

Every item of evidence recovered must be listed on the scene examination report. This record forms part of the evidence chain and helps in any issues that may arise regarding 'integrity' and 'continuity'. The evidence types fall into four categories and, as previously described, will generally be recovered in a particular order. Although used more for the purposes of scene recording images captured on videotape, photographic film and compact disc are all considered as evidential items in their own right and will be recorded as such. Because recording the scene is the first task at a crime scene then the photographic evidence comes first in chronological terms. Then items recovered for scientific examination will be recorded next, followed by material taken for later chemical or technical fingerprint examination. Then last, but by no means least, will be fingerprints developed with powder and recovered from the scene during the examination. It can be seen from the example crime scene examination form that the four different types of evidence are intentionally segregated.

Each item is given its own reference number. This comprises of the initials of the person who first identifies or deals with the item as potential evidence, followed by a consecutive number. Therefore, if the crime scene examiner is named John SMITH and the first task undertaken is to record the scene by taking a series of photographs this will be recorded as follows:

Ref. no.	Photographs taken
JS/1	Master copy of CD recording the scene of burglary at 12, High Street, Anytown.

3.11.1 Diagrams showing the location of evidential items

Rough or thumbnail diagrams and sketches are made by SOCO mainly as an aide memoire. However, like any other notation or record made and kept in relation to a specific crime, its existence may be required to be disclosed to the legal process and it can, therefore, become an exhibit in its own right. This means that it has to conform to all the rules of evidence. Even if the crime scene examination report is computer-generated paper diagrams may still be made.

3.11.2 Current location of evidential items

Knowing the location of an individual evidential item at any particular time is important when considering issues of integrity and continuity. The various agencies that receive and deal with evidence for the court process have always maintained paper records to show the location and movement of any item in its care. This has been made extremely easy by using computerized systems that involve the use of bar codes and scanners. Now, at any given time, items can be tracked making it easier to maintain and prove their continuity.

3.11.3 Results of submissions

Obviously, once an item of evidence has been submitted to an agency for an examination to be carried out all officers involved in the investigation will be keen to know and understand the results. This information, if urgent, can be relayed to interested parties verbally. A report or statement will be compiled later to confirm the findings. Results are rarely acted upon until they are in written form. This is to try and avoid mistakes being made during the arrest and search procedures. Computer systems have greatly helped to speed up the process by allowing reports to be forwarded electronically if required.

3.12 Integrity, continuity and contamination

In the preceding text several references have been made regarding the importance placed on maintaining and proving the *integrity and continuity* of all evidential items and ensuring the evidence does not become *contaminated*. Without these safeguards being in place the evidence in question may not be accepted by a court.

The term *integrity* may be defined as follows:

> Integrity proves the honesty and accountability of an exhibit. It shows that an
> evidential item has been dealt with correctly and demonstrates that no
> interference, addition or loss of material could have either deliberately or
> accidentally taken place.

The term *continuity* may be defined as follows:

> The continuity of an item commences from the moment it is recognized as
> being potential evidence. From then on its location and movement must be
> accountable and documented until it is presented before court and until its
> disposal is authorized.

Within every operational department of the police service procedures have
been implemented that are intended to ensure that evidence handling is accurately recorded. The procedures involve the completion of various documents,
registers and log books. Some are handwritten and others are computer generated. Whichever the case the purpose is the same, to prove to a court that the
evidence adduced before it has been properly dealt with and may be relied upon
when decisions are made regarding the guilt or otherwise of an accused person.
Once identified as potential evidence an exhibit label must accompany each
exhibit. This single document contains the reference number, full details of the
item itself, when and where it was found and by whom it was found. It also
records reference numbers that relate to other relevant documentation, such as
property registers and so on. The exhibit label is then signed and dated by the
finder. Subsequently every other person who handles the evidence will also sign
and date the label. Thus the evidence chain or continuity of the item is
maintained. Further information explaining the content of an exhibit label in
detail is given in Chapter 11.

3.12.1 Contamination of evidence

Contamination of scientific evidence is very real and can have serious consequences
on criminal proceedings. Advances in technology mean that even the most minus-
cule piece of scientific evidence may be located and identified. This increases the
possibility and suggestion that the evidence has somehow been contaminated and
therefore cannot be trusted or relied upon. It is, therefore, extremely important to
be able to prove that the issue of contamination has been considered and does not,
in fact, exist.

Contamination can occur for any of the following reasons:

- secondary transfer of material;
- inappropriate practices when dealing with evidential items;
- incorrect or poor packaging of evidential items.

3.12.2 Secondary transfer of material

There are several ways that this could occur. The most likely circumstance is when a police officer attends a crime scene as the FOA (see Chapter 2). If you consider the implications of Locard's Theory, there is a possibility that certain types of contact traces may adhere to the officer's clothing. Under normal circumstances that will not cause a problem unless that same officer, for operational reasons, then becomes involved in the arrest of a person suspected of being responsible for committing the crime. It could then be argued that any trace material recovered from the clothing of the suspect may have been inadvertently transferred to them from the clothing of the police officer. Another scenario, where this transfer could take place, is where a person under arrest is conveyed to the police station in the same vehicle that has transported the complainant in the crime. Any trace material may have been transferred from the complainant to the seat of the car and then onto the clothing of the suspect. In either of these situations the problem can be resolved. Such situations will require the scene examiner to declare the situation to the forensic scientist and request that, in addition to the suspect's clothing being examined for trace material, it is recorded how the material was distributed on the suspect's clothing. This information, as described previously in this chapter when explaining control and questioned samples, will add strength to the prosecution case.

3.12.3 Inappropriate practices

When dealing with contact trace evidence certain practices have been introduced to the process of recovery, packaging and storage of scientific material that will, if complied with, totally eliminate the chances of contamination. These practices need to be constantly reviewed, especially during major investigations. It will be seen from the preceding paragraph that, where operationally possible, any officer attending the crime scene should not become involved in the arrest of a person suspected of committing that crime. All officers, including pathologists and scientists, and so on, attending any scene that has been designated a major crime are equipped with disposable coveralls (including hair covers), gloves, overshoes and masks. It is the responsibility of the Crime Scene Manager to ensure that this protective clothing is worn at all times until the possibility of contamination has been totally alleviated (this equipment also provides a barrier for Health and Safety purposes and so may still be worn after the contamination issues have been dealt with).

During the investigation, of any category of crime, there will always be instances where evidential items are seized from both the scene and suspect and taken to the same police station. For operational reasons this situation is generally unavoidable. Therefore, items recovered at the scene should always be packaged at the scene. Items seized from suspected persons, under terms of the Police and Criminal Evidence Act, should either be packaged at the time and place of arrest, or as soon as possible after the individual arrives at a police station. Any variation to this procedure must be carefully monitored. Under no circumstances whatsoever should items from the scene come into contact with items from a suspect, even when packaged, until all relevant scientific tests have been carried out and the issues of contamination have, again, been totally alleviated.

3.12.4 Incorrect packaging

Because of the complexities that can be involved when a myriad of evidential items may be left at a variety of different crime scenes, the whole subject of packaging and storage can be quite complicated. It is; therefore, appropriate to explain in simple terms the more basic principles that form the foundation of evidence recovery, packaging and storage.

It appears that whole ranges of different containers and packaging materials are available to police officers and SOCO. However, when rationalized, they fall under only three main headings and the variation actually relates to the different sizes of the containers.

The three main types of packaging material are:

- paper (including cardboard boxes);
- polythene (including rigid polythene); and
- nylon bags.

When deciding what type of packaging is most appropriate under a particular circumstance, quite a number of considerations need to be made. Listed below are the main examples.

1. Is there a health hazard involved?
2. Will the contents leak or filter through the material?
3. Will the contents decompose inside the container?
4. Is the packaging material suitable to freeze?

5. Will the item or sample puncture the container?

6. Does the item inside the container need to be seen by witnesses?

The above considerations will now be examined individually in more detail.

3.12.5 Health hazards

In every case involving the spillage or distribution of any bodily fluid there is always a potential health hazard. That hazard can be increased if the wrong packaging is used for storage. There are occasions, however, where the wrong packaging is used intentionally to temporarily alleviate the hazard. This anomaly will be explained later. However, in all occasions, adhesive tape bearing the logo health hazard must be attached to the outer packaging.

3.12.6 Leakages and filtration

Paper or cardboard packaging will obviously allow the liquid from wet or even damp items to leak. This greatly increases the possibility of contamination between items especially if they are stored closely together. For this reason wet or damp items must be air-dried before this type of packaging material can be considered as suitable. Some samples are taken, especially at crime scenes where arson is suspected, to establish the presence of hydrocarbons. Using the wrong packaging for these samples will allow the hydrocarbons (from petrol) to filter through. This again provides a high risk of contamination.

3.12.7 Decomposition

Bodily fluids, once they have left the body, very quickly begin to decompose. DNA recovery, at any crime scene where bodily fluids are involved, is normally a priority. If the wrong packaging material is used or storage is inappropriate decomposition will continue, so degrading or destroying any DNA and increasing the health hazard greatly. The degradation can be stopped by either air drying or freezing the item.

3.12.8 Freezing

As described above, if the circumstances at the crime scene are such that a sample is required to be examined for the presence of DNA, one option is that it can be stored in a frozen state. This then will determine the need to use a polythene container. Ordinary paper or cardboard containers are obviously not suitable for freezing. In a frozen state they could fracture, or when thawed they might disintegrate. Either situation would increase the possibility of contaminating other items stored nearby.

3.12.9 Puncturing the container

Sharp instruments, such as knives and syringes, are regularly recovered during crime scene examinations. If such an item caused the packaging to become punctured, not only will contamination become an issue, everyone's health and safety will be at risk. Such instruments must be packaged in suitable rigid containers. Deciding whether a cardboard box or a rigid clear plastic container is used will depend upon the type of contact trace evidence that could be found during any subsequent examination. Considerations as described above for DNA examination will therefore also apply to sharp instruments.

3.12.10 Items to be seen by a witness

Once an item of evidence has been sealed inside any packaging material, to avoid the possibility of contamination, it is advisable that it remains so preserved until the relevant examination takes place. However, as part of the enquiry it may be extremely important that a witness be shown the item to identify it. This could be necessary when, for instance, the description of clothing being worn by an offender, is a key element to the investigation. In such circumstances, if destruction of contact trace evidence is not an issue, then a transparent packaging material may be preferred to one that is opaque. A better alternative would be to take photographs of the item before packaging and make them available to all interested parties under the rules of disclosure of evidence. This allows an identification to be made without the other inherent problems.

3.13 Packaging materials

Having outlined the issues that can be alleviated by using appropriate packaging the materials themselves now need to be explored.

3.13.1 Paper and cardboard boxes

Paper bags are used mainly to store items of clothing, shoes and bedding and so on that have been *air-dried* to stop the degradation of body fluids. Paper allows air to circulate while, if properly sealed, preventing any possibility of contamination.

Cardboard boxes are used to contain such items as firearms and sharp instruments. Again, if body fluids are to be considered a box will allow the circulation of air. The disadvantage that these materials are opaque is overcome by introducing polythene viewing strips in the bags and clear vinyl windows in the boxes. Storage should be in a cool and dry environment.

3.13.2 Polythene bags and rigid containers

If an item, of any description, is dry and no body fluids are involved, and no other material is present that may decompose, then properly sealed and airtight polythene packaging and containers including knife tubes can be used. Storage should be in a cool and dry environment.

Where the item is wet from body fluids and a DNA examination is required then a properly sealed container should be used and stored frozen with a health hazard warning (normally a tape).

3.13.3 Polythene bags followed by paper bags

Because of their size, very large or bulky items that are saturated with body fluids cannot, easily, be stored frozen. The fact that the item is saturated makes it inappropriate to use a paper container. Circumstances such as these require a compromise. There are two ways to deal with this situation. The item may be allowed to air dry in place at the scene and then packaged in a paper sack and sealed. Alternatively, the item can be temporarily sealed into a polythene bag for transportation to a cabinet made especially for the purpose of air-drying scientific exhibits. The original polythene packaging should also be included in the drying process. Once dry the item and original packaging can be sealed into a paper sack and stored in a cool dry environment. Either method overcomes both contamination and health and safety problems.

3.13.4 Nylon packaging

As mentioned previously, nylon packaging is specific to samples that have been taken to ascertain the presence of hydrocarbons. The evaporated gases from hydrocarbons will not permeate through properly sealed nylon bags. The bag should be large enough to allow plenty of space in the bag. This allows any vapours emanating from the exhibit to collect and be drawn off for analysis. Nylon is, by its nature, prone to being easily punctured. Debris from fire scenes can be made up of predominantly sharp material. To prevent a situation where the packaging splits, the item should be double bagged with a swan neck seal and then placed into a rigid outer container. The item should then be stored in a cool dry environment.

Obviously the variety of items that may be found and recovered from crime scenes is endless (a chart listing some of the exhibits that are more frequently recovered from crime scenes can be found in Table 3.1).

Table 3.1   Exhibit Packaging and Storage. The chart below shows a small selection of items that are commonly recovered from crime scenes or suspected persons.

Exhibit	Packaging Material	Storage
Dry clothing and bedding, etc.	Brown paper bag	Cool, dry environment
Wet or damp clothing and bedding, etc.	Initially in polythene bag until it can be dried then in brown paper.	If item cannot be dried it should be stored frozen. If item can be dried it should be packaged in brown paper and stored as above. NB The original packaging should also be included with item.
Footwear.	Brown paper bags.	Each item of footwear should be packaged separately and stored in a cool dry environment.
Fibre tape lifts.	Each strip of adhesive to be sealed down onto a clear vinyl sheet, marked with the location from where it came and placed into a polythene bag.	Dry environment.
Dry blood sample swabbed from a surface using distilled water.	Original plastic sleeve from swab and re-sealed. Sealed into polythene bag with control swabs.	Freeze.
Wet blood removed from surface with swab or pipette.	Swab dealt with as above. Pipette sealed into a polythene bag.	Freeze.
Cigarette ends	Rigid polythene container.	Freeze.
Saliva swabbed from a drinking vessel. 1st swab	Swabs returned to original sleeves and re-sealed. Sealed	Freeze.

moist with distilled water 2nd swab dry.	into polythene bag with control swab.	
Glass. Control sample from scene.	Strong, rigid cardboard box	Dry environment.
Tool or instrument marks. The whole item Cast of the mark.	1. Strong rigid container 2. Rigid container	Dry environment. NB. Scale photographs need to be included.
Tools or instruments	Protect blade or tip with polythene, then seal in a strong rigid container	Dry environment.
Material cut by tools	Any suitable container that will prevent damage to cut ends. Item should be packaged to prevent loss of any other material that is paint, fibres and so on adhering to it.	Dry environment. Action should be taken to prevent cut ends rusting or degrading.
Paint flakes	Flakes should be folded into a piece of clean paper and then placed into a polythene bag. The paper wrap will prevent any problems caused by static electricity when the bag is opened.	Dry environment. NB. When scraping an area for a paint sample a new, clean blade should be used and submitted with the paint. Packaging to be suitably marked with 'Cut Hazard' warning.
Fire debris to ascertain the presence of accelerant that may be either: Hydrocarbon based Alcohol based	1. Nylon bag. Using 'swan neck' method to seal. Ensure large airspace above sample. 2. Method as above then place into polythene bag and seal. If there is a danger that the packaging could be punctured by sharp debris, first place debris into a strong cardboard box before securing in nylon and polythene.	Fire debris should be submitted for analysis as soon as possible. To make a 'swan neck' seal twist the neck of the bag tightly and then fold over. Secure the resulting swan neck with numbered security tag or strong adhesive tape. Control samples of packaging materials should be submitted with exhibits.

3.13.5 Poor packaging

Even if the correct packaging material is used there is still a danger that if it is left open or poorly sealed contamination will still be a concern. The term 'properly sealed' has been used in the above text when describing the various packaging

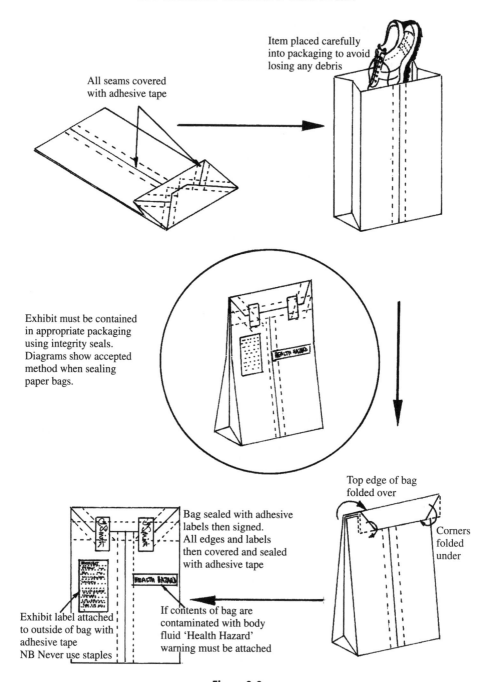

All seams covered with adhesive tape

Item placed carefully into packaging to avoid losing any debris

Exhibit must be contained in appropriate packaging using integrity seals. Diagrams show accepted method when sealing paper bags.

Top edge of bag folded over

Corners folded under

Bag sealed with adhesive labels then signed. All edges and labels then covered and sealed with adhesive tape

Exhibit label attached to outside of bag with adhesive tape NB Never use staples

If contents of bag are contaminated with body fluid 'Health Hazard' warning must be attached

Figure 3.2

materials. Properly sealed means that when a packaged item arrives at a laboratory the scientist will be able to endorse that:

- The packaging material is suitable for its purpose (as described above).
- The packaging has been integrity sealed.
- The continuity of the evidence is intact.

Integrity or tamper evident seals

Whatever type of packaging has been used, it must be demonstrated that since the item was sealed in the container it could not have become contaminated, nor could the contents have contaminated anything else. Also it must be shown that nothing has happened that may jeopardize its integrity. Forensic scientists aid this process by recording the fact that upon receipt of the item the packaging itself was undamaged, all seals were unbroken and intact and that in their opinion contamination is unlikely to be a factor.

Some packaging can be purchased with self-adhesive integrity or tamper evident seals. Other packaging material requires the use of signatures with adhesive labels and tape to form 'do it yourself' tamper evident seals (a diagram showing how to form a tamper evident seal can be seen in Figure 3.2).

3.13.6 Proving the continuity

Similarly to inspecting the integrity of the packaging the forensic scientist will check any relevant documentation. This will include exhibit labels that are the mainstay in proving the *continuity* of an item. The scientist, like anyone else handling the evidence, is also required to prove their involvement by signing and dating the continuity documents.

3.14 Conclusion

That then concludes the whole role and responsibility of the scenes of crime officer. From being tasked to attend the crime scene up to delivery of the evidence to a forensic scientist and that is where, generally, SOCO involvement stops.

It is worth reiterating here that the whole process is designed and intended that any fingerprint or scientific evidence presented before a criminal court will be accepted and that there can be no doubt that a conviction obtained on the basis of it is sound. It can be appreciated that this is a heavy burden of responsibility.

Self-assessed questions

3.1   What do the acronyms CSE, SOCO, CSM, CSC, SIO and CRFP represent?

3.2   What may be classed as 'key evidence' areas?

3.3   What are 'key evidence' types?

3.4   What is the meaning of the word 'Forensic'?

3.5   What three criteria affect the transference of material at crime scenes?

3.6   What are the four general categories of trace material?

3.7   What important criteria should be included during the initial assessment of a potential crime scene?

3.8   How may 'Integrity' be defined?

3.9   When does the continuity of an item of potential evidence begin?

3.10 How may the contamination of an item occur?

4
Police Photography

Chris Crowe

4.1 Introduction

The theory and practice of photography is a vast and complex subject. Photography is both an art and technical form and the aim of most professional photographers is to produce an image that is aesthetic and pleasing to the viewer. To achieve this the photographer will employ many different techniques needed to adjust the camera, its lenses, lighting and subject matter. Police photographers are no different. Although they have little control of the subject matter, they too must understand the mechanics of their craft in order to produce properly exposed images that are in sharp focus.

A good background text for students embarking on a career as a SOCO is Langford's *Starting Photography* by Michael Langford and Philip Andrews.

This chapter is aimed at students who already appreciate the principles of photography, and seeks to provide them with additional practical advice and guidance. This information will assist those who are required to make a photographic recording of crime scenes and other incidents being investigated by the police. Technical information is only provided where it is seen as necessary to ensure that evidence is properly recorded, as this is particularly relevant to police photography. Those students who wish to study the whole topic of photography should read publications that specialize in the subject and attend one of the many recognized courses conducted by Further Education Colleges or Higher Education Institutions.

Crime Scene Management: Scene Specific Methods   Edited by Raul Sutton and Keith Trueman
© 2009 John Wiley & Sons, Ltd

When carrying out an examination of a crime scene it is essential that a photographic record is made before exhibits are moved or disturbed. Courts will often ask where, for example, the knife was found and where it was in relation to the scene. Recording the exact location of fingerprints or footwear marks may be vital to prove the suspect's involvement in the offence. Detailed photographs taken at the scene will provide the Senior Investigation Officer (SIO) with a visual record that can be referred to without the need to revisit the crime scene. Photographs can help juries to understand the nature and severity of the offence and provide clarity in complex cases. Some evidence can only be recovered by photography; for example fingerprints or footwear marks deposited in blood.

In the police service recording a crime scene photographically is mostly carried out by Scenes of Crime Officers (SOCO). The duties and responsibilities of a SOCO are fully explained in Chapter 3. The principal that:

> Photography or light drawing is essentially a combination of technique and visual observation.

Langford (1997) applies accurately to the crime scene photographer. SOCOs are trained observers so, with the added knowledge of photography and lighting techniques, they make excellent crime scene photographers. During the Initial Crime Scene Investigation Course at the NPIA Training Centre in Durham the SOCO receives three weeks' training in photography. This provides officers with the basic skills to enable them to capture good quality images in most situations.

4.2 General guidelines

Health and safety is an important issue as every crime scene poses potential hazards for the SOCO. In an effort to address and deal with hazards, all known and recognized risks have been assessed by trained staff. These are compiled into one 'Generic Health Assessment' document that is available to the SOCO for reference purposes. However, this does not alleviate the requirement for a dynamic risk assessment to be carried out at each scene to identify and manage hazards not covered by the generic assessment.

Crime scenes are variable by their nature and SOCO need to be appraised of the circumstances surrounding the case before embarking on photography. So before taking a camera out of its case officers must be briefed about the incident and look at the scene to make an assessment as to what is required.

The purpose of taking photographs is to make a visual record that describes the event in pictures. Wide-angle views of the general scene are most useful and provide the SIO and the court with an overview, enabling them to become familiar with the scene. Close-up photographs of specific evidence and exhibits must also be taken. This process will be ongoing for the whole time during the scene examination. Wherever possible, the photographs should be taken in a logical order so that when they are printed and presented in an album the viewer is visually taken through the scene in the order in which the events happened. It is important to remember that a poorly taken photograph will give little information and could compromise any investigation by calling into question the evidence gathering process. Conversely good photographs will enhance the process. It is therefore important to concentrate on quality not quantity. An album containing a small number of photographs that fully illustrate the scene and includes evidential items, all properly described with an index, are far more use than dozens of photographs randomly taken.

4.3 Equipment

With improvements in quality and reductions in price the Digital Single Lens Reflex (D-SLR) camera is the choice of many police forces. Typically SOCO will have the following equipment available to them for use at the crime scene:

- D-SLR camera body;
- 18–35 mm zoom lens (35 mm equivalent is 27–52 mm, see below);
- 60 mm macro lens (35 mm is equivalent 90 mm);
- flash gun;
- tripod;
- remote release cable;
- scales marked in millimetres;
- spare batteries.

Photographs taken for police purposes should be correctly exposed and in sharp focus. The D-SLR is a good choice as these cameras incorporate accurate through the lens metering systems and a choice of manual or auto focus lenses. The sensor in the D-SLR camera is generally smaller than a 35 mm frame although some high end cameras are produced with full frame sensors. Sensors in D-SLR cameras are approximately 24×16 mm which when measured diagonally across the frame is about 1/3 smaller than a 35 mm frame. Lenses made for 35 mm cameras can in many cases be used on a D-SLR of the same make, but because the sensor is smaller the image will be cropped. Manufacturers now produce lenses specifically for digital cameras and typically a standard zoom lens supplied as part of a digital camera kit will have a focal length of 18–35 mm which is equivalent to a 27–52 mm on a 35 mm camera. When comparing lens coverage on a 35 mm frame with a 24×16 mm D-SLR sensor, the focal length should be multiplied by 1.5 to take into account the cropping that occurs with the D-SLR.

Self-assessed questions

4.1   What types of photographs are best taken with a 60 mm macro lens?

4.4 Exposure

Exposure is the product of the intensity of image forming light reflecting from the subject and passing through the lens and the time this light is allowed to impinge on the film or sensor. Therefore the formulae for exposure can be expressed as:

$$E = I \times T$$

where E is the exposure, I the intensity of the light and T is time (shutter speed).

The intensity of light is controlled by changing the lens aperture (*f-number*) and the time controlled by the shutter speed. These factors determine the exposure for a given subject. Allowing too much light to pass through the lens or too long an exposure will produce an image that is too light with no detail in the high light intensity regions (over exposed). Allowing too little light to pass through the lens or too short an exposure will produce an image that appears too dark with no shadow detail, (underexposed). With very accurate metering systems on most D-SLR cameras the correct exposure is easy to determine.

Self-assessed questions

4.2   What will be the effect on an image that is overexposed?

4.4.1 Histogram

Setting the correct exposure is important when capturing images with a digital camera. An underexposed image will lack shadow detail and look dark whereas an overexposed image will loose detail in the highlights and the image will appear washed out. Detail lost due to overexposure cannot be recovered. The quality of the image can be checked on the camera monitor; however, it is difficult to make an assessment because variations in the ambient light can make it difficult to see the image clearly on the monitor.

The histogram shows the range of tones in the captured image as a graph. The horizontal axis shows 256 brightness levels, 0 (black) on the left to 255 (white) on the right. The vertical axis shows the number of pixels for each brightness value. On most cameras the histogram is superimposed over the image. A low contrast image will produce a histogram with the tones concentrated in the middle of the graph while a high contrast image may produce a graph with the deep shadows and highlights clipped. Try and obtain an image where the histogram shows a small gap between the brightest highlight and the edge of the graph to ensure that the highlight detail is captured. Over exposure must be avoided because, as explained above, highlights lost cannot be recovered, however, images that are slightly underexposed can be corrected. Checking the histogram as well as looking at the image on the monitor is the best way to achieve the correct exposure. The histogram can be checked whatever the ambient light conditions (Figure 4.1).

Self-assessed questions

4.3 How many brightness levels are shown on the histogram?

(a)

Figure 4.1 Photographic image and exposure histogram (a) correct exposure (b) underexposure. Note that the histogram has moved to the left (c) overexposure note that the histogram has moved to the right.

(b)

Figure 4.1 (Continued)

4.4.2 Lens aperture (F-STOP)

The camera lens transmits light reflected from the subject and forms an image on the sensor or film. The lens has an iris diaphragm which can be adjusted to allow more or less light through the lens. These adjustments are called f-stops or apertures. In effect they control the intensity or brightness of the light passing through the lens. Closing the lens aperture by one stop reduces the exposure by half while opening the lens aperture by one stop doubles the expose. The values of the apertures are engraved on most lenses and where the camera has an LCD display the value is also displayed there. Typically aperture values are f-2.8, f-3.5, f-4, f-5.6, f-8, f-11, f-16 and f-22. Depending on the type and quality of the lens some will have a larger or smaller range of apertures or f-stops. The higher numbers are small apertures that reduce the intensity of the light passing through the lens and the

(c)

Figure 4.1 (Continued)

small numbers indicate a larger aperture that allows more light through the lens. The value of the f-stop is the same on every lens because it is a measure of the brightness or intensity of the light passing through the lens at a given *f- stop*, not the actual size of the aperture and is therefore referred to as the relative aperture.

Self-assessed questions

4.4   If the correct exposure as indicated by the camera meter is 1/125th second at f-8 what will be the effect on the exposure if the aperture is changed to f-11?

4.4.3 Shutter

The shutter in a D-SLR camera sits in front of the sensor and usually comprises of a series of thin metal blades that open vertically across the focal plane. The shutter is usually in two parts with one set of blades opening to reveal the sensor and another set of blades that follows to close the shutter and terminate the exposure.

The shutter dial on the camera is rotated to select the shutter speed required. D-SLR cameras will have a range of shutter speeds from about 30 seconds to 1/8000th of a second and a position marked Brief. When Brief is selected the shutter will stay open for as long as the shutter release is pressed. The shutter works in harmony with the apertures by doubling and halving the exposure. For example if the shutter dial is moved from 1/125th second to 1/250th second the exposure is halved and if moved to 1/60th second the exposure is doubled. All D-SLR cameras will have electronically controlled apertures and shutter speeds providing intermediate setting to give much greater exposure control.

Self-assessed questions

4.5 If the correct exposure as indicated by the camera meter is 1/125th second at f-8 what will be the effect on the exposure if the shutter speed is changed to 1/250th second?

4.4.4 Sensor sensitivity

Sensors in digital cameras, like film, have sensitivity to light which, like film, is measured using ISO[1] speed ratings. Speed ratings for digital camera sensors are referred to as ISO equivalent because manufacturers have adopted the film speed rating for the sensors used in their cameras. Most sensors are rated at 100 or 200 ISO, higher speeds are achieved by amplifying the signal reaching the sensor.

  ISO is a measure of the sensitivity of film to light with low speed colour films rated at 100 ISO and high speed films rated at 400 ISO and above. When using high speed films the quality is reduced due to the large grain structure of the film. When using a D-SLR camera, the ISO equivalent can be raised to as much as 3200, but this increase in sensitivity will produce visible noise on the image. The best quality images will be obtained at ISO 100 or 200; however acceptable images can be obtained using higher ISO ratings for low light scenes. Not all sensors are the same and some perform better at higher ISO ratings than others. It is best practice to shoot test photographs at different ISO settings to determine the point where an increase in ISO produces unacceptable noise levels.

Self-assessed questions

4.6 High ISO settings may be chosen when shooting in low light conditions. What affect will this have on the image quality?

---

[1] ISO stands for the International Organization for Standardization. This organization ensures that there is international comparability in technical products.

4.4.5 Reciprocity

Changing the aperture by one f-stop, or doubling or halving the shutter speed, or doubling or halving the ISO value all have the same effect on the exposure. This reciprocal arrangement with the shutter speeds and apertures halving and doubling the exposure by opening and closing the aperture by one stop and or, by doubling or halving the shutter speeds is at the heart of setting the correct exposure. When using film this reciprocal arrangement breaks down with exposures longer than one second due to the way film emulsion reacts to long exposure times. Using shutter speeds of one second or longer may not produce a correctly exposed image because of this failure of reciprocity. At an indicated shutter speed of one second the difference may not be noticed but longer exposures times will dramatically increase the error. When using film in low light conditions where long exposure times are required the only way to ensure the correct exposure is to take several photographs using different shutter speeds to compensate for this failure in reciprocity. This phenomenon known as reciprocity failure does not occur with digital cameras making them the preferred camera for low light or night photography. Digital sensors do not suffer from this and therefore it is relatively easy to obtain the correct exposure using the TTL (through the lens) meters in the D-SLR.

Self-assessed questions

4.7   What is reciprocity?

4.8   When using film when will reciprocity start to fail?

4.5 Image quality/size

D-SLR cameras have a choice of quality and size settings. There are two image quality options available on most cameras: RAW and JPEG. A third type, TIFF, is an option on some cameras.

RAW files, as the name implies, is image data stored directly to the memory card. These files are large, specific to each camera manufacturer, and require specialist software to enable them to be viewed on a computer. Many professional photographers choose to capture images in RAW because they are able to apply settings such as white balance post image capture and prefer to undertake image processing themselves.

JPEG (Joint Photographic Experts Group) images are a universal file format used on all digital cameras and can be viewed on most computers without using special software. JPEG images are compressed at a choice of three quality settings: fine, compression ratio (1 : 4), Normal (1 : 8) and basic (1 : 16). The compression process creates artefacts that can be seen as blocks of pixels at high compression settings and some detail is discarded. More images can be stored on the memory card at the basic setting but this will greatly affect the quality of the image. For all police photography JPEG fine should be chosen.

TIFF (Tagged Image File Format) is a universal graphics file format that can be viewed on most computers. TIFF files are compressed without loss of data but the files are large. The TIFF file format is generally available only on high end professional D-SLR cameras. Where available, images of fingerprints should be captured using TIFF to ensure that there is no loss of fine detail.

The image size is measured in pixels and most D-SLR cameras offer the choice of three sizes: large, medium and small. For maximum quality large image size is selected for all police photography tasks.

Self-assessed questions

4.9   What does JPEG stand for?

4.10   When taking photographs for police purposes what JPEG quality setting is recommended?

4.6 Depth of field

When taking photographs for evidential purposes it is important to produce images that are in sharp focus to show as much detail as possible. An image that is not sharp or is blurred does not reflect well on the ability and professionalism of the photographer, nor does it look good in court where clear well presented pictures are expected. To ensure that the image is in sharp focus the SOCO must have a basic understanding of depth of field and the factors that control depth of field.

Light reflecting from the subject passes through the lens and forms an image on the sensor. Most D-SLR cameras have lenses that can be focused manually or automatically. Before making an exposure on the D-SLR camera the lens should be focused to ensure that the subject appears sharp in the viewfinder. Images are formed by focusing points of light reflected from the subject onto the sensor. Points of light reflecting from those parts of the subject that are closer or further away from the plane of focus will appear as out of focus discs of light. A camera lens can only be focused on one point but when the picture is taken parts of the subject in front and behind the point of focus will appear to be in sharp focus. The reason for this is that the discs of light are so small that the eye cannot distinguish between them and the points of light that are in sharp focus. When the eye is able to distinguish between the points of light that are in sharp focus from those that appear as discs the image formed by the discs of light will appear out of focus. The distance between the nearest and furthest points of sharp focus is known as *depth of field*. There are a number of factors that affect depth of field:

- The size of the lens aperture. A large aperture (small f-number) reduces depth of field. Small apertures (large f-number) increases depth of field.

- Wide angle lenses (short focal length) increase depth of field and telephoto lenses (long focal length) reduce depth of field.

- The distance from the subject to the camera. As the camera is moved closer to the subject the depth of field is reduced. Moving the camera further away increases depth of field.

- The size of the finished print affects depth of field because areas that are out of focus become more noticeable at large print sizes.

For general scene photography, including room scenes, focus about one-third into the scene for maximum depth of field. This is because depth of field extends further behind the subject than in front except when taking close-up photographs when the depth of field is about the same in front as it is behind the subject.

Depth of field can be used creatively to improve image quality for example when taking portrait photographs choosing a telephoto lens with a large aperture will produce an image that has a shallow depth of field. This can be used to deliberately create an out of focus background drawing the eyes of the viewer to the subject (Figure 4.2).

(a)   (b)

Figure 4.2 Depth of field at large and small apertures (a) captured at F32 (b) captured at F3.2.

Self-assessed questions

4.11   Define the term Depth of Field?

4.12   Explain how depth of field is affected when choosing a large aperture (small f number) and a small aperture (large f number).

4.13   Explain two of the other three factors that affect depth of field.

4.7 White balance

Colour temperature is the colour of the light source at a given temperature measured on the Kelvin scale. This scientific principle is derived at by heating a theoretical black body with radiant heat. The colour of the light emitted from this black body at a given temperature is referred to as the colour temperature. For example, artificial or incandescent light is produced at a temperature of about 3000 K and daylight at between 5000 and 8000 K. Whatever the colour temperature of the light source we see white as white because our brain adapts to the changes in colour temperature. When using a digital camera the colour temperature or white balance has to be set to match the colour temperature of the light source.

The white balance settings on D-SLR cameras range from about 2500 to 10 000 K with pre set values for known light sources and automatic which measures the colour temperature using a built in RGB sensor. The auto white balance setting works well with daylight and with the camera's built in flash but more accurate results are obtained by setting the white balance manually. Settings available on most D-SLR cameras are:

- A (Auto) 3500–8000 K

- incandescent 3000 K

- fluorescent 4200 K

- direct sunlight 5200 K

- flash 5400 K

- cloudy 6000 K

- shade 8000 K

- K (manually set Value) 2500–10 000.

When choosing one of the above settings except K (manually set value) most quality D-SLR cameras have a fine tune control that allows further adjustment to the white balance setting by increasing the value to make the image appear cooler (blue) or reducing the value to make the image appear warmer (reddish).

In addition to these settings most D-SLR cameras will have a setting that allows the photographer to pre set the white balance using a grey or white card. This is done by taking a photograph of the card under the light that will be used for the finished photograph. This is the most accurate way to achieve the correct white balance especially when shooting under mixed lighting conditions. Follow the instructions supplied with the camera to set the white balance this way.

There are some light sources where setting the correct white balance is impossible. One type that the SOCO will come across on a regular basis is Low Pressure Sodium Vapour streetlights. The light produced by these street lamps is yellow of a particular wavelength that will not produce a value for white balance. In these circumstances it is best to experiment with a few test shots to see what setting produces the best results. A setting of between 2500 and 3000 K is probably the best compromise.

Mixed lighting is another tricky area for the SOCO and once again this is likely to happen when taking photographs of scenes lit by street lamps and there are areas of the picture that are unlit that will require some additional lighting such as electronic flash. If the white balance is set to 2500–3000 K and flash is used to illuminate dark areas then the areas illuminated with the flash will be blue and look unnatural. The answer here is to put a gel filter over the flash head to change the colour temperature of the flash to match the white balance setting on the camera.

Self-assessed questions

4.14 How is white balance measured?

4.15 What is the approximate colour temperature of?
(1) Fluorescent light.
(2) Direct sunlight.
(3) Electronic flash.

4.8 Image data

Information about the image captured such as the date, time and camera settings is stored on the memory card. This is very useful when reviewing images to confirm the settings used and is subject to disclosure rules. This means that the SOCO is required to make this information available to the court if required to do so. It is therefore very important that the date and time is set accurately on the camera and from time to time checked again for accuracy. It is also important to remember to change the time in the summer and the autumn when the clocks change.

Self-assessed questions

4.16   What settings in respect to image data should be checked by the SOCO
before using a D-SLR camera to capture images at crime scenes?

4.9 Flash photography

Much of the photography undertaken by the SOCO will involve using a flash gun.
Some D-SLR cameras have small pop up flash guns incorporated into the camera.
These have limited uses in crime scene photography due to their low power and
coverage. They are useful for close-up shots but a good quality powerful flash gun is
an essential tool for general scene and night photography.

Flash guns are attached to the camera using the camera hot shoe or by a bracket
and connected to the camera with a synchronizing lead plugged into a socket on the
camera body if one is fitted. Flashguns made by the camera manufacturer and by
some independents are dedicated to the camera. This means that information such
as *f* numbers, shutter speed, ISO, zoom lens position etc are automatically transmitted from the camera to the flash gun. The correct exposure is achieved by a TTL
sensor in the camera that controls the output of the flash. The camera and flash gun
will have an exposure compensation control to increase or decrease the flash output
to take into account the reflectivity of the subject. Non-dedicated flashguns can be
used on most D-SLR cameras but will have to be set manually. The flash gun will
have a sensor to control the output of the flash in a similar way to the TTL sensor.
Flashguns also have a separate button to allow the gun to be fired off the camera; this
is known as open flash. The duration of the flash is very short so it is important to
choose a shutter speed that synchronizes with the flash. Most D-SLR cameras
incorporate a focal plane shutter with speeds from 30 seconds to 1/8000th second
and brief. When set on brief the shutter will stay open while the shutter release is
pressed. The flash will synchronize with all speeds up to 1/250th but refer to the
camera manual for flash synchronization speeds as these can vary. When using a
dedicated flash the camera will normally prevent a shutter speed being selected that
does not synchronize with the flash.

Some lighting situations require the use of balanced flash to obtain even
exposures, for example when taking a photograph of a vehicle inside a garage or
when taking an interior photograph that includes a view of the outside. In these
situations it is necessary to balance the flash with the available light. To achieve a
correctly exposed image, set the camera shutter speed and aperture to the exposure
required for the ambient light making sure that the shutter speed selected is within
the range that will synchronize with the flash. Set the aperture on the flash gun to
the same as the aperture on the camera and after taking the picture check the

quality on the camera monitor or by the histogram. Be sure to use a tripod when the ambient light levels are low to avoid camera shake. This task is easier when using a dedicated flash gun as the aperture set on the camera is automatically set on the flash gun.

Fill-in flash is much the same as balanced flash except that the main exposure is obtained using available light and the flash is used to fill in the shadow areas. Normally the flash exposure is set to one or two stops less than the main exposure to give a natural look to the picture.

When using flash to photograph injuries to victims it is recommended to use a 60 mm lens. This lens will give the same angle of view as a 90 mm lens on a 35 mm SLR. This will enable the photographer to capture close detail without being too close to the subject. The flash will be more evenly spread, diffused, and the victim will feel more comfortable not having the camera lens so close to them.

Open flash is a technique used to photograph large scenes such as arson or vehicles at night where there is insufficient available light. The camera must be mounted on a sturdy tripod and the shutter set to brief. Set the camera to the required aperture and lock open the shutter with the cable release. Fire the flash as many times as necessary from different positions to evenly illuminate the area, then close the shutter taking care not to move the camera. The area that can be photographed is limited by the distance that the flash will operate. It is important to understand *Newton's Inverse Square Law* as it affects electronic flash to appreciate limitations of the electronic flash gun. The Inverse Square Law states that when a surface is illuminated by a point source of light, the intensity of illumination produced is inversely proportional to the square of the distance separating them. In simple terms this means that if the flash to subject distance is doubled the amount of light falling on the subject is reduced by a factor of four (Figure 4.3).

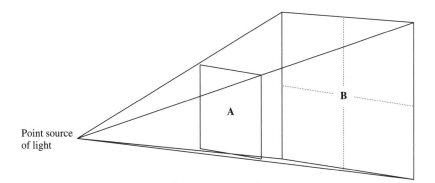

Figure 4.3 Inverse square law. Area A is illuminated by a point source of light. If the distance is doubled the area covered by the same point of light B is four times larger.

Self-assessed questions

4.17   Explain in simple terms Newton's Inverse Square Law as it affects flash photography.

4.18   When using flash to take photographs of victims' injuries how will the exposure be affected by changing the shutter speed from 1/60th to 1/125th second?

4.19   An interior photograph of a room taken using flash with the camera aperture set at f-16 produces an image that is too dark (under exposed). What adjustment is necessary to produce an image that is correctly exposed?

4.10 Room interiors

When photographing room interiors, it is important to take wide angle views from each corner of the room to record maximum detail before any item or exhibit is moved. Each photograph should overlap to ensure that no detail is missed. Where the room has an irregular shape, it may be necessary to take additional photographs to ensure full coverage. Use a good quality flash gun mounted on the camera and set the lens aperture to f-8 or f-11. Select a shutter speed that will synchronize with the flash, e.g. 1/125th second. Check the quality of the captured images on the camera monitor and by viewing the histogram.

Self-assessed questions

4.20   Why is it necessary to take overlapping photographs of room interiors?

4.11 Vehicles

A vehicle may be a crime scene in its own right or an exhibit. Take a three-quarter view from the front and from the rear of the vehicle to include both the front and rear number plates. Take a photograph of the vehicle identification number (VIN) plate. This plate is often located at the base of the door pillar on either the drivers or passengers side of the vehicle and can be seen when the doors are open. Sometimes, the VIN plate is located under the bonnet or can be seen at the back of the bulkhead through the windscreen. Photograph any obvious damage and marks or scratches that may assist identification. Take interior photographs using a wide angle lens and flash.

Self-assessed questions

4.21   Identify three places where the VIN plate may be found on a vehicle?

4.12 Exhibits

It is normal practice to photograph exhibits such as knives, weapons, etc. at the crime scene before being recovered showing the exact location and in close-up. Once the exhibit has been recovered, it may be necessary to take further detailed photographs. The exhibit should be placed on a plain background and a scale included in the photograph. Good quality photographs can be taken using a DSLR and a flash gun. If the exhibit has a serial number or other features that will assist identification, they should be photographed in close-up so that the features or numbers can be seen clearly. Use the 60-mm macro lens for the close-up shots, and where possible, mount the camera on a tripod and position the lens a right angles to the serial number. Choose a small aperture to increase depth of field. Position the flash at 45° to the subject to avoid unwanted reflections. To do this, you will need to attach an extension cord to the flash and connect it to the camera hot shoe. This will allow the flash to be operated off the camera.

Self-assessed questions

4.22   How would you avoid unwanted reflections when taking close-up photographs of exhibits?

4.13 Assaults and woundings

It is important to photograph injuries because they will in many cases be completely healed by the time the case is taken to court so greater emphasis is placed on photographic evidence, particularly in cases of domestic violence. It is accepted that injury photographs taken in a properly equipped studio will produce the best results; however in most cases this is impractical. With care and attention to detail good quality photographs can be produced using a D-SLR and a flash gun.

Photographs can only be taken with the consent of the subject and this is particularly important when photographing parts of the body normally covered by clothing. In the case of a minor the consent of the parent or guardian is needed. The photographs should be taken by a photographer of the same sex as the subject. If this is not possible then a witness of the same sex as the subject must be present, ideally a police officer or relative of the subject. When working in hospitals the permission of the doctor must be obtained as well as the patient before any photographs are taken.

Use a 60 mm lens to obtain close-up detail without the need to invade the subject's personal space and use a diffuser to soften the flash. Set the white balance to auto and the ISO to 100 or 200.

When photographing facial injuries it is important to avoid firing the flash directly into the subject's eyes. Tell the subject to look away and not to look directly at the camera or flashgun.

Be sure to avoid clutter or people showing in the background. This distracts from the subject and looks unprofessional. A plain white sheet or light grey material can provide a satisfactory background for the photographs. Always use a scale when reproduction to actual size is required. Check the image quality and histogram on the camera monitor.

Self-assessed questions

4.23   What important considerations need to be taken into account before taking photographs of a person's injuries in hospital?

4.13.1 Photographing bite marks

Good quality photographs of bite marks can in some cases be matched to the offender. The identification is made by a Forensic Odontologist who compares the detail on the photographs with a dental impression from the suspect. The photographs must be of the highest quality for a successful outcome. The following tips will maximize the chance of a positive identification:

- In cases where the bite mark is fresh and has not been cleaned in any way a swab should be taken so that any residual salivary deposits can be submitted for DNA profiling.

- Take a photograph of the injury without scales and a photograph showing the injury location. Also take a photograph of the face of the victim for identification purposes.

- A scale must be placed around the bite mark to facilitate the accurate reproduction to actual size.

- The camera must be at right angles and parallel to the bite mark.

- Where the bite mark is on a curved surface such as the arm take several overlapping photographs to minimize distortion.

- Photographs should be taken in colour. If a black and white image with enhanced contrast is required then this is easily achieved in the police photographic laboratory equipped with a digital mini lab. The photographs should be repeated at 24 hour intervals until the bruises are fully developed. Each new set of photographs to be taken from the same positions using the same scale and reproduced to actual size.

- Position the flash carefully to avoid shadows and reflections.

It is possible to obtain bite mark images using ultra violet (UV) photography. There are, however, health and safety considerations when using UV sources, and so this should only be carried out by appropriately qualified personnel in strictly controlled environments (Figure 4.4).

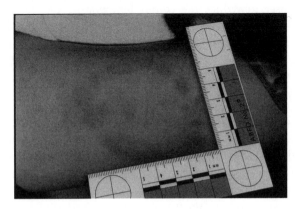

Figure 4.4 Bite mark photography.

Self-assessed questions

4.24   When must a scale be included in the photograph of an injured person?

4.14 Night photography

The SOCO officer will be required to take photographs at all times of the day and night and in all weathers. Lighting conditions vary considerably and the SOCO will need to take care to ensure the correct exposure, as the camera meter may not function correctly in low light conditions. During the early mornings or evenings when there is some daylight the camera meter should indicate the correct exposure. Good quality photographs can be taken of street scenes illuminated by street lights but care must be taken to ensure the correct white balance is set. For low pressure yellow sodium vapour lights set a white balance of between 2500–3000 K. Set the ISO to 400 or higher if the camera used is capable of producing good quality images at higher ISO settings. The correct exposure can be determined using the camera TTL meter. However, some adjustments may be needed if street lights are in the frame as they can upset the readings. The following settings are a good guide and should produce acceptable quality images:

- Main roads illuminated by sodium vapour discharge lamps provide sufficient illumination to obtain good photographs. Set the white balance to incandescent or manually to a value of 2500–3000 K whichever produces the best results. As a guide an exposure of 2–8 seconds at f-8 using an ISO setting of 400 will give good results. If the image is too dark increase the exposure and reduce the exposure if the image is too light. Flash will not be much help except to illuminate areas in the foreground that are in shadow. When using flash place an incandescent gel filter over the diffuser to reduce the colour temperature of the flash. If a colour correction filter is not used then the areas illuminated by the flash will appear unnaturally blue. The picture will have a yellow/orange appearance because of the colour of the street lamps but this is normal. Other well-lit roads will require an exposure of 15–30 seconds at f-8 using an ISO setting of 400. Once again flash exposure is only effective to add light to those dark areas in the foreground.

- Unlit streets or scenes where there is no ambient light can only be photographed using flash. Set the white balance to Auto and the shutter to B (brief) then walk around painting the scene with flash. Overlap the flashes to ensure proper coverage. This will not cause overexposure, as flash is not accumulative. Stay outside the angle of view of the camera lens and avoid firing the flash towards the lens. Where possible re-take the photographs in daylight hours (Figure 4.5).

(a)   (b)

Figure 4.5 Image of a street scene at night (a) one second at f-8, ISO 400 (b) two seconds at f-8, ISI 400.

Self-assessed questions

4.25 When taking photographs of street scenes illuminated by street lamps and using flash what white balance setting would you use and how would you deal with the mixed lighting that is street lamps and flash?

4.26 When taking photographs of an outside scene at night not illuminated by street lamps and using flash, which of the following statements is true?
(1) Set the shutter to brief and the aperture to f-8 and during the time exposure paint the scene with flash and overlap the flashes to ensure coverage of the scene.
(2) Set the shutter to brief and the aperture to f-8 and during the time exposure paint the scene with flash taking care not to overlap the flashes to avoid over exposure.

4.15 Footwear impressions

Footwear impressions recovered from crime scenes provide useful evidence and intelligence that can greatly assist the investigation. Even a partial footwear impression is useful because if there is detail present, the sole pattern can be identified providing good intelligence and if the impression has unique wear characteristics then a positive link to the suspect is possible. To achieve a positive link the suspect's shoes must be seized for comparison with the impression recovered from the crime scene. The suspect's shoes and footwear impressions recovered from the crime scene will be compared by a Forensic Scientist who will report in writing to the SIO as to the probability of a match.

It is always good practice to photograph footwear impressions before using any other recovery technique. Always use a tripod and set the camera at right angles and

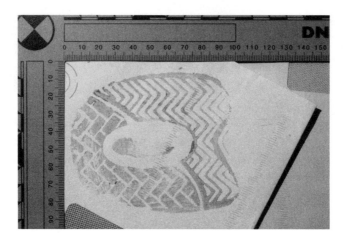

Figure 4.6   Image of shoe mark.

parallel to the impression. Place scales along at least two sides and, if the mark is clearly visible, take the photograph using available light or flash. Use a long synchronization lead to allow the flashgun to be angled at approximately 45 degrees to the impression. This will greatly enhance the detail and avoid unwanted reflections from shiny floors and surfaces.

The use of special lighting such as the Crime Lite 80 L high intensity forensic light source is useful for searching for and highlighting shoe marks and is supplied with red, green, blue and yellow filters for improving contrast where the mark is on a coloured background. For best results when using this light source block out any ambient light and switch off any room lights. The camera meter may not indicate the correct exposure so it is good practice to take several photographs using different exposures to ensure maximum detail is captured. Photographing a whole footwear mark in sections is considered best practice to ensure maximum detail is captured (Figure 4.6).

Self-assessed questions

4.27   When setting up the camera to take a photograph of a visible footwear mark why is it important to use a tripod to ensure that the camera is set at right angles and parallel to the mark and that scales are included on two sides?

4.16 Fingerprints

Fingerprint powders are used successfully as a method of developing latent fingerprints (also referred to as a mark or marks) from smooth, clean, dry and non-porous surfaces. However, unless a flake powder has been used the finger-print must be photographed before any attempt is made to lift it from the surface. Also there are many visible fingerprints left at crime scenes by offenders that are not suitable for treatment with powder. These may have been deposited by an offender from a contaminant, such as grease or blood present on their hand. Fingerprints can also be formed in liquid that is already on a surface such as wet blood or drying paint. In addition to these there are latent fingerprints that can only be developed with the application of certain chemicals. In all of these cases photography is, essentially, the only method by which the fingerprint can be recovered successfully.

At major crime scenes specially trained technicians are deployed to recover any of the above described fingerprints deemed not suitable for treatment with powder. The technician will use a variety of chemical processes to develop latent fingerprints then recover marks found using photographic techniques (details of the chemicals and their application can be found in Chapter 5). At all crime scenes the SOCO should have the equipment and skills to recover fingerprints using non-destructive photographic techniques. This provides an opportunity for an early identification to be made without compromising the mark so leaving it available for further treat-ment if necessary.

As stated above fingerprints in grease or blood are not suitable for treatment with powder, but if ridge detail can be seen then it can be photographed. In order to prove the integrity and continuity a label should be placed next to the mark showing as much detail as possible. At the very least it should be endorsed with the time, date, crime number and the SOCO reference number. An indicator should also be drawn somewhere in the frame from which the fingerprint may be oriented. On a vertical surface this is normally an arrow pointing to the ground and is commonly termed the 'gravity mark'. Obviously on horizontal surfaces or moveable objects a gravity mark would be inappropriate. In these cases some other sign that provides orientation may be made at the discretion of the photographer. The only proviso being that the photographer must be able to explain the symbol and its purpose when requested. An entirety photograph, showing the location of the fingerprint is also advisable. Showing the exact position of the mark can be as important as capturing the visible ridge detail, especially when trying to prove a person's involvement in an offence. Fingerprints deposited at crime scenes are not always in the most accessible places. However, for the very best results it is advised that, wherever possible, a tripod should be used. Mounted on a tripod the camera can be accurately placed at right angles to and parallel to the mark. A macro lens is needed for close-up photography and choosing a corresponding small lens aperture depth of field can be kept at an optimum. Move the cameras as close to the mark as possible filling the frame with the fingerprint and label. Check again to make sure that the

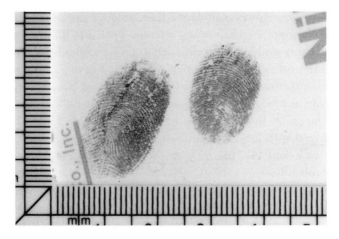

Figure 4.7   Image of fingerprint.

camera is at right angles to and parallel to the mark. This is essential because at such close distances even slight misalignment will affect depth of field. Where possible use available light as this provides an even illumination with no high-lights to adversely affect the ridge detail. When sufficient ambient light is not available an ordinary hand held torch will provide a flat even illumination, again avoiding highlights. However, if using a flashgun is the only option then by attaching a long synchronization lead the flash head can be held at an angle to provide oblique illumination. When using this method of illumination care must be taken not to cast a shadow over the fingerprint. Check each photograph on the camera monitor to ensure that all the detail is captured and is in sharp focus (Figure 4.7).

Self-assessed questions

4.28   When taking a photograph of a visible fingerprint a label is always paced next to the mark and included in the photograph. What information should be written on the label?

4.17 Recording video evidence at crime scenes

It is common practice at the scenes of major crimes to make a video recording for use by the SIO for briefing purposes. The video recording of crime scenes is normally the responsibility of the Scenes of Crime Department.

4.17.1 Equipment

It is not necessary to use professional video cameras to produce videos of crime scenes; good results can easily be obtained using a compact semi professional camera or high specification domestic camcorder. The objective is to capture images of the scene that include wide angle views and close views of specific evidence and exhibits taken in the right order to complement the briefing given by the SIO.

The following points should be considered when choosing a camcorder:

- Choose a camera with a good wide angle lens as many scenes are inside houses and buildings with limited space.

- A camera that produces good quality results in low light conditions is desirable.

- A camera with a large LCD screen is useful as the SOCO suited up and wearing a face mask and glasses may find it difficult to use the camera viewfinder.

- Always carry a spare battery.

- A tripod or mono pod is useful to avoid camera shake and other unplanned movements that can be distracting when viewing the film.

- Built in video lights have limited use and an external battery powered video light source is an essential piece of equipment.

4.17.2 Preparation

The SOCO must ensure that the equipment is serviceable and that batteries are fully charged. It is essential that the SOCO is briefed before commencing filming and that notes are taken to ensure that nothing is missed out. The best way to do this is to make a list or story board of the scenes and close-ups that need to be taken. Videos shot for briefing purposes are normally not edited due to time constraints and it is for this reason that the scenes should be filmed in a logical order that follows the events that occurred. A short commentary by the SOCO recorded for each scene adds clarity to the briefing video and is a specific requirement in some police forces. As a general rule the video should be no longer than ten to fifteen minutes. Before starting to film ask anyone present to keep quiet to avoid unwanted sounds and voices being recorded.

Wherever possible use a tripod and avoid zooming in and out as this looks unprofessional. Zooming out from a close-up to a wide view is more effective than zooming in. Where it is necessary to pan across a scene, use a tripod and pan slowly.

Original tapes should be labelled as the master tape and secured following force procedures. Copies of the master tape can be made onto DVD or VHS tape as required.

Self-assessed questions

4.29   What is the primary reason for making a video recording of a crime scene?

4.18 The use of digital images in court

The Science and Technology Committee of the House of Lords produced a report in 1998 concerning the use of digital images and stated that while it is accepted that digital images can be manipulated no problems in court had been experienced. In March 2002 the Home Office Scientific Development Branch produced a document entitled *Digital Imaging Procedure* which sets out guidelines on the capture and preservation of evidential images from still and video recordings and recommends these guidelines be incorporated into police procedures. The National Policing Improvement Agency in 2007 produced on behalf of ACPO an updated document entitled *Practice Advice on Police Use of Digital Images*. The following is a brief summary of the main points that need to be adhered to by the SOCO when engaged on photographic duties:

1. Authority must be obtained before photography assignments are undertaken.

2. Commence audit trail to establish and maintain continuity.

3. It is the responsibility of the SOCO to check that the photographic equipment is serviceable.

4. Images captured must not be deleted.

5. Images will be recorded on removable medium, for example, compact flash card. It is good practice to use one memory card for each job.

6. Images to be copied to WORM for example CD-R or secure server.

7. Define master CD and produce working copies as required.

8. The master CD must be documented and stored in a secure location.

9. Master CD must be retained as an exhibit.

10. Any further copies or prints should be produced from the copy CD.

11. Exhibits to be retained for the statutory period.

12. Exhibits should be disposed of after the statutory period and the audit trail completed.

The retention period is determined by the seriousness of the offence and the length of sentences and can in some cases be as long as 50 years. It is therefore essential to have a strategy for archive storage that ensures that the media does not degrade over this period. CDs and DVDs are considered to be suitable only for short-to-medium storage and to ensure the integrity of the data files need to be transferred to new media every five years. Consideration should be given to archive storage on a secure server under the control of the force ICT department.

Suggested further reading

Andrews, P. (2007) *Langford's Starting Photography: the Guide to Great Images with Digital or Film*, 5th edn, Focal Press.
Langford, M.A. and FoxSmith, R.S. (2007) *Langford's BASIC Photography: the Guide for Serious Photographers*, 8th edn, Focal Press.
Robinson, E.M. (2007) *Crime Scene Photography*, Academic Press.
Stewart, G.B. (2008) *The Crime Scene Photographer*, Lucent Books.

Some of the documents cited in this chapter are restricted and cannot be obtained by members of the general public.

PART II

Evidence Gathering Techniques

5
Fingerprints

David Charlton

5.1 Introduction

Fingerprints represent important evidence at scenes of crime. Not only are they used to establish the presence of an individual at that scene but also, when their orientation is interpreted correctly, they can be used to determine the actions of the criminal. In this chapter we are going to investigate some of the requirements and considerations of maximizing forensic potential for fingerprints when assessing a scene of crime.

We will look at the way a SOCO investigates a crime scene (see Figure 5.1), how to recognize a finger mark for what it is through an understanding of the biological underpinning of friction ridge skin formation. Then, we will assess how best to recover latent finger marks and what implications certain treatments may have for other forensic considerations. Finally, we will look at some of the more novel future treatments that may be available to scenes of crime specialists and laboratory scientists in the next few years.

A wide range of optical, physical and chemical techniques are available for the detection and enhancement of latent finger marks. The best results are obtained if a methodical and logical sequence of techniques is applied. The application of many different techniques or reagents will often increase the number of prints detected, and/or improve upon the quality of those already developed. It is vital that each process is applied in a pre-planned order as the incorrect choice of one method over another could adversely effect use of another technique and diminish its usefulness.

Crime Scene Management: Scene Specific Methods   Edited by Raul Sutton and Keith Trueman
© 2009 John Wiley & Sons, Ltd

Figure 5.1   A SOCO examines a scene for potential fingerprint evidence (Picture courtesy of Sussex police).

The choice of the best sequence of techniques will depend on several factors that include:

- the nature of the surface and the presence of any particular contaminants;

- environmental factors;

- the likely age of any evidential finger marks (Figure 5.2).

Figure 5.2   A SOCO examines a car using traditional brush and powder technique. (Picture courtesy of Sussex police).

Emphasis should always be placed on optical techniques, as these are non-destructive. Optical methods will improve the results obtained by physical or chemical methods. The chosen techniques should always be applied with caution, and developed prints recorded at *every* opportunity as finger marks are fragile and easily destroyed.

Recently, emphasis has been put on other techniques for personal identification. For example, the effect of different treatments on the success of DNA profiling is always to be considered. For finger marks in blood, only a small number of detection methods will cause serious problems. The prolonged use of UV light could degrade or even destroy DNA evidence. The reagent, physical developer, will also reduce the likelihood of successful DNA profiling simply because of the number of washing steps involved in the process. Magnetic powder may interfere with DNA amplification. The best advice is always to consult with a forensic biologist before proceeding if you are not sure and, if possible, collect a biological sample before processing the item for fingerprints.

5.2 The nature of friction ridge skin

Fingerprint evidence has been core to the detection of criminal activity for well over 100 years. The science behind the collection and interpretation of friction ridge skin is well established. The uniqueness of the friction ridges on the fingers, palms and feet is well rooted in the biological sciences, which we will discuss further on in this chapter. But before we progress, it would be prudent to examine the very nature of what friction ridge skin is, and why it is such a valuable tool in the identification and detection of individuals.

The majority of the skin on the human body is smooth and relatively featureless in personal identification terms apart from the occasional tattoo, scar, crease and dimple. However, the same cannot be said of the palms of the hands, the fingers, toes and the soles of the feet. These areas of the human body are covered with a system of raised ridges, associated furrows, containing creases and many sweat pores. The reasons for the presence of such features can be attributed to our evolutionary past, which suggests that we were tree dwelling apes that slowly evolved into the upright *Homo sapiens*. While not as important today as it may have been in those early days of our evolution, friction ridge skin gave an evolutionary advantage for the arboreal dweller. A human still needs to grasp items in order to maintain an everyday existence. Without friction ridge skin the ability to grip items is reduced, so that the simple physical action of holding something would be more difficult.

Friction ridge skin is made up of a number of ridge 'units' each corresponding to one primary epidermal ridge (glandular fold) formed directly beneath each sweat pore opening There are approximately 2700 ridge 'units' per square inch of friction skin. The pore openings are clear and visible in many instances along the upper surface of friction ridges and are fairly evenly spaced. This is because for each ridge 'unit', one pore opening and one sweat gland will be present.

Friction ridges form before birth. The blueprint for the friction ridge skin config-uration is established very early on in the human embryo's development. The stratum basale (generating layer) of the epidermis forms prior to birth, and it does not change except for injury, disease or decomposition after death. Injury to the generating layer will affect the skin's ability to regenerate tissue and scars will form as a result.

5.3 The structure of friction ridge skin

Thick skin (which includes friction skin) has two principal layers. The epidermis is a layered, flat epithelial tissue five layers thick. The dermis is much thicker than the epidermis and consists of two layers, the papillary layer, an area of loose connective tissue extending up into the epidermis as dermal pegs and the deeper reticular layer (Figure 5.3).

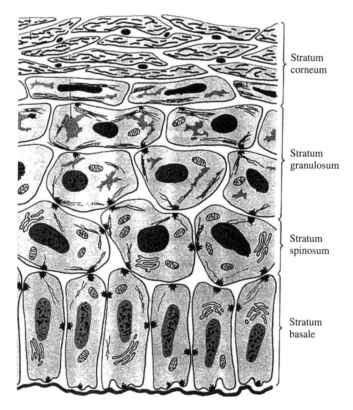

Stratum corneum

Stratum granulosum

Stratum spinosum

Stratum basale

Figure 5.3   Layers of the fully formed epidermis (courtesy NPIA fingerprint training manual).

The epidermal layers are:

stratum corneum	25–30 layers of stratified (layered) squamous (flattened) dead keratinocytes (skin cells) that are constantly shed.
Stratum lucidum	present only in thick skin (lips, soles of feet and palms of hands) with little or no cell detail is visible.
Stratum granulosum	3–4 layers of cell thickness deep and consists of flattened keratinocytes. At this level the cells are effectively dying.
Stratum spinosum	several layers thick, consisting mostly of keratinocytes. Together with the stratum basale it is sometimes referred to as the Malpighian layer (living layer).
Stratum basale	a single layer of cells in contact with the basement membrane. These cells are mitotically active and reproducing which is the reason why it is often referred to as the generating layer.

The dermis sustains the epidermis. The papillary layer is made up of connective tissue with fine elastic fibres. The surface area of this layer is supplemented by the dermal papillae. These formations increase the surface area to facilitate the exchange of oxygen, nutrients and waste products between the dermis and the epidermis.

The boundary between the dermis and epidermis is a point of potential weakness. The two tissues can be separated from each other. This can be evident in cases of decomposition and long immersion in water where the outer layer of friction ridge skin can slough off.

5.4 Friction ridge growth

Understanding friction skin growth during foetal development is important as this underpins the persistency and uniqueness of friction skin. Scientific research shows us why fingerprints are persistent and unique.

The development of epidermal ridges are preceded by the formation of volar pads (swelling of mesenchymal tissue) that first appear as elevations on the palm around six weeks after egg fertilization, followed by the five digits about one week later. Volar pads exhibit rapid growth between 6.5 and 10.5 weeks. Initially the pads appear uniform and rounded. However, by the ninth week, the pads begin to vary in position and shape. Volar pad development has a direct influence on friction ridge path configuration and pattern formation. The shape of the volar pad and the genetic timing of the regression of these pads will influence the pattern and configuration of friction ridge skin. This is why similarities in overall pattern design can be seen quite often in siblings, especially identical twins. Identical twins have the same DNA, but different overall friction ridge patterns. It is believed to be caused by external pressures and stresses (differential growth) which have altered the volar pad shape during foetal development.

In 1929, Harold Cummins describes how the growth of epidermal (friction) ridges is dependent on:

"two major development circumstances, namely, variations in the histology of different regions and differential growth incident to the production of irregular reliefs of the volar surfaces."

He goes on to say:

"The various configurations are not determined by self-limited mechanism within the skin. The skin possesses the capacity to form ridges, but the alignments of these ridges are as responsive to stresses in growth as are the alignments of sand to sweeping by wind or wave."

In other words, friction ridge patterns are not just the result of genetic factors but also random physical stresses and tensions.

5.5 Principles of friction ridge identification

A detailed examination of friction ridge skin under a magnifying glass will show that friction ridges are not uniform in configuration, nor do they necessarily flow in straight lines. Friction ridge skin has fractures and interruptions within the structure known as Galton details, after Sir Francis Galton, also known as ridge characteristics or minutiae.

It was Galton who estimated the probability of two persons having the same fingerprints. He studied the heritability and racial differences in fingerprints. He wrote about the technique for identifying common pattern in fingerprints and devising a classification system that survives to this day. This is why features such as ridge endings and bifurcations are to this day known as Galton details (Figure 5.4).

It is these characteristics that, when visible to the examiner, enable a determination of individualization of a latent crime scene finger mark against a suspect's ten-print

Figure 5.4 Sir Francis Galton 1822–1911.

card. There are two primary classifications of the characteristics to be found, namely, ridge endings (A), where ridges stop abruptly, and bifurcations, where a ridge divides into two (B) (Figure 5.5).

In a bifurcation, the ridges running parallel to this feature diverge to accommodate the ridge division. There are variations on the theme for these primary characteristics. For example, a lake (C) is where two bifurcations join together; an independent ridge (D) is a short ridge that is divorced from any other ridge. A spur (E) is a combination of a small independent ridge and a bifurcation and a cross-over (F) as the name suggests is a small ridge joined at each end to two parallel ridges.

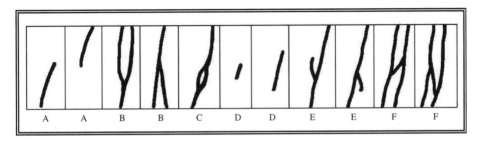

Figure 5.5 The types of features identified by Galton can be classified into two types, endings and bifurcation (Courtesy of NPIA training manual).

1st Level   2nd Level   3rd Level

Figure 5.6 The levels of fingerprint detail (Pictures courtesy of NPIA training manual).

For comparison purposes latent print examiners will assess holistically all features within a fingerprint from which a personal identification is made. These features are broken down into three levels of detail (see Figure 5.6). Level one refers to the basic pattern of the print, level two refers primarily to the Galton details described earlier, and level three refers to the configuration of sweat pores, shapes of the ridge edges and so on.

5.6 Comparison methodology

Every feature and characteristic in a sample of friction ridge skin is readily recognizable and identifiable and an identification can be made so long as there are sufficient characteristics of acceptable quality. It is possible to match very small amounts of friction ridge skin from a crime scene against a suspect, so long as there is sufficient clarity upon which to rely upon the permanence and reproducibility of visible features.

When comparing detail between a crime scene mark and a ten-print exemplar, a generic methodology has been adopted known as ACE-V. That is to say, in order to make a value judgment on any individualization, one must first *assess* the friction ridge detail in the scene mark so that useful reference points can be identified in the next phase, *comparison* of the mark features with that of features within the reference print. Then there must be an *evaluation* of the findings, from which conclusions as to identity must be derived. Finally, as in all scientific endeavours, there must be an element of peer review, known as *verification*, to repeat the ACE process independently to hopefully reach the same conclusions as that of a colleague.

During an assessment, the fingerprint examiner will look for:

- distortion;
- development methods and medium used to visualize latent material (chemicals and powders, etc.);

- deposition pressure to highlight areas of possible distortion;

- anatomical attributes (features);

- clarity.

During the comparison, the examiner will look for similarities in:

- pattern;

- ridge path;

- ridge shape;

- pore positioning.

During the evaluation, the examiner will look to form an opinion:

- Can the mark be eliminated as it belongs to someone having legitimate access to the crime scene?

- Is there sufficient information available to individualize?

During verification, an independent assessment of the casework is undertaken to see whether the ACE process has been correctly carried out and that the conclusions reached are consistent with the original findings. In the United Kingdom, for a crime scene mark to be identified, the comparison must be undertaken three times. One check will be made by the original examiner, then verification by two further experts who must come to the same conclusions independently.

Before any analysis of fingerprint evidence is possible there has to be some material to work with in the first place. The latent finger marks must be found at a crime scene before they can be compared against ten-print cards held nationally. It is all too easy to assume that finger marks can be readily found at a crime scene by SOCO, but this is not the case. Forensic examination is painstaking work, often producing no positive outcome. It requires careful planning and risk assessment to make sure that officer safety is paramount. This requires assessment of risk to individual officers and assessment of the risk to others. Some health and safety considerations in the enhancement and recovery of finger marks are discussed later.

5.7 Chemical composition of latent prints

A latent finger mark is a complex mixture of natural secretions and contaminations from the environment. Three types of glands are responsible for the natural secretions of the skin, the sudoriferous *eccrine* and *apocrine* glands, and the *sebaceous* glands. Eccrine sweat is approximately 98.5% water, the remainder being principally made up of mineral salts, for example sodium chloride, organic acids, urea and sugars (see Table 5.1).

The palms of the hands and the soles of the feet produce only eccrine gland secretions, whereas the apocrine glands are located in the groin, in the arm pits and in the perianal regions, where they generally open at the hair follicles.

Sebaceous glands are found on the chest and the back, where they are associated with hair roots, and on the forehead, the lips of the vagina and the glans of the penis. These glands secrete oil, the sebum, which serves to protect the skin and hair against water and act as a lubricant.

As the ridges of the hands are covered exclusively by eccrine glands, eccrine gland secretions are present to some degree in every latent fingerprint. Contamination by sebaceous gland secretions is also very common, whereas that from the apocrine glands is much rarer but may be important in certain crimes, for example crimes of a sexual nature. Sebaceous material is transferred onto the hands by contact between the hand and the forehead, the nose and the eye region of the head.

Contaminants from the workplace which dirty the hands are also valuable when detecting latent prints. This means that there will be two types of mark left at the

Table 5.1 The major chemical constituents of the glandular secretions.

Source	Constituents	
	Inorganic	**Organic**
Eccrine glands	Chlorides	Amino acids
	Metal ions	Urea
	Sulphates	Uric acid
	Phosphates	Lactic acid
	Ammonia	Sugars
	Water (>98%)	Creatinine
		Choline
Apocrine glands	Iron	Proteins
	Water	Carbohydrates
		Sterols
Sebaceous glands		Fatty acids
		Glycerides
		Hydrocarbons
		Alcohols

scene, a latent (barely visible/invisible mark) print that needs its visibility enhanced, or patent print that is clearly visible to the naked eye.

5.8 Identification of common locations for prints

Police officers are often disappointed with the lack of the irrefutable evidence of the suspect's fingerprints on a particular item of evidence. It is unfortunate that, unlike on television, the 'suspect's' prints don't always appear where you want them too. Factors influencing the chances of obtaining prints assist us in understanding the fragile and elusive nature of latent impressions. Each of the following factors independently or in combination can account for the lack of prints on any given surface:

- Individuals don't always have a sufficient quantity of perspiration and/or contaminates on their hands to be deposited.

- When someone touches something, they may handle it in a manner which causes the prints to smear.

- The surface may not be suitable for retaining the minute traces of moisture in a form representative of the ridge detail.

- The environment may cause the latent print to deteriorate.

- The perpetrator may be wearing gloves.

The most important fact when considering a lack of fingerprints found at a crime scene is that it does not suggest, imply, or establish necessarily that any person did or did not touch an item of evidence.

Having established that not everyone is capable of leaving behind a latent finger mark that can be found by an examiner at a crime scene, we also have to consider environmental conditions too. Humidity can also influence the ability for latent material to survive at a crime scene. Indeed, in the right conditions latent finger marks could survive for years before being powdered or treated with chemicals. However, a hot dry surface, such as you might find on a windshield of a car in summer may degrade a viable finger mark in a matter of minutes or even seconds to a point where the material in question can never be recovered, by whatever means.

Having discussed the likelihood of latent mark survival, and assuming there is a finger mark at the crime scene, then what can a SOCO do to maximize the potential to recover such marks? Generally speaking, experience is the key to being a successful SOCO. A useful paradigm to follow is to 'think like a criminal'.

In this case it is important to have some idea of what might have happened at the scene of crime. Reconstruction of the events pertaining to the crime will enable identification of the likely areas where prints may be deposited. Consider a routine burglary scene:

- SOCOs first establish the points of entry and egress. This is because such areas are common places for prints to be deposited and their relative position may also provide evidence of the criminal's actions.

- The development of latent prints with powder should be left to the end of the examination (see Chapter 3, section 8). Exception to this might be receptive external surfaces if there is a risk of rain, for example. Surfaces that are particularly receptive to powders include those that are smooth or shiny to the touch. These surfaces will include such materials as glass and plastics, for example see Figure 5.7.

- The SOCO should talk to the occupier, assess items that seem out of place and that could have been moved. This may indicate items handled by our intruder and may have retained finger marks.

- Consider what is suitable for treatment at the crime scene, and what items may need to be recovered for further work in the laboratory.

- If items are recovered, ensure appropriate packaging to avoid unnecessary damage to fragile latent finger marks that may be present. In a scenario where it may be necessary to send into the lab a smoke damaged glass bottle from an

Figure 5.7 Person developing a latent fingerprint on a plastic bottle. (Picture courtesy of Sussex police).

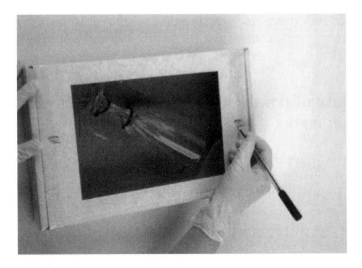

Figure 5.8   A Correctly packaged item (Picture courtesy of Sussex police).

arson scene, it will be important to avoid transporting the item in a way that will adversely impact upon the evidential potential of the exhibit (Figure 5.8).

In other words, protect any potential latent finger marks. This can be achieved by, as far as is possible, immobilizing the item to avoid any slippage or bumping in transit in packaging that preserves the evidence, such as an exhibit box. Transportation of such an item as the one described in a plastic exhibit bag may seem on first impressions to be a prudent action, but in fact the friction between the exhibit and the bag as it is in transit, will inevitably damage and sometimes completely remove any latent finger marks present. Packaging of exhibits will always be a fine balance between the need for evidential integrity and what is best to preserve the item for maximum evidential yield. It should always be remembered that continuity issues can always be explained in the courtroom. Inappropriate packaging can result in no evidence, and thus no case with which to present to a jury.

- Where possible, always recover as many elimination prints from the injured party and those with legitimate access. This is an often overlooked area of crime scene examination that can have a real bearing on the likely success rate of search hits on automated fingerprint searching systems such as the IDENT1 system employed in the United Kingdom. Recovery of elimination prints also reduces significantly the disclosure of unidentified material, which can only be of benefit in any court hearing.

• Remember, with the appropriate treatment, whether it is powder or chemical, many surfaces can and should be considered for treatment to enhance latent finger marks.

5.9 The use of powdering techniques to enhance latent finger marks

There are a multitude of different powders available to the crime scene examiner today that simply did not exist 50 years ago. Developments in the range and diversity of powders such as magnetic and fluorescent, as well as more traditional applications mean that powders can be applied to an ever increasing range of surfaces that may yield enhanced latent finger marks.

Within a fresh finger mark, that is, one recently deposited, it is the aqueous content within the finger mark upon which the powder adheres. In older finger marks where most of the water has evaporated powders adhere primarily to the fatty part of sebaceous sweat. The relative effectiveness of the powder application will depend not only on the chemical and physical make up of the powder, but also, and not unimportantly, the experience and skill of the operative and the type of applicator used. Under most circumstances it is the powders made up of flakes, which are far more sensitive, that produce consistently good results on most applicable surfaces. These can be lifted and placed onto plastic sheets for recovery to a central laboratory. Other less sensitive powders can be used at crime scenes. Black and white powders can be readily used, but they will, to a point, depend on the skill and expertise of photographers to get the best possible enhancement of the latent finger mark developed for the examiners in fingerprint bureau to work with.

Powders can be used on any surface that is relatively smooth and clean. Powders are easy to deploy and use. The most obvious example of where powders are extremely effective is glass. It should be noted that the use of powders is undesirable where the target surface is wet, or where the surface is very dirty, rough or covered in other unspecified contaminants. It is important to note that the application of powders on older finger marks is not nearly as effective. Also, powders require adequate illumination to highlight enhanced material. When using powders at any time, the crime scene examiner must always be mindful of the destructive properties of powders, in that their use may preclude or inhibit further sequential treatments and processes. For example, if there is to be a consideration of other evidence present on the target surface such as handwriting, indented writing, body fluids that may provide DNA samples, or perhaps fibres, then powders should be used with caution, or advice sought as to what priority should be apportioned to each evidential strand.

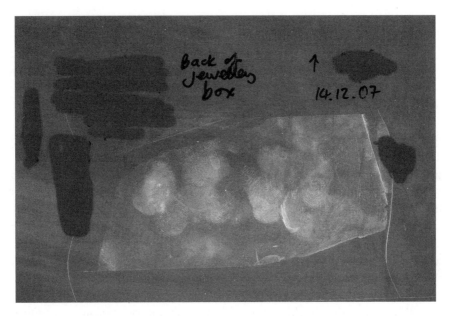

Figure 5.9   A Latent set of finger marks developed with aluminium powder (Picture courtesy of Sussex police).

Powdering technique is very important to achieving good results (as seen in Figure 5.9). Poor technique will result in finger marks that are possibly of insufficient quality for fingerprint examiners to use effectively, or evidence may be destroyed altogether. A pot of aluminium powder will last a long time. A pot of aluminium powder should never be full. A pot containing a few centimetres of powder will be sufficient, in the context of the average workload of an operational SOCO, to last several weeks.

There are a variety of applicators at the disposal of the crime scene examiner.

- Glass fibre should be used whenever aluminium powder is applied. The very fine fibres of the brush do far less damage to the latent finger mark in situ.

- Carbon fibre brushes are of a similar design to the glass equivalent and can be used with aluminium powder. However, these brushes are susceptible to break up with use, which can be problematic for obvious reasons.

- Animal hair brushes can be used so long as care is taken in application. Many examiners use better quality squirrel hair brushes.

In short though, when applying aluminium powder, the glass fibre brush is considered to be the brush of choice by not only most users, but also police agencies and the Home Office Scientific Development Branch.

The powdering of a window is not to be considered in the same way in which you might expect to paint emulsion onto a wall. If the brush used to apply the powder is too heavily 'charged', then the latent finger mark will be 'flooded' and all ridge detail will be obliterated. It should be remembered that a latent finger mark can be 'built up' with fresh applications of powder, but it is far more problematic to 'clean' a mark out that has been over powdered.

There are two schools of thought about how to apply powder. Some SOCO will apply powder with a sweeping motion of the brush (much like painting), while others prefer the 'twizzle' method, whereby the brush is rotated and spun in the hand. While it is open to debate which method provides the safest and most reliable results, it is just as important to learn and master how to 'charge' the brush. Charging is the loading of the brush with the powder ready for application. After loading the brush with powder, it is usually desirable to 'shake out' the brush away from the area of interest so that excess powder can be removed from the brush to prevent any possibility of over powdering. This is a process that is usually learned with experience and the amount of powder required to obtain optimum results is more an art than a science and is a practice best learned through trial and error (preferably on practice exhibits in a controlled laboratory environment). Once a mark has been developed using either of the above described methods it is sometimes necessary to 'clear' the mark using an unsoiled animal fur brush. To do this, short strokes that follow the ridge line should be used.

As with all airborne particulates, powders used at crime scenes carry their own unique health risks. The most common powder in use today is comprised of aluminium flakes. Aluminium, being the third most abundant element in the earth's crust, can be found naturally in the human body. It must be considered an occupational hazard for the SOCO, entering our bodies via inhalation. Small amounts of aluminium absorbed into the body is rapidly excreted as urine by the kidneys. However, it is believed that aluminium could play a role in the cause of leukaemia, some cancers and there is also some debate as to whether aluminium is a causative agent of some forms of Alzheimer's disease. The results of a project carried out by Richard Curruthers, a Crime Scene Examiner working for the Leicestershire Constabulary suggests there is no convincing scientific evidence for a link between aluminium and mental illness, and that the use of aluminium powder in the field of scenes of crime shows there is little risk to officers. Carruthers does highlight the importance of safety procedures when using aluminium powder in scene examination.

When using any powder, inform all staff of the correct use of the material and correct processes via the 'Safe System of Work'. At a crime scene that is poorly ventilated, or during very long examinations, high concentrations of powder will accumulate. If this is the case, then respiratory protective equipment should be considered. Of course, safety should not be an issue confined to the examiner. The injured party may be in the property while powdering takes place. In my experience it is always better to ask the occupant to 'go and make a cup of tea' while examination takes place. Firstly, it is inadvisable for a member of the public to be present while powdering takes place as they will always try to influence what you do and how you examine the property. More importantly, the health and safety of the public is also your responsibility when using a potentially hazardous substance. So where possible, only commence powdering when you are sure that all persons within the area of interest are wearing both protective clothing including respirators.

So how does a crime scene examiner get the best from the use of powders and maximize the potential for the successful recovery of finger marks? While every crime scene is different and will have unique attributes, there are some generic rules of thumb that will give the examiner the best chance of retrieving useful fingerprint evidence.

The magnetic application of powders on rough, grained or porous surfaces is a possible consideration, though it should be remembered that the powder used is often mixed with metals and oxides to aid magnetic properties. Because these metals will have larger particulate properties, this may inevitably lead to a reduction in the sensitivity of the powdering technique.

5.10 Chemical development techniques

There are a number of chemical development techniques that are suitable for use at scenes of crime, though some are more specialized and will need to be applied in a laboratory setting. Some of these are very useful for enhancing marks present in bodily fluids such as blood whereas others can be used on latent marks.

5.10.1 Primarily laboratory based

Gentian Violet (GV) is a dye that stains the fatty components of sebaceous sweaty deposits producing a very strong purple image. This treatment is extremely effective when applying to adhesive surfaces like tapes and protective films. It will also be effective on occasions when treating surfaces that are contaminated with oils and grease. GV should not be used in large quantities. Phenolic compounds present in the chemical makeup of GV are toxic.

Small Particle Reagent (SPR) is a suspension of fine molybdenum disulfide particles within a detergent solution. Latent finger marks contain fatty constituents that SPR adheres to. It is a simple process and should marks develop will result in a grey deposit. This method tends to be more effective on older rather than newly deposited finger marks. There is a spray application that can be employed but it has a far lower success rate and any consideration to deploy such techniques should only be undertaken when all other options have been exhausted. One interesting thing to note about this treatment is that the grey deposit can in theory be lifted in the same way as a powdered latent finger mark. This simplifies the photographic process considerably.

Physical Developer (PD) is silver based, and reacts with components within sebaceous sweat leaving a grey silver deposit (see Figure 5.10). Normally used on paper, it can be applied to other surfaces and is especially useful when treating items that have been wetted and is usually used after DFO and Ninhydrin (see later) treatments have concluded. While this treatment is effective, it is consuming both in terms of time, and also the human resources required to process evidence using this method. It usually takes about 45 minutes to process an item of evidence using PD as there are several individual processes within the overall treatment including immersion in acidic solutions and subsequent wash solutions.

Vacuum Metal Deposition (VMD) is arguably the most sensitive technique for fingerprint detection on non-porous surfaces such as glass and plastic. Although, this is not in itself a scene technique, when gathering evidence at scenes the SOCO must be aware that the technique exists so that suitable items will be collected for

Figure 5.10 Fingerprints developed with physical developer (Picture courtesy of Sussex Police).

later laboratory treatment. In this process, exhibits are placed within vacuum environment and coated with thin layers of gold and zinc. The deposited gold penetrates the latent fingerprint deposit producing a uniform layer. The zinc will generally deposit on the substrate but not on the finger mark.

VMD units are expensive and their use requires significant experience for optimum results. When applied correctly however, excellent results can be obtained even on old, degraded finger marks. VMD is effective on problematic surfaces where other techniques fail.

5.11 Laboratory and scene applications

Ninhydrin and 1, 8-diazafluoren-9-one (DFO) are very effective treatments for items such as paper and cardboard and their use will be dependent on many associated factors. For example:

- In optimum conditions DFO may prove more effective in enhancing latent material than ninhydrin.

- Ninhydrin is cheap and easy to use and produces easily visible finger marks.

- DFO is more costly and requires light source examination after the initial DFO treatment.

- If Ninhydrin is used after DFO there will almost certainly be additional finger marks developed.

Both DFO and Ninhydrin will react with blood and may be used to develop blood contaminated latent finger marks. DFO is only recommended to be used on papers and more porous surfaces for the purpose of enhancing blood marks whereas Ninhydrin can work equally well on non-porous surfaces as well.

DFO is very effective on paper and other porous surfaces. Reacting with amino acids and other components within a latent finger mark, the resultant product is highly fluorescent and will have a pink/purple colouration. High intensity light sources must be used to augment this process. Originally this process used formulations that contained CFC-based solvents, but these have been replaced by new CFC-free formulations such as HFE7100 that are far more eco-friendly.

Ninhydrin is also a very effective treatment on paper and other porous surfaces. It reacts with amino acids and produces an immediate purple coloured product, the results of such treatment on finger marks can be seen in Figure 5.11, especially if used in conjunction with a humidifier. Caution should be exercised in assessing success when using Ninhydrin, however. There is always the chance that marks will

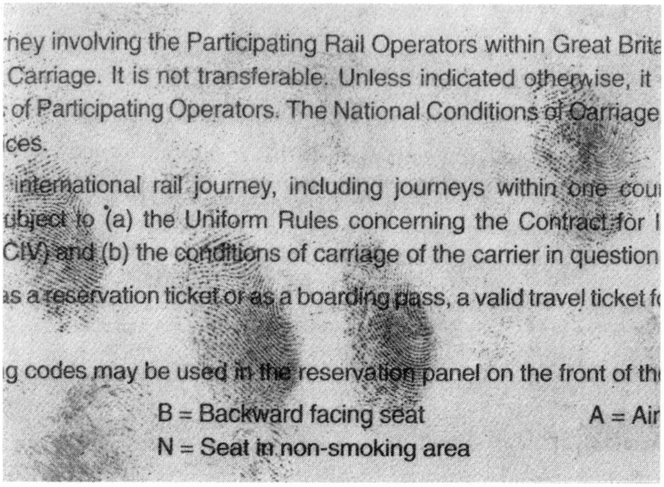

...hey involving the Participating Rail Operators within Great Brita...
...Carriage. It is not transferable. Unless indicated otherwise, it...
...of Participating Operators. The National Conditions of Carriage...
...ces.

...international rail journey, including journeys within one cou...
...ubject to (a) the Uniform Rules concerning the Contract for I...
CIV) and (b) the conditions of carriage of the carrier in question...

...as a reservation ticket or as a boarding pass, a valid travel ticket f...

...g codes may be used in the reservation panel on the front of the...
          B = Backward facing seat   A = Air...
          N = Seat in non-smoking area

Figure 5.11   Ninhydrin developed latent marks on paper (Picture courtesy of Sussex Police).

continue to develop for weeks after the initial treatment so in-house policy and procedure should possibly include a buffer time between initial treatment and result notification to allow for such occurrences. This will, of course, be at the discretion of the individual laboratory and will be dependent on the individual circumstances of the investigation. As with DFO, originally this process used CFC-based solvents, which have now been replaced with CFC-free solvents such as HFE7100.

Solvent Black 3 is a dye that reacts with fatty components of sebaceous sweat and produces a blue-black image. It is a very useful solvent to use on items such as dried soft drink deposits, grease or other foodstuff stains. It can also on some occasions be used to augment the superglue fuming technique, though there are other, more effective solutions in this regard. There are two different formulations for SB3. There is a formulation based on an ethanol ingredient, which is recommended for use in the laboratory, which must never be used at a crime scene. There is also another formulation based on 1-methoxy-2-propanol that was developed for more general use at crime scenes. It should be noted that the methoxy-propanol solution is flammable but can be used at crime scenes with few restrictions so long as the surface or ambient temperature remains below 48°C.

Superglue fuming (Cyanoacrylate Vapour) is one technique that is probably best applied in the laboratory setting, but it is possible to apply the technique at a crime scene and to achieve excellent results. This is especially useful where the item to be treated is too large or bulky for transportation or where the item in question is too fragile to risk moving. Clearly, the health and safety implications of conducting this technique outside of the normal controls within a laboratory should not be

Figure 5.12 Superglue and basic red 14 dye developed latent fingerprints (Picture courtesy of Sussex Police).

underestimated. In addition, the fluorescent dye (water based Basic Red 14 as in Figure 5.12), recommended for use at crime scenes, is less effective than alcohol based dyes such as Basic Yellow and so where possible consideration should be made to remove the item to the laboratory.

The superglue vapour polymerizes on some latent finger marks to produce a white deposit. This reaction is thought to occur as a result of water and other constituents present within latent finger marks. There are many ways of applying this technique at crime scenes and current technology is now both easy to use and portable. As described earlier in this chapter, a safe system of work must be defined and agreed upon. The safe removal of vapours and the potential for other hazardous gases resulting from the gradual decomposition of the superglue into other toxic substances require many risk reducing measures to ensure the safe use of the process. It cannot be underestimated how potentially dangerous this technique is at any time, especially in an environment like a crime scene, where considerations such as correct application of the technique and the need to be mindful of the proximity of other people such as victims, members of the public and other law enforcement officers.

The usefulness of the technique will depend on the right environmental factors. Ideally, a relative humidity of 80% should be accompanied by heating the superglue to about 120°C to facilitate evaporation of the substance. It is the humidity that enables the chlorides present to take up water which in turn leads to polymerization. The result is a fibrous matted deposit. This technique is especially useful on a range of non porous surfaces but the examiner should always use a fluorescent dye which should be applied to the deposits because this will, under a light source, highlight the maximum number of finger marks.

It should be noted that this technique can interfere with other forensic examinations. For example, handwriting and indented impressions, DNA profiling and fibre analysis amongst other forensic considerations can be compromised through the use of superglue so the examiner must be mindful of the operational priorities before embarking on this treatment.

5.12 Fingerprints in bodily fluids

Finger marks in bodily fluid, most commonly blood, are by their very nature fragile and easily damaged. It is perhaps not surprising that when an examiner comes across such evidence, often the best way of recovering evidence that the fingerprint bureau will involve enhancement techniques used in situ. It must be emphasized that where possible photography and visual examination should always precede any potentially destructive chemical enhancement process. Using blood as the most obvious body fluid that an examiner may encounter, one should aim where possible to allow the blood to dry naturally in its location before a photographic record is made. Using artificial blowers may be worth considering, but care should be taken to avoid drying at too high a temperature as this can cause the evidential material to flake and disintegrate. Direct photography of the finger mark in any bodily fluid is always preferable so long as the mark is readily visible as there will be greater contrast and clarity observable in the crime scene mark for use by the fingerprint examiner.

On more porous surfaces DFO is a very useful chemical treatment that will also react with any latent finger mark deposits that may be present with the visible finger mark in blood. Similarly, consideration should be given to the use of Ninhydrin also, but as with DFO, one should take into consideration that both processes may well impact upon the effectiveness of Acid Black 1 and Acid Violet 17 dye formulations. Physical developer should also be considered after the preceding treatments have been attempted and as with all the treatments mentioned thus far, visual, fluorescent and photographic examinations should be carried out before embarking on any new enhancement technique.

On non porous surfaces latent material in bodily fluids are subject to different techniques which may be considered after the initial drying and visual examination phase. For example, vacuum metal deposition could be considered, which is more sensitive than powders or superglue, though the examiner is limited by what size of exhibit will fit into the vacuum chamber. For this reason, the examination may well progress to powders, whereby any visible material should be photographed post treatment and should *never* be lifted. Conversely, superglue treatment could also be considered at this stage for articles which have not been wetted previously, however, as no dye solution should be used, the examiner should aim to photograph the resultant visual material. It should be noted that as with Ninhydrin and DFO, superglue treatments may likewise impact upon the overall effectiveness of fluorescent treatments such as Acid Yellow 7 and Acid Violet 17. As with porous surfaces, physical developer is another option and where there are heavy greasy contaminants the option to use Solvent Black 3 should be considered.

Luminol can locate traces of blood, even if it has been cleaned or removed. A solution of luminol can be sprayed throughout the area under investigation. The iron present in any blood in the area catalyzes the chemical reaction that leads to luminescence revealing the location of the blood. The glow lasts for about 30 seconds and is blue. Detecting the glow requires a fairly dark room. Any glow detected may be documented by taking a long exposure photograph.

Luminol has some drawbacks that may limit its use in a crime scene investigation:

- Luminol also fluoresces in the presence of copper or an alloy of copper, horse-radish and certain bleaches; and, as a result, if a crime scene is thoroughly cleaned with a bleach solution, residual bleach will cause the entire crime scene to fluoresce, effectively camouflaging any evidence, such as blood.

- Luminol will also detect the small amounts of blood present in urine and it can be distorted if animal blood is present in the room that is being tested.

- Luminol's presence may prevent other tests from being performed on a piece of evidence. However, it has been shown that DNA can be successfully extracted from samples treated with luminol reagent.

DAB (Diaminobenzidine) is used to develop latent prints and enhance visible prints that have been deposited in blood. DAB can be applied by two methods—the submersion method and the tissue method.

Cyanoacrylate fuming can be detrimental to all blood DAB processing and DAB processing must be completed before processing with cyanoacrylate.

Acid Black 1, Acid Black/Amido Black is a dye stain which reacts with proteins in the blood and other body fluids. Because it will not react with the normal associated contaminants present in a latent finger mark, care must be taken to use this method in strict adherence to sequential protocol. Otherwise there will be a serious risk of losing vital forensic opportunity. Care should also be taken with the substrate as the treatment of some porous surfaces will sometimes result in the production of a uniform dark background colour.

Acid Violet 17, Acid Violet, also reacts with proteins in blood and other body fluids. It gives off a violet fluorescent product. It too will not react with the normal associated contaminants present in a latent finger mark; care must be taken to use this method in strict adherence to sequential protocol. Otherwise there will be a serious risk of losing vital forensic opportunity. Care should also be taken with the substrate as the treatment of some porous surfaces will sometimes result in the production of a uniform dark background colour.

Acid Yellow 7, Acid Yellow, also reacts with proteins in blood and other body fluids. It gives off a yellow fluorescent product. It too will not react with the normal associated contaminants present in a latent finger mark; care must be taken to use this method in strict adherence to sequential protocol. Otherwise there will be a serious risk of losing vital forensic opportunity. This dye should only be used on non porous surfaces as it cannot be removed from porous backgrounds making it impossible to detect latent material.

The baseline with any enhancement technique is photograph, photograph, photograph! Never assume that the enhanced material visible to the examiner will persist beyond the next phase of the sequential treatment. All too often the delicate nature of latent material is manifest in the way one particular chemical treatment will irrevocably damage the underlying detail.

5.13 Scenes of fire

It may be assumed that fire scenes will destroy finger marks, or at least expose them to conditions where the retrieval of fingerprint evidence is made considerably more difficult. However a number of recent studies demonstrate that usable evidence may survive. Finger marks may well survive if the exhibit has not been exposed to temperatures greater than 300°C. Survival rates for finger marks are higher if the surface has been protected in some way from the direct effects of heat and smoke. Finger marks may develop on articles that are relatively clean and show only minor smoke damage.

Techniques are available for the removal of heavy smoke damage, but in general such techniques significantly reduce the chances of finding marks. Articles or regions of articles that have not been wet may well be useful sources of latent finger mark material, so evidence retrieval in this instance should focus on areas that have been protected from the direct effects of water. No article or surface should be entirely discounted. Marks have been found on articles with heavy smoke damage that have been exposed to temperatures in excess of 700°C and soaked in water.

Sodium hydroxide solution has been used effectively in operational work by several police forces. The process involves immersion of the exhibit in sodium hydroxide (or washing sodium hydroxide solution down the surface of the sample), followed by a water wash. This process loosens heavy soot deposits from the surface of articles, or has the effect of making the wetted soot more 'transparent' for photography. The use of sodium hydroxide is detrimental to DNA evidence, and its use may not be desirable if subsequent DNA analysis is required.

Collaboration with fire investigators is essential at arson scenes to provide guidance on the temperatures to which different regions of the scene have been exposed. This knowledge will help the crime scene examiner in deciding which examination technique is likely to be effective. Most existing fingerprint development techniques are effective to some extent for exposure temperatures up to 200°C. Above this temperature, the choice of development process becomes much more limited.

The most effective soot removal techniques for light/medium sooted non-porous surfaces are likely to be lifting tape and silicone rubber casting compounds. These remove much of the loose surface soot without damaging underlying marks. The best soot removal process for porous surfaces is believed to be the commercial product 'Absorene'. The most effective fingerprint development process for general use on non-porous surfaces is powder suspension. This can be applied both at a scene and in the laboratory if so desired.

The Home Office Scientific Development Branch is developing a formulation for a Black Powder Suspension for fingerprint development after fire damage. An optimized White Powder Suspension formulation is also being produced. Operational work by police forces suggests that of the commercial White Powder Suspension products, 'WhiteWop' appears to give the best results. Physical Developer was found to develop the most marks on porous surfaces, possibly because most porous exhibits become wetted when fires are extinguished.

5.14 Optical methods to reveal fingerprints (laser and other light sources)

Optical detection methods are non-destructive with respect to latent finger marks. Such techniques do not preclude the later application of conventional fingerprint development procedures (Figure 5.13).

The simple observation of an object under white light may disclose finger marks that can be photographed without any further treatment. On the other hand, more

Figure 5.13   Scene-based optical enhancement of latent fingermarks (Picture courtesy of Sussex police).

complex optical detection methods may reveal prints that may not be developed by other techniques. A sequential fingerprint analysis should intuitively commence with one or more of the following methods.

5.14.1 Photoluminescence

Lasers have, for many years, been proposed for the luminescence detection of untreated fingerprints on non-luminescent surfaces as shown in Figure 5.14.

Figure 5.14   Identification of scene marks using photoluminescence (Picture courtesy of Sussex police).

Three types of lasers have been employed to detect luminescent fingerprints – the argon ionic, the copper vapour and the Nd: YAG laser. Positive results have been obtained on many surfaces, including metal, firearms and human skin.

A search for luminescent fingerprints should always precede the application of a destructive detection method. The evidential object should be illuminated at different wavelengths using a suitable high-intensity light source while observing through appropriately filtered goggles.

Ultraviolet absorption and luminescence

Japanese workers have proposed the optical detection of latent fingerprints by short-wave UV reflection. This technique requires the use of a UV-sensitive CCD camera, equipped with a quartz lens, and a source of UV light. The technique is based on obtaining a contrast between the surface, which may absorb or reflect UV light, and the fingerprint deposit which absorbs some UV radiation and diffusely reflects the remainder. The angle of incidence of the UV illumination is critical for obtaining satisfactory results.

The Serious Crimes Unit (SCU) in London routinely uses reflection techniques in both the long and short-wave UV region. The SCU has reported that the illumination of latent prints on paper using the Nd: YAG laser, with photographic detection of their luminescence emission in the long-wave UV region, can produce images with good ridge detail as shown in Figure 5.15.

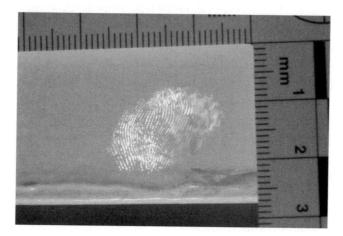

Figure 5.15 Identification of scene marks using Nd: YAG laser, with photographic detection of finger marks through their luminescence (Picture courtesy of Sussex police).

Episcopic coaxial illumination

Latent fingerprints on smooth non-porous surfaces, such as glass, plastic and polished metal, can often be detected using episcopic coaxial illumination. The technique involves the use of a semi-transparent mirror to observe the reflection of light perpendicular to the surface. The light is diffused by the fingerprint deposit but specularly reflected by the surface, the print is therefore visible as dark ridges against a light background. As well as detecting untreated latent prints, the technique also gives excellent results after cyanoacrylate treatment.

5.15 New and emerging techniques

Oil Red O(ORO).   ORO has been proposed as an alternative solution for Physical Developer for marks on paper that have been wetted. Research is ongoing in the United States, Australia and the United Kingdom into the method and its effectiveness when compared to PD. Results thus far indicate that while it has fewer process elements than that of PD, it tends to be a longer treatment overall and it is considered less effective on older deposits and those marks that have been wetted for extended periods of time. It has also been noted that the solvents used in other treatments like Ninhydrin and DFO may remove some of the constituents upon which ORO reacts. So its general use within established sequential treatments may be questionable.

Nanoparticles.   In India, United Kingdom, Israel, Australia and Switzerland there are several research groups currently assessing and developing novel and new fingerprint reagents utilizing nano-technology to both initiate other chemical processes, as very fine powders, or as suspensions with fluorescent properties. Many of these research efforts are still in the laboratory development stage though there are some encouraging results being obtained.

Indanediones.   The replacement of Ninhydrin and DFO with indanediones for fingerprint detection on porous surfaces is being investigated. Indanediones are as easy to use as Ninhydrin and have the sensitivity of DFO but importantly can be applied at a potentially lower cost.

Optical Techniques.   On-site optical and chemical enhancement techniques are likely to feature heavily in future crime scene examination with greater reliance on high-intensity specialized light sources and UV-imaging equipment. These advances will be complimented by better information technology to facilitate the remote, real-time transmission and searching of scene finger marks against automated fingerprint identification systems using wireless broadband infrastructures using virtual private networks.

Scenes of Crime Officers will rarely, if ever, know the exact composition of the latent impression which is being developed. The amount of secretion, pressure and length of contact, temperature, humidity, air flow, reaction with the specific substrate etc are all unknown variables that the examiner has to both consider and account for when deciding on an appropriate treatment. The chances of successfully developing a fingerprint will vary dependent on the time which has elapsed since it was deposited. It is essential to attend scenes of crime as soon as possible after the event.

5.16 Summary

This chapter gives a brief overview of the complexities of friction ridge skin, its deposition as well as discussing some of the available enhancement processes that can maximize forensic yield from a crime scene. As in any discipline, the vast majority of the skills and understanding of the domain of latent print enhancement, detection and recovery come from many years of tried and tested experience, married with an insatiable appetite to find new, novel and exciting ways to apply latest technology and chemistry to the task of finding latent finger mark evidence. If there is any message to come out of this chapter it is as follows:

- Only by understanding what friction ridge skin is and how it is constructed is it possible to investigate ways to enhance and recover such evidence.

- Remember, any evidence, (and latent finger marks are no different), is fragile and easily destroyed. You will probably only ever get one chance to get the best possible evidence. The wrong choices in powdering technique or chemical treatment could be fatal to this process.

- Always record evidence through photography after every sequential treatment process has been attempted. The next step in the treatment process may destroy the exhibit and/or the latent material.

- If you are not sure about a particular process, then take advice. Don't embark on a treatment that may leave the evidence redundant. To destroy evidence through carelessness or neglect is the cardinal sin of all those involved in the crime scene to court process.

- Working at a crime scene, especially with chemicals and other high intensity light sources can be dangerous if conducted by ill trained staff. Health and safety considerations must be paramount in the minds of the examiners. Supervision to protect examiners, and also law enforcement and multi-agency personnel is a core task of any responsible forensic examiner. Risk assess the scene and ensure nominated staff know how to use technology and chemicals and that they are aware of their risk management responsibilities.

- Be aware that you may need to justify your actions in a court of law. Always document your processes and ensure that evidence recovered is appropriately accounted for, packaged and signed off. Continuity is one of the most important attributes of effective forensic evidence. Evidential provenance is vital to evidential integrity.

In following many of the suggestions within this chapter it should be possible to both locate and enhance latent finger mark material to a point where a finger print examiner will be able to compare the evidence with known exemplars to identify the perpetrator of the crime under investigation. A 'match' on a finger mark provides no greater satisfaction to all within the scientific support environment and represents an effective professional partnership between all the disciplines within a forensic department.

Self-assessed questions

5.1   The choice of the best sequence of enhancement techniques will depend on what factors?

5.2   Emphasis should always be placed on optical techniques. Why?

5.3   What are the implications of applying enhancement techniques on other evidence such as DNA for example?

5.4   What are the different layers that make up the structure of friction ridge skin?

5.5   What are the implications to the regeneration of friction ridge skin of deep seated injury to the sub dermal skin tissue?

5.6   What is ACE-V methodology as it pertains to fingerprint identification?

5.7   What types of information will the examiner assess during a finger mark comparison?

5.8   What sorts of health and safety considerations should be made prior to commencing an examination?

5.9   What factors may explain an inability to find usable friction ridge evidence at a crime scene?

5.10   What does a lack of friction ridge evidence on an exhibit at a crime scene NOT imply?

5.11 What strategy should a SOCO adopt to maximize the chances of finding useful trace evidence?

5.12 Name five typical treatment processes at a crime scene.

5.13 When might you use Physical Developer?

5.14 What would a Yag Laser be used for?

51.5 What action should you take when unsure about which treatment process is appropriate?

Acknowledgments

The author is grateful for the assistance and support from the following specialists:
Roger Crowley, Head of Scene of Crime, Derbyshire Police.
Karen Stow, SSM, Derbyshire Police.
Tracy Stocker, SOCO Trainer, Sussex Police.
Brian Cook, SSM, Sussex Police.
Dr Itiel Dror, Senior Lecturer, University of Southampton.
Martin Bloomfield, Imaging and Laboratory Services Manager, Sussex Police.

The author also wishes to extend grateful thanks to Sussex Police, The NPIA Police National Training School and to the Home Office Scientific Development Branch for the re-print use of certain photographs and illustrations within this chapter.

Some photographs subject to Crown Copyright are re-printed with kind permission of the controller of HMSO and the Queens Printer for Scotland and are originally to be found in the Fingerprint Development Handbook of the Home Office Policing and Crime Reduction Group Publication no. 3/00.

Other photographs and illustrations re-printed with kind permission of Sussex Police and are originally to be found in the Sussex Police Forensic Trainer Handbook (Student Officer Course).

Selected further reading

Ashbaugh, D. (1999). *Quantitative-Qualitative Friction Ridge Analysis: an Introduction to Basic and Advanced Ridgeology*, CRC Press Inc, ISBN: 9780849370076.
Bleay, S.M., Bradshaw, G. and Moore, J.E. (2006). Fingerprint Development and Imaging Newsletter: Special Edition, Pub Nos 26/06.
Carruthers, R.S. (2002). The effects of aluminium fingerprinting powder on the health of Scenes of Crime Officers, PGCE Diploma in scientific support skills project, University of Durham.
Charlton, D., Del Manso, H. and Dror, I.E. (2007). Expert error: the mind trap. *Fingerprint Whorld*, **33**, 151–5.

Cummins, H. (1929). The topographic history of the volar pads in the human embryo (walking pads: Tastballen), *Contributions to Embryology*, **20**, 103–26.

Dror, I.E. and Charlton, D. (2006). Why experts make errors. *Journal of Forensic Identification*, **56** (4), 600–16.

Dror, I.E., Charlton, D. and Peron, A. (2006). Contextual information renders experts vulnerable to making erroneous identifications. *Forensic Science International*, **156** (1), 74–8.

Dror, I.E. and Charlton, D. (2007). Improving perception and judgment: an examination of expert performance. *Fingerprint Whorld*, **33** (129), P232.

Dror, I.E. and Charlton, D. (2007). Methodological and conceptual problems in measuring and enhancing expert performance. *Fingerprint Whorld*, **33** (129), P235.

Fairweather-Tait, S., Hickson, K., McGaw, B. and Reid, M. (1994). Orange juice enhances aluminium absorption from antacid preparation. *European Journal of Clinical Nutrition*, **48**, 71–3.

Good, P. (1987). Uptake of aluminium into CNS lung nasal-olfactory pathway. *The Lancet.*, P1028.

Jaques, A. (1998). *Understanding Dementia*, Churchill Livingstone, New York.

Kent, T. (1993). Fingerprint development handbook (abridged from *The Manual of Fingerprint Development Techniques*, PSDB).

LjunggrenLidums, K.G.V. and Sjogren, B. (1991). Blood and urine concentrations of aluminium among workers exposed to aluminium flake powders. *British Journal of Industrial Medicine*, **48**, 106–9.

Massey, R. and Taylor, D. (1989). Aluminium in food and the environment. *Royal Society of Chemistry, Spec. Publication.* **73**, 14–6.

McLaughinKazantzisKing, A.G.E., TearePorter, D.R. and Owen, R. (1962). Pulmonary fibrosis and encephalopathy associated in the inhalation of aluminium dust. *British Journal of Industrial Medicine*, **19**, 253–63.

Roberts, E. (1986). Alzheimer's disease may begin in the nose and may be caused by aluminosilicates. *Neurobiology Aging*, **7**, 561–7.

Selkoe, D. (1990). Deciphering aluminium disease: the amyloid precursor protein yields new clues. *Science*, **248**, 1058–60.

Sherwood, L. (1993). *Human Physiology: From Cells to Systems*, 2nd edn, West Publishing Company, New York.

Stocker, T. (2007). *Forensic training handbook*, 1st edn, Sussex Police.

Triplett, M. (2007). http://ridgesandfurrows.homestead.com/friction_skin.html

Victoria Forensic Science Centre (2002). Structure of Skin, Module 3, Fingerprint Branch, FPB Training.

6

DNA-Rich Evidence

Terry Bartlett

6.1 Introduction

In 1869, 23 years before fingerprints were first used to solve a murder, Friedrich Miescher discovered 'nuclein', the component of cell nuclei which today we call nucleic acids. More than a century later, deoxyribose nucleic acid (DNA) fingerprints[1] were first used to bring a killer to justice.

The purpose of this chapter is to provide a brief history of DNA and DNA profiling and to review the sources of DNA rich evidence, how they are tested for and how the evidence is collected and stored. By the end of this chapter you should be aware of the limitations of each type of evidence with respect to ease of recovery and evidential value.

6.2 Historical background

The rape and murder of Lynda Mann in 1983 and Dawn Ashworth in 1986 in Narborough, Leicestershire prompted the local police to employ a new technique called restriction fragment length polymorphism (RFLP) analysis of minisatellite DNA, developed by Alec Jeffreys at Leicester University, to try to identify the killer.

---

[1] Whilst the term DNA 'fingerprint' was coined by Alec Jeffreys, the accepted terminology today is DNA profiling.

Crime Scene Management: Scene Specific Methods   Edited by Raul Sutton and Keith Trueman
© 2009 John Wiley & Sons, Ltd

This resulted in DNA evidence excluding from the investigation a local mental hospital employee who had confessed to the assault of Dawn Ashworth. Subsequently, a mass screen of 1400 local men led to the arrest of Colin Pitchfork. He was caught after it was discovered that he had convinced another man to provide a DNA sample for him. Analysis of Pitchfork's DNA led to his conviction for the rape and murder of both victims.

6.3 The structure and properties of DNA

A model for the structure of DNA was proposed in 1953 by James Watson and Francis Crick, based on the X-ray crystallographic data obtained by Maurice Wilkins and Rosalind Franklin (see Figure 6.1). Their model answered questions about its structure and explained how DNA could be replicated.

DNA is a double helix with a deoxyribose sugar-phosphate backbone surrounding a core of nitrogenous bases (Adenine, Cytosine, Guanine and Thymine, or A, C, G and T). The sequence of bases in the DNA strands code for the various genes which make up an individual. The arrangement of the two strands of the helix, and the specific way in which bases 'pair up' (A=T and C≡G), which is dictated by the molecular constraints of the structure of DNA, mean that each strand is able to provide a template for the synthesis of a new daughter strand, thus preserving the sequence of bases between generations. This also provides the means by which DNA profiles can be produced.

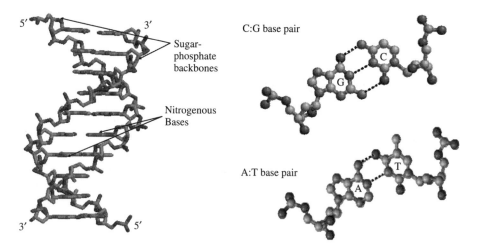

Figure 6.1 The structure of DNA. Three-dimensional structure of DNA. Hydrogen atoms are not shown. Note that the directionality (5′→3′) of the two strands is antiparallel. Dashed lines = hydrogen bonds between base pairs.

6.3.1 DNA profiling

DNA is present in most cells in all living organisms. It can be found in the nucleus of animal, plant and fungal cells, as well as in mitochondria and (in plants) chloroplasts. In humans, nuclear DNA is organized into 46 chromosomes, arranged as 22 autosomal pairs, plus 2 sex determination chromosomes (X, Y or X, X for male or female, respectively). During meiosis, the chromosomes are divided up so that each egg or sperm cell (gamete) receives one copy of each autosomal pair and a sex chromosome. At this time, genetic information can be 'shuffled' between chromosomes. Offspring receive half of their chromosomes from each parent, therefore with each subsequent generation there is a possibility for genetic reorganization, making the DNA of all but identical twins different from any other persons. In humans, mitochondrial DNA is inherited solely from the mother. Whilst it has proven useful in forensic identification (see later) the discriminatory power of mitochondrial DNA is less than for nuclear DNA.

6.4 DNA analysis

Chromosomes in eukaryotes contain a vast amount of DNA which does not code for proteins. Within these regions, there is a greater frequency of mutation, duplication and repetition of short sequences. It is these regions which are exploited by modern DNA profiling methodologies. DNA profiling relies upon stretches of DNA which are repeated many times. These 'tandem repeat' regions can vary between individuals. The length of the repeat can range from a few base pairs up to several thousand base pairs in length. Depending upon the type of screening procedure used, variations in both types can be detected.

6.5 Types of DNA testing

6.5.1 Restriction fragment length polymorphism (RFLP) based techniques

This is the original method developed by Alec Jeffreys. The technique detects regions known as variable number tandem repeats (VNTRs), 'minisatellite' DNA sequences of 14 to 100 base pairs which are repeated between 4 and 40 times. Whilst it was revolutionary at the time, and proved conclusive in securing the conviction of a number of high profile cases, including that of Colin Pitchfork (see above), it proved of limited usefulness because large quantities of intact DNA are required. With crime scene samples the DNA may be degraded and undetectable using VNTR analysis. The procedure is also time consuming. Use of Southern blotting procedures for DNA analysis means that suspect and evidence samples need to be directly compared. In addition, it is difficult to compare samples using automated methods.

6.5.2 Polymerase chain reaction (PCR) based techniques

Around the same time that RFLP was first used in a forensic context, Kary Mullis reported the development of a means of amplifying specific DNA sequences. Small oligonucleotides complementary to regions of DNA which flank the target sequence of interest are used as primers to initiate synthesis of a copy of the target sequence. By using a thermostable DNA polymerase, the newly synthesized DNA copies can be used as templates for further rounds of DNA synthesis. After 30 cycles of PCR, the target sequence can be amplified more than 500 000 000 times. The PCR technique was rapidly adapted to profile DNA recovered from forensic samples using HLA DQα polymorphisms. The use of PCR to obtain a DNA profile that helped to secure a conviction was first presented in court in the United Kingdom in 1991.

The key advantage of PCR based profiling is that smaller quantities of DNA are required. Consequently, samples that were too small to be considered previously can now be used to develop a profile (see Box 6.1). A blood drop the size of a pinhead may contain sufficient DNA to recover a profile if the DNA has not been degraded (see later). Because of the difficulty in analyzing VNTR sequences in crime scene samples, regions (called loci, singular locus) containing short tandem repeat (STR) sequences are used. These loci contain sequences between 2 and 10 base pairs which are repeated several times. The number of repeats at a given locus can be highly variable. Analysis of the number of repeats at several different loci increases the discriminating power of the technique. Testing and identification of DNA patterns specific to an individual can be used by forensic experts to exclude or include individuals as possible sources of biological evidence recovered from crime scene or victim. In the United Kingdom, SGM+ (second generation multiplex, plus sex determination) is currently used to develop profiles for analysis. Because the size of the amplified product is small, the technique lends itself to analysis of highly degraded samples. It is also easy to automate the analysis of samples. Because the data obtained can be entered as a string of numbers it is also possible to store the information electronically in a searchable database, which is another advantage of the technique. DNA profiles generated using SGM+ consist of a string of 20 numbers and an indicator of the gender of the subject. The probability of a match between the SGM+ profiles of two unrelated subjects is on average less than one in 1 billion, although the discriminatory power decreases for related individuals.

Box 6.1. The Lynette White case

Thanks to DNA evidence, a 15-year-old case was finally laid to rest in 2003 after Jeffrey Gafoor was convicted of the murder of Lynette White. Lynette was stabbed more than 50 times in her Cardiff flat on Valentine's Day in 1988. Three men wrongfully convicted for her murder in 1990 had been released after a successful appeal in 1992 and the case was reopened after an independent review prompted a new enquiry. This resulted in the discovery of blood spots on the skirting board in the flat. Because of the time that had elapsed, this new evidence had been painted over but was discovered upon a later reexamination of the crime scene. The DNA in the bloodstain was preserved by this overpainting. Due to the violence of the attack and the amount of blood at the scene, police always believed that the killer had left traces of his blood there and that DNA evidence would eventually catch the killer.

Comparison of the DNA profile obtained from this new evidence with that of Lynette White proved that the blood did not originate from her, and was likely to be that of the killer. The profile didn't match any held on the National DNA Database (NDNADB), but was shown to be a partial match to a subject who had not been born at the time of the murder. Routine questioning of the boy's relatives in Cardiff resulted in the arrest and prosecution of his uncle.

The most recent advances in PCR techniques (low copy number, or LCN) mean that a profile can be recovered from DNA present in microscopic amounts of sample (even sweat droplets can produce a DNA profile). Because of the increased sensitivity of the method, great care must be taken during evidence collection to avoid contamination of the sample (see later).

6.5.3 The National DNA Database

The first database of profiles generated by PCR based profiling methods, the National DNA Database (NDNADB) was established in the United Kingdom in 1995. Similar databases (such as the Combined DNA index system – CODIS – in the United States of America) followed soon afterwards. After changes to the police and criminal justice act in 2003 to allow samples to be taken from anyone arrested for a recordable offence, by the end of March 2005 there were over 3 million subject samples and more than 232 000 crime scene samples stored on the NDNADB. Since May 2001, nearly 196 000 crime scene profiles have been matched with just over 157 000 separate individuals. Most crime scene to subject matches return a single suspect, with the remainder (about 69 000) producing a list of suspects. This is probably due to the fact that crime scene samples are more likely to produce a partial profile because the DNA in the sample is degraded.

6.5.4 Mitochondrial DNA analysis

In humans, most cells contain many mitochondria. These all contain a circular strand of DNA consisting of more than 16 500 base pairs. Mitochondria are inherited solely from the mother, and therefore provide an important means of tracking matrilineage. Because mutation rates in mitochondrial DNA are higher than for nuclear DNA, there is sufficient variation for mitochondrial sequences to be used for forensic purposes, although it has to be borne in mind that the discriminating power is lower, and there is no discrimination between siblings and close maternal relatives. However, this conservation of sequence similarity between closely related individuals over a few generations has been useful in solving some of the mysteries of the early twentieth century (e.g. the fate of the Romanov's, the true identity of 'Anastasia' Romanov and the identification of the remains of Joseph Mengele, to name a few).

Mitochondrial DNA is analyzed by a different method than the STRs in nuclear DNA. Certain regions of the mitochondrial genome have higher mutation rates than others, and are designated hypervariable regions (HVRs). The DNA in these regions accumulates point mutations at approximately 10 times the rate of nuclear DNA. Two regions (HVR1 and HVR2), both around 500 base pairs in length, are sequenced and the degree of divergence from a reference sequence is noted.

Self-assessed questions

6.1   Why is VNTR analysis no longer used?

6.2   What are the advantages of analyzing STRs?

6.3   How does mitochondrial DNA analysis differ from STR profiling?

6.4   What are the advantages and limitations of analyzing mitochondrial DNA?

6.6 Biological evidence

This is defined as a type of physical evidence which contains biological material. Prior to DNA analysis, biological evidence would be analyzed for blood type (ABO, Rhesus, etc.) or specific isoenzymes (e.g. phosphoglucomutase and erythrocyte acid phosphatase, to name two), which was of limited usefulness in linking suspects to crimes because of the frequency with which these markers could be found in the general population. Also, relatively large samples needed to be analyzed, which limited its usefulness as evidence to blood and semen samples left on victims or at the scene of crime. With the advent of DNA analysis of forensic samples, biological evidence has become an increasingly important source of information about potential suspects if a DNA profile can be generated from it. The collection and preservation of biological evidence has therefore become a key aspect of processing crime scenes, victims and potential suspects. It is therefore essential that an accurate assessment of the scene is carried out as soon as possible to enable potential evidence to be correctly preserved and interpreted.

The types of biological evidence which can be useful in solving a crime are not always visible to the naked eye. The most useful sources are blood and semen, or other body fluids that may contain DNA (e.g. saliva, mucus, sweat, urine, etc. that can have epithelial cells present), hair, bones and teeth and tissue samples (e.g. skin and muscle tissue on weapons used for assault). Gastric contents and faecal material can also provide sources of DNA, but generating profiles from them can be difficult due to sample degradation. The quantity of DNA that can be recovered from these sources varies (see Table 6.1), and it must be borne in mind that crime scene samples will contain less usable DNA depending upon the local conditions in which they are found, and the length of time between deposition and collection.

Table 6.1 DNA content of biological samples.

Type of sample	Amount of DNA
Blood (liquid)	20 000–40 000 ng/mL
Blood (stain)	250–500 ng/cm^2
Semen (liquid)	150 000–300 000 ng/mL
Post-coital vaginal swab	10–3 000 ng/swab
Hair (with root) – Plucked	1–750 ng/root
Hair (with root) – Shed	1–10 ng/root
Saliva (liquid)	1 000–10 000 ng/mL
Saliva (oral swab)	100–1 500 ng/swab
Urine	1–20 ng/mL
Bone	3–10 ng/mg
Tissue	50–500 ng/mg

From Lee and Ladd (2001).

Table 6.2 Sources of biological evidence.

Evidence	Possible location of DNA on the evidence	Source of DNA
Baseball bat or similar weapon	Handle, end	Sweat, skin, blood, tissue
Hat, bandanna or mask	Inside surfaces	Sweat, hair, dandruff, saliva
Eyeglasses	Nose or ear pieces, lens	Sweat, skin
Facial tissue, cotton swab	Surface area	Blood, semen, saliva, sweat, mucus, ear wax
Dirty laundry	Surface area	Blood, semen, saliva, sweat
Toothbrush	Brush, handle	Saliva, sweat
Toothpick	Tips	Saliva
Used cigarette	Cigarette end	Saliva
Cigarette lighter	Body	Sweat
Stamp or envelope	Licked area	Saliva
Tape or ligature	Inside/outside surface	Skin, sweat
Watchstrap	Inside/outside surface	Skin, sweat
Bottle, can, or glass	Sides, mouthpiece	Saliva, sweat
Used condom	Inside/outside surface	Semen, vaginal or rectal cells
Blanket, pillow, sheet	Surface area	Sweat, hair, semen, urine, saliva
'Through and through' bullet	Outside surface	Blood, tissue
Bite mark	Person's skin or clothing	Saliva
Fingernail	Partial fingernail scrapings	Blood, sweat, tissue

National Commission on the future of DNA evidence (1999).

The most likely sources of biological evidence have been listed by the National Institute of Justice (see Table 6.2). Different types of sample yield different success rates in the recovery of a full DNA profile. Subject samples are usually high quality and have a high success rate, because the sample (blood, hair or buccal swab) is collected directly from the subject and stored in such a way as to preserve DNA. Crime scene samples are another matter. Usually, they are in a poorer state, possibly degraded (due to environmental conditions at the scene and the length of time they have been there) or contaminated by materials from the crime scene (e.g. fabric dyes, humic acid in soil) which affect DNA recovery or profiling methodologies. According to the Association of Chief Police officers, about 50% of samples recovered from crime scenes yield a partial profile at best. Many of them yield no DNA profile at all. They recommend that sample processing is tailored to suit the type of sample and the substrate it is recovered from in order to improve success rates. For this reason, it is good practice to note the substrate material on documentation submitted to the laboratory so

Table 6.3 Recovery of DNA profile from various sources.

Evidence types	Success rates (%)
Chewing gum	94
Semen	90
Blood	85
Cigarette butts	75
Fingernail clippings	69
Comb/Razor/Toothbrush	53
Hair with roots	50
Saliva	40
Cigarette lighter	23
Watch strap	18
Hair without visible roots	15

Association of Chief Police Officers (2003).

that the best extraction method is employed. Figures for success rates for recovery of a DNA profile from various types of crime scene sample are given below (see Table 6.3).

Self-assessed questions

6.5   What type of biological evidence contains the most DNA?

6.6   What type of biological evidence is least likely to produce a DNA profile?

6.7   What components of gastric and faecal material cause sample degradation?

6.7 Procedures for collection of biological evidence: general considerations

6.7.1 Health and safety considerations

Any biological evidence is a potential source of infection, and as such should be handled with care. It is important that you do not eat, drink, smoke or touch your face whilst handling samples. If biological material originates from a person known or suspected to have hepatitis, tuberculosis or HIV/AIDS, this information must be included on the submission forms accompanying the evidence. Biohazard tape or labels must be used. If evidence is to be stored frozen, glass containers should not be used, as there is a possibility that they could shatter upon thawing.

Certain items of evidence may have sharp edges (needles, broken glass, etc.) and these should be packaged in solid containers resistant to puncture. Sharps should be handled wearing Kevlar impregnated gloves. Evidence bags should never be sealed with staples. Not only does this introduce holes through which contaminants may pass, but there is a risk of injury and possible infection to persons handling the bag.

6.7.2 Protection of scene of crime

As noted in Chapter 3, protection of evidence is fundamental to successful prosecution of a case. It is important to accurately document evidence at the scene. The location, type of evidence and the physical state (e.g. whether it is wet or dry at time of collection) must be carefully noted at the time it is collected. This is especially important for blood spatter evidence.

6.7.3 Contamination

DNA evidence can be contaminated when DNA from another source is mixed with DNA relevant to the case. Because only very small samples are required as evidence, great care must be taken to avoid contamination when identifying collecting and preserving DNA evidence. It is equally important to determine possible sources of contamination if necessary. Evidence processing by as few persons as necessary minimizes the possibility of contamination.

The following should be avoided when collecting evidence:

1. touching areas where you suspect the presence of DNA evidence when you are inspecting a scene;

2. touching your face, nose hair and mouth when collecting and packaging evidence;

3. sneezing or coughing. Even if you are wearing a mask, air loaded with saliva or mucus (and therefore containing your DNA) can escape around the edges of the mask.

6.7.4 Minimizing contamination of potential sources of DNA

In order to minimize contamination, use suitable protective clothing. This not only minimizes the possibility of accidental contamination but also protects you from possible health risks. Wearing two pairs of sterile gloves and a full body coverall (including hair cover) is recommended. Double gloving makes changing the top pair of gloves easier. The top pair should be changed often (ideally, after each sample is recovered) to minimize contamination. Wearing a face mask to cover nose and mouth is also necessary, whilst talking should be kept to a minimum. When recovering sharp objects, consideration must be given to wearing suitable protective gloves. These should in turn be covered by a pair of sterile gloves.

Ancillary activities at the scene should be restricted. Actions that could compromise the scene, such as smoking, eating or drinking, or actions resulting in littering should be avoided. Actions which alter the state of the scene should also be limited. Doors or windows should only be opened or closed when absolutely necessary (e.g. to ventilate a smoke filled room, or to prevent wind and rain from disturbing the scene). Any actions taken which alter the physical appearance of the scene should be carefully documented. Although this is less important today with the prevalence of mobile phones, do not use telephones present at the scene, as there could be important DNA evidence on the ear or mouthpiece. In cases where mobile phone reception is poor, police radio should be used for communications. You should only move evidence prior to documentation and collection if there is a risk it will be lost or destroyed if left in its original location. Detailed notes of the actions taken to preserve the evidence should be made.

Should they require medical examination, victims and suspects of assault should be transported in such a way as to minimize the loss or contamination of possible evidence on their skin, hair or clothes. Prior to transport, it is recommended that they be enclosed in a clean covering, ideally a disposable paper suit with head covering. Their hands should be covered with paper bags taped at the wrists to preserve evidence under fingernails. Consideration should be given to evidence recovery from victims.

Self-assessed questions

6.8 Why should biological evidence be handled with care?

6.9 Why should you avoid touching exposed areas of your face when collecting biological evidence?

6.7.5 Sample collection and storage

As discussed earlier, the chances of producing a full DNA profile from biological samples recovered from a crime scene is variable, therefore the way in which the evidence is recovered and processed is very important to ensure that the DNA present does not become degraded or contaminated. For all biological evidence, each item should be packaged separately using a suitable, properly sealed container (e.g. sealed paper bags or a stout paper sack, cardboard box, etc.). All sides of the packaging should be sealed with tape to minimize contamination and items should be sealed on a clean surface. The recommended method is to use a fresh polythene bag, cut and opened out, so that the clean inner surface becomes the work surface for packaging. When recovering large items, for example bed linen, the orientation of the item should be recorded. Mark the item in such a way that evidence recovered from it in the laboratory can be related to its original position in the scene. Typically, upper and lower surfaces are clearly marked and orientation (e.g. top or bottom, left or right side) are clearly indicated on the item using permanent marker.

Depending upon how recently they were deposited and the volume present, samples at the scene will be either wet or dry. For samples on removable items (e.g. clothing, upholstery, etc.) the whole item should be submitted for analysis (if possible). Wet samples should be allowed to dry completely before packaging. This should be a natural process. **No** attempt should be made to accelerate drying (e.g. use of an oven or hair dryer). You should make a note on the submission form if any stains were wet when the items were collected. If they cannot be dried at the scene, they should be packaged carefully folded with impervious layers between contacting surfaces, to avoid transfer of wet stains to non-stained surfaces (this is important for interpretation of the events that occurred, especially for bloodstain pattern analysis. See Chapter 7). If items are to be transported wet, they should be placed into a plastic bag and sealed. If this is done, it should be noted that significant degradation of the sample can occur, so samples should be stored cold and transported to the police examination room as soon as possible. The items should be dried thoroughly as soon as possible once returned. They should be dried separately to avoid contamination and repackaged in clean packaging. The original packaging should also be dried (if necessary) and included for continuity purposes. Drying cabinets (e.g. Astec) are ideal for drying samples at the laboratory, as they can accommodate several small items at once or larger items singly. They dry samples using a stream of filtered cold air. The outflow is also filtered, protecting the room from contamination and they are self-cleaning, thus minimizing the chance of contamination between samples.

Self-assessed questions

6.10   Why is it important that evidence samples are dried?

6.11   Why is it not recommended to accelerate the drying process?

6.7.6 Collection of blood evidence

In addition to being evidence of the events that have taken place at the scene (see Chapter 7), blood is a very good source of DNA. There is an 85% success rate in recovering a profile from blood found at a crime scene. Prior to collection, a presumptive test should be performed in order to determine that the stain is likely to be blood and not some other material (e.g. coffee, chocolate, vegetable juices) which has the same appearance as blood. Presumptive tests rely upon the fact that haemoglobin in blood possesses a 'pseudoperoxidase' activity. In the presence of hydrogen peroxide, haemoglobin is able to oxidize certain molecules to form coloured products (see Figure 6.2).

6.7.7 Presumptive testing for blood

Tests which are routinely performed are the Leucomalachite green (LMG) and Kastel-Meyer (KM) tests. The basic principle of these tests is shown in Figure 6.2. A variation on these colorimetric tests is the Luminol test, in which photons are released as an end product of the haemoglobin catalyzed reaction of hydrogen

- General peroxidase reaction:

$$AH_2 \text{ (donor)} + ROOH \rightleftharpoons A + ROH + H_2O$$
(reduced)   (peroxide)   (oxidised)

$$H_2O_2 \xrightarrow{\text{In presence of haem}} 2[OH^-]$$

$$AH_2 + 2[OH^-] \longrightarrow A + 2H_2O$$

- AH_2 = reduced, colourless substrate
  - Yields coloured product when oxidised

- Hydrogen peroxide (H_2O_2) generally used as peroxide in reaction

The Kastle-Meyer test

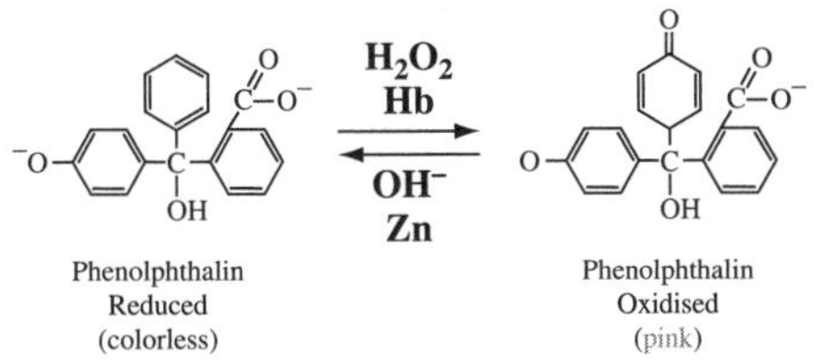

Phenolphthalin
Reduced
(colorless)

Phenolphthalin
Oxidised
(pink)

Figure 6.2   Presumptive testing for blood.

peroxide with luminol (3-aminophthalhydrazide). This reaction is highly sensitive, able to detect blood diluted up to 5 000 000 times. It is very useful for detection of traces of blood on dark surfaces. However, because the luminescence is transient, results need to be viewed in a darkened room and photographed to provide a record of blood spatter at the scene. Care should be taken when using Luminol, as the chemicals used can result in degradation of DNA. Hemastix can also be used for presumptive testing. These are supplied as a bottle of 50 test strips, so an advantage of using them is that there is no need to prepare fresh reagents and carry several bottles to the scene. The simple test involves recovering some of the sample with a moistened swab and then touching the swab to the tip of the hemastix strip. A colour change from yellow to dark green (depending upon the amount of blood present) occurs within seconds and is compared to a colour chart on the bottle to confirm a positive test result.

One drawback of these tests is that they are all susceptible to contaminants at the scene that interfere with the reaction. Peroxidases present in some plant extracts can return false positives, whilst bleach and certain transition group metals (e.g. iron and copper) also return false positives. For this reason, these tests are deemed to be presumptive tests for the presence of blood. Any actual blood present would need to be confirmed by specific tests. One such test is the 'Hexagon OBTI' test, originally developed to detect faecal occult blood, which detects human haemoglobin (hHb) in the sample. The test involves reaction of hHb with specific antibodies and is highly sensitive, being able to detect whole blood up to a dilution of 1 : 1 000 000. The Hb from as few as 500 erythrocytes will return a positive result.

If the suspected blood spot is very small, presumptive testing can result in the removal of a significant portion of the stain, leaving insufficient material to recover DNA for profiling. In these cases, a sample for profiling should be recovered first and the area where it was recovered from is then swabbed for presumptive testing.

6.7.8 Evidence collection and storage

If blood is present it may (or may not) have clotted (see Chapter 7 for differences in the visual appearance of these), which can influence the methods used for collection. Collection procedures for blood on removable items have already been covered (see Section 6.7.5). For bloodstains on immovable items, collection procedures vary. Pools of blood can be collected with a pipette or syringe and placed in a clean, dry screw-cap bottle. Alternatively, the syringe or pipette can be sealed and submitted as they are. Partially clotted blood can be lifted with a sterile knife or swab and stored in the same way. All wet or semi-solid blood samples should be kept in a cool place and transported to the laboratory as soon as possible. If a delay is unavoidable, store samples in a deep freeze (-20°C or lower) prior to transport.

If a large volume of blood is dried onto the surface (e.g. wallpaper or plywood), cut away the surface bearing the bloodstain (if possible). A non-stained piece of the surface material should be taken as a control before the bloodstain is collected to avoid contamination. Place each item in a separate, properly sealed container suitable for storage (e.g. stout paper sack or cardboard box). Alternatively, scrape dry blood onto a sheet of paper and package by folding carefully (e.g. medical 'Beechams' wraps) and seal in a labelled envelope. For smaller dried blood spots, collect the sample by lightly moistening a swab tip with sterile cold water. Swab the stain until the swab appears dark brown/red (or, for very small samples, until the whole stain has been removed) to obtain a high concentration of blood. Chisel tipped swabs are best for recovery of small blood spots, as this minimizes dilution of the stain on recovery. Before sampling, a blank control swab should be obtained from the surface near to, but not in contact with, the blood. Samples should be frozen as soon as possible after collection and stored at −20°C (or lower if possible) until required for DNA recovery.

Self-assessed questions

6.12   What are the advantages and disadvantages of presumptive blood tests?

6.13   How is the presence of blood confirmed?

6.14   Why is it recommended that the tests are performed after the evidence has been collected?

6.7.9 Semen samples

Semen is a very good source of DNA and represents strong evidence of the events that have occurred during sexual assault. It can help to confirm or refute the accounts given by suspect and victim, therefore establishing the presence (and location) of semen and its collection from the scene are of high importance.

6.7.10 Presumptive testing for semen

Visual inspection of items (e.g. clothing, bed linen, carpets and upholstery) using a good light source can reveal the presence of white or off-white stains, which could indicate the presence of semen. Analysis with UV or blue light (e.g. polilight) can show fluorescence, indicating that the stain may be semen. Other fluids may also fluoresce or have a similar appearance to semen, so again it is recommended that a presumptive test is carried out. For semen, the test relies on the presence of an enzyme in seminal fluid known as prostatic acid phosphatase. To carry out the test, moistened blotting paper or a cotton swab is used to pick up soluble materials from the suspect stain. A few drops of reagent (α-naphthyl phosphate and fast blue B) are then added and a rapid (<30 sec) development of a purple colour is indicative of the presence of acid phosphatase. Again, this test is only presumptive for the presence of semen, since phosphatase activity from other sources (e.g. vaginal secretions) can return a false positive result. Also, false negative results are possible, as no phosphatase activity may be detected depending upon the age of the stain. Another drawback of the test is that the reagents are toxic and it is not recommended for use at the scene. Samples should be recovered and a laboratory test requested.

A confirmatory test for seminal fluid involves detection of prostate specific antigen (PSA, or p30) using immunoassay. The test is similar in principle to the OBTI blood test (see above), and was developed for clinical screening for the presence of PSA to diagnose prostate cancer. It has since been validated for detection of PSA in semen samples stored at room temperature for 30 years, and is therefore sensitive enough for most routine testing at a scene or on a victim of sexual assault. Another confirmatory test for semen is microscopic examination. Suspect areas can be swabbed and stained (haematoxylin and eosin, 'Christmas tree' or alkaline fuchsin staining) and examined using a microscope. It can be difficult to perform this test in the field, but if necessary it can be requested as a laboratory test. One disadvantage of this test is that it will not confirm the presence of semen with azoospermic (e.g. samples from vasectomized or infertile males) samples.

6.7.11 Evidence collection and storage

To collect semen stained samples, ideally, the whole item should be submitted to the laboratory. Wet stains should be dried before packaging (see above). If it is not possible to dry the item, small items (e.g. underpants and tampons) may be frozen and submitted to the laboratory as soon as possible. Swabs of stains on immovable items can be taken in the same way as for blood and should be stored frozen prior to submission. A note should be made on the submission form (and medical examination form for victims) of any stains that were wet when the items were obtained. If condoms are recovered, they should be stored frozen in rigid plastic containers. The end of the condom should be sealed in order to prevent contamination of DNA evidence (e.g. from the victim) on the outside by seminal fluid inside the condom. Use a freezer bag clip, rather than tie the end of the condom, as this will preserve potential fingerprint evidence and is less likely to leak condom contents during transport and storage. Condom collection kits are available that contain a clip, plastic container and evidence bag for documentation purposes.

Self-assessed questions

6.15 Why is presumptive testing for acid phosphatase at the scene not recommended?

6.16 How long does semen remain detectable on evidence items?

6.17 Why is it recommended that specific collection kits are used to recover condoms?

6.7.12 Saliva samples

Epithelial cells shed from the buccal lining of the mouth end up in saliva and therefore DNA can be found on any items that have been in contact with saliva. Chewing gum, cigarette ends, the rims of drinking glasses, cans and bottles, balaclavas (or other facemasks), handkerchiefs, toothbrushes, etc. can all be used to recover DNA profiles. An example of the importance of saliva samples comes following a successful pilot scheme in Scotland, where saliva recovery kits were issued to staff of a number of rail businesses to help catch those who spit at them. These kits are intended for staff to collect the saliva and hand this in with their statement for subsequent analysis. This resulted in several trials for assault as a result of the DNA evidence recovered from the saliva and subsequently, the numbers of such assaults dropped during the pilot scheme, resulting in the adoption of the scheme nationwide. Another example of the importance of saliva evidence comes from toothbrushes recovered at cannabis factories, which has resulted in specific individuals being linked with several different factories, often in widespread locations.

6.7.13 Presumptive testing for saliva

If the saliva sample is sufficiently large, a presumptive test for salivary amylase can be performed. Several reagents are commercially available (e.g. SALIgAE, Phadebas) to detect breakdown of starch or a chromogenic substrate, with the release of a coloured product indicative of the presence of saliva. The limitation of these presumptive tests is that they do not differentiate between salivary amylase and other amylase sources (e.g. pancreatic amylase or amylases of non-human origin). More recently, immunological methods to detect salivary alpha amylase using test strips similar to the OBTI blood test kits have been developed. These are specific for human salivary amylase, are quick to perform (results are available in less than ten minutes) and are sensitive, being able to detect the amylase present in one microlitre of saliva.

6.7.14 Evidence collection and storage

To obtain a DNA profile from an individual, buccal swabs are usually taken. However, if it is necessary to establish the presence of other evidential material (e.g. semen in cases of sexual assault), liquid saliva samples should be collected in sterile 25 mL plastic vials. About 10 mL should be collected. It is important that the donor does not wash their mouths out before the sample is provided. Sometimes, collection of a mouth rinse and/or swabs from around teeth and gums can reveal presence of foreign DNA rich material. All samples recovered should be clearly labelled with the donor's name and the date and time taken. Samples should be frozen as soon as possible.

To recover saliva samples from stains, the whole item should be recovered and allowed to dry completely as before. Avoid talking over the item, to minimize possible contamination with saliva from investigators. If wet stains are present on a victim's body (e.g. from kissing or biting), the area should be swabbed using a dry, sterile swab. If the area is dry, double swabbing should be used. Swab the area with a circular motion, firstly using a moistened swab, followed by a dry swab. Swabs should be labelled with the exact location they were taken from as well as the order in which the swabs were used. They should be frozen as soon as possible.

Cigarette ends should be packaged separately in rigid containers (to preserve the condition of the cigarette end itself). If they are wet or recently smoked, they should be frozen as soon as possible. Bottles or cans should be submitted, along with any contents (which should be transferred to a separate plastic container, avoiding wetting the opening of the container). Bottles with 'sports' caps are a good source of DNA, as there are surfaces that can abrade the inside of the lip, thus picking up epithelial cells, and the top can be unscrewed and packaged easily. Alternatively, the rim of the vessel can be swabbed (using the double swab method as before if necessary). Any foodstuffs (e.g. chewing gum, apple cores, etc.) should be stored in sterile plastic containers and frozen as soon as possible.

Self-assessed questions

6.18   What components of saliva contain DNA?

6.19   Why are toothbrushes becoming increasingly important evidence items?

6.20   When should liquid saliva samples be recovered from victims or suspects?

6.7.15 Faecal samples

Faeces can be found at scenes for a number of reasons. Burglars can be nervous and may need to defecate, or may simply leave faeces as an act of defiance. Anal intercourse may also result in deposition of faecal material on clothing or surfaces. Faeces can be a source of DNA (both nuclear and – more commonly – mitochondrial) from epithelial cells lining the gut.

6.7.16 Evidence collection and storage

If possible, the entire stool sample should be submitted using suitable sterile rigid plastic containers. For faecal smears on clothing or other moveable items, submit the whole item, suitably packaged. Small stains on immovable items should be cut from the surface, leaving an unstained area (about 2–3 cm) around the stain. Larger stains should be scraped (using medical wraps as before) or swabbed, using sterile water if required. In these cases, a control swab should also be submitted. It is possible that drug wraps that have been passed through the body may be recovered. It is recommended that these are submitted in their entirety for examination. All faecal samples, swabs and wraps should be stored frozen as soon as possible.

6.7.17 Other biological evidence

As can be seen in Table 6.2, a variety of other biological materials can yield DNA evidence. Sweat is a common source. Distraction burglaries often involve criminals posing as utility company employees. When investigating such scenes, consider swabbing gas taps and stop-cocks, as these areas are unlikely to have been touched for some time and the presence of a suspect's DNA is unlikely to have an innocent explanation. Similarly, window latches in inaccessible areas may have been tempered with so it is important to establish from the victims of such crimes areas the perpetrator may have touched. This extends to boxes or old handbags in wardrobes or under beds (or other places where money may have been hidden) that are unlikely to have picked up a perpetrator's DNA through innocent transfer. Recover evidence from such locations using the double swabbing method as described previously.

Hair, skin, muscle and bone can be left at scenes of violent struggle, especially upon the ends of implements used for assault. If possible, submit the whole item for analysis, but in cases where evidence from sweat may be recovered (e.g. the handle of a bat or hammer), swab these areas first or securely fasten a polythene bag over these areas to prevent contamination. Fingernail clippings from assault victims can provide the assailant's DNA profile. It is recommended that the fingernails are trimmed, rather than scrapings taken from underneath, because current profiling methodologies are so sensitive to contamination. Use DNA free sterile nail clippers if possible, or thoroughly cleaned sharp scissors. If nails are too short to clip, scrapings with fingernail quills should be taken. In both cases, perform this over a pre-folded paper packet then seal inside a polythene bag or sterile plastic container.

Plant material can be a potential source of DNA evidence linking a suspect with a scene. Cannabis leaves should be stored in paper envelopes or bags in a cool dry environment. Small perforations should be made in the packaging to prevent degradation. If whole cannabis plants are recovered, they should be stored individually in paper sacks (do not strip leaves from the plants to be stored separately). Roots should be retained (excess soil may be shaken off before packaging). Do not water plants after seizure, but store them so that they dry naturally. Seeds may also be recovered and packaged in the same way as for leaves.

Self-assessed questions

6.21   Why is DNA recovered from perspiration important as evidence?

6.22   Where should you look for such potential evidence?

6.7.18 Sources of DNA: limitations

DNA evidence can be used to identify victims, perpetrators, witnesses and possible suspects or accomplices. Due to its longevity (unless degraded by one of the factors previously discussed), DNA evidence cannot be used to determine when a suspect handled an item of evidence (e.g. a gun or other weapon used in an assault) or was present at a scene. However, presence of a suspect's DNA in unlikely areas is a useful intelligence tool (see above).

6.8 Limitations of DNA evidence

Identical twins have identical DNA profiles, whilst close relatives can have similar profiles, making absolute identification in such cases difficult. Medical conditions, such as chimaerism or bone marrow transplantation, can result in different profiles being deposited depending upon the type of biological evidence left at the scene.

Environmental factors which lead to DNA degradation (sunlight, bacterial/ mould activity, strong bleaches) can limit its usefulness. Factors which preserve DNA also mean that a timeline for the deposition of the DNA sample cannot be established, although the longevity of DNA evidence has proven highly successful in solving many high profile 'cold' cases, for example, during the analysis of the scene of the rape and murder of Lynette White (see Box 1).

6.9 Elimination and reference samples

These are often required to determine whether evidence originated from a suspect or from another individual unrelated to the case. Collection of reference and elimination samples will differ depending upon the type of crime committed.

For murder and serious assault, it is common practice to document all individuals who have legal access to the scene. Reference samples (typically buccal swabs) should be obtained from all individuals normally present for elimination purposes.

For sexual assault cases, the identity of recent consensual partners (i.e. from the last four days) may be required due to the longevity of DNA evidence on the victim. A DNA sample from the victim is also required for clarification of laboratory results.

Self-assessed questions

6.23 What are the limitations of DNA evidence?

6.24 What sort of environmental factors result in DNA degradation? Why is this an important consideration in police evidence stores?

6.10 Summary

Advances in our understanding of DNA structure and function have led to major advances in the way biological evidence is used. Typing of short tandem repeat loci is the current method of choice for linking suspects to crime scene samples. These sensitive typing methods mean that sample collection and preservation is of paramount importance if a sample is to yield a full profile.

Various sources of biological evidence can be found at a scene. The most important types are blood, semen and saliva. Presumptive testing can help differentiate between the types of sample found. Specific, antibody-based test strips are also available for the main sources of evidence. Once identified, evidence needs to be recovered, packaged and stored correctly to minimize contamination and degradation.

Whilst DNA evidence has advanced forensic science, it has its limitations. It is not possible to differentiate between identical twins, nor is it possible to establish precisely when a DNA sample is left at a scene.

References

Gill, P., Jeffreys, A.J. and Werrett, D.J. (1985) Forensic application of DNA 'fingerprints'. *Nature*, **318** (6046), 577–9.

Hochmeister, M.N., Budowle, B., Sparkes, R., et al. (1999) Evaluation of prostate-specific antigen (PSA) membrane tests for the forensic identification of semen. *Journal of Forensic Science*, **44** (5), 1057–60.

Hochmeister, M.N., Budowle, B., Sparkes, R., et al. (1999) Validation studies of an immunochromatographic 1-step test for the forensic identification of human blood. *Journal of Forensic Science*, **44** (3), 597–602.

Jeffreys, A.J., Wilson, V. and Thein, S.L. (1985) Individual-specific 'fingerprints' of human DNA. *Nature*, **316** (6023), 76–9.

Lee, H.C. and Ladd, C. (2001) Preservation and collection of biological evidence. *Croatian Medical Journal*, **42** (3), 225–8.

Martin, P.D., Schmitter, H. and Schneider, P.M. (2001) A brief history of the formation of DNA databases in forensic science within Europe. *Forensic Science International*, **119** (2), 225–31.

Quarino, L., Dang, Q., Hartmann, J. and Moynihan, J.N. (2005) An ELISA method for the identification of salivary amylase. *Journal of Forensic Science*, **50** (4), 873–6.

Saiki, R.K., Scharf, S., Faloona, F., et al. (1985) Enzymatic amplification of beta-globin genomic sequences and restriction site analysis for diagnosis of sickle cell anemia. *Science*, **230** (4732), 1350–4.

7
Blood Pattern Analysis

Terry Bartlett and Raul Sutton

The voice of your brother's blood is crying to me from the ground
Genesis 4 : 10–12

7.1 Introduction

Some people interpret the above verse from the story of Cain and Abel as a reference to bloodstain pattern analysis (BPA). Whilst this is contentious, there have been numerous historical reports about the uses of BPA. What is clear is that blood patterns have excited the imagination of authors and investigators for many years. This is because the presence of enough blood at the scene of a suspected crime will often be associated with a crime of violence and as such will attract the attention of the media. As a consequence, the crimes are often given a high profile.

The nature of blood pattern analysis is complicated and so the interpretation of blood patterns at the scene is usually the realm of a blood pattern specialist. However, knowledge of simple blood distribution patterns will aid the recovery of other items of evidence, since the sequence of events that gave rise to the particular distribution at the scene can often be elucidated and will direct any search for evidence to appropriate areas. An illustration of this is the identification of a footmark in blood pointing away from a door. This may guide the investigator to adopt due care when entering a room that may be the primary scene of crime.

Crime Scene Management: Scene Specific Methods   Edited by Raul Sutton and Keith Trueman
© 2009 John Wiley & Sons, Ltd

7.2 History of the development of blood spatter as a scientific discipline

Apart from the biblical reference above, there is evidence from records in China around 250 BC of an appreciation of the importance of bloodstain patterns in medico-legal proceedings. Experimentation on bloodstain pattern interpretation has been carried out over the centuries, but it was not well documented until 1895 when a paper published by Eduard Piotrowski examined the effect of impact spatter using anaesthetized rabbits. In the early twentieth century, the use of bloodstain pattern interpretation in criminal investigations was documented by the German forensic chemist Paul Jeserich. Also, in 1901, E.S. Wood made observations on several key aspects of BPA, including the form of bloodstains and drying times for blood, whilst in 1910 the role of BPA in scene examination was discussed by Otto Leers. Victor Balthazard wrote a seminal work on bloodstain pattern experiments in 1939, but a major advance in BPA came with the testimony of Dr Paul Kirk In 1955. He used bloodstain evidence in the case of the *State of Ohio v Samuel Sheppard*, the result being that Sheppard's appeal against his conviction for murder was successful. This case was of key importance in getting bloodstain evidence accepted by the legal system. Bloodstain pattern interpretation was further refined by Herbert MacDonell, who devised experiments to replicate the bloodstain patterns observed at crime scenes. His work, published in 1971 as 'Flight Characteristics and Stain Patterns of Human Blood' represented the first modern research on the subject and the use of bloodstain pattern interpretation and its acceptance by the courts have been improved as a result. MacDonnell held the first advanced course in BPA in 1983. The participants of that course went on to establish the International Association of Bloodstain Pattern Analysts (IABPA) in that year. The IABPA publish a quarterly newsletter in which BPA research is published. BPA work is also frequently published in journals such as *Journal of Forensic Sciences, Journal of the Canadian Society of Forensic Science, American Journal of Forensic Medicine and Pathology* and *Forensic Science International* among others. More recent developments in the 1990s have seen the advent of computer programs to analyze blood spatter and determine areas of origin of impact, as well as Anita Wonder's development of 'keys' for pattern morphology to enable the characterization of impact, cast-off and arterial stain patterns. Most recently, methods using laser based mapping of crime scenes have been adapted to detect and measure bloodstain patterns.

The above account is by no means an exhaustive list of the work that has led to the application of BPA today. It is intended merely to highlight the key events in the development of BPA as a scientific discipline. The sections that follow will cover composition and flight characteristics of blood, and how this is important in the development and interpretation of bloodstain patterns.

7.3 Composition of blood

An understanding of blood distribution patterns will need some basic introduction to the nature of blood. Blood is a liquid with unusual properties. This is because it is an extremely complex mixture of components containing salts and a diverse array of biological molecules, ranging in size from quite small components (such as the adrenal hormones) to extremely large molecules (for example the proteins involved in the clotting process). In addition, blood contains a variety of cells (in particular red and white blood cells) which play an important physiological role and also affect the fluid behaviour of blood. An understanding of some of the components of blood is necessary if we are going to be able to understand some of the chemical methods that are used to reveal blood patterns at crime scenes.

Red Blood Cells (erythrocytes).   These highly specialized cells, shaped like a biconcave disc, occupy a significant proportion of blood volume. Their primary function is transport of oxygen from the lungs to the tissues where it is used. Red cells carry oxygen by binding it to a protein called haemoglobin. Haemoglobin contains a pigment molecule (haem) that is closely involved in oxygen binding and gives blood its characteristic red colour. An unusual property of haemoglobin is that it can also act as an enzyme with a 'peroxidase' like activity. This means it can catalyze (speed up) the following chemical reaction:

$$H_2O_2 + AH_2 \rightarrow 2H_2O + A$$
Hydrogen peroxide + reduced compound $\rightarrow$ water + oxidized compound

The molecule A in its reduced form (AH_2) can be any one of a number of dyes (e.g. phenolphthalein or leucomalachite green) that change colour in response to peroxidases (or in this case, haemoglobin). This property of haemoglobin forms the basis of many of the chemical enhancement methods for visualizing blood patterns at scenes of crime.

White blood cells.   These are also known as leucocytes and are divided into a number of different cells. These cells are involved in a variety of different immune responses within the body. Leucocytes have forensic significance as they contain a nucleus, which can serve as a source of nuclear DNA for DNA profiling.

Platelets.   These are tiny colourless irregularly shaped cells that are closely involved in the blood clotting process (along with other important factors in plasma, such as vitamin K and fibrinogen). Blood clotting is an important factor in blood pattern analysis as the shape of the pattern may change significantly after blood clots.

Plasma.   This straw-coloured liquid occupies about 55% of the blood volume. It is about 90% water, with the remainder of the content being composed of salts, hormones, fatty bodies and proteins. Methods for detection of protein content of both plasma and cellular constituents of blood can also be used in visual enhancement of blood patterns.

Infectious agents.   Blood may contain infectious agents, such as bacteria, viruses and prions (small proteins responsible for diseases such as Creutzfeld–Jacob disease). These render blood present at scenes of crime a potential biohazard and precautions must be taken when examining blood patterns in view of the potential risk of infection from transmissible diseases.

Self-assessed questions

7.1   What fraction of blood contains haemoglobin?

7.2   (a) Name the enzymic activity possessed by haemoglobin.
(b) How do forensic scientists make use of this activity?

7.3   Which constituent of plasma is useful for colour enhancement of blood patterns?

7.4   Why must care be taken if blood deposits are found at the scene of crime?

7.4 Physical properties of blood

Blood is a complex fluid. It has all the properties of that you would expect of a fluid, such as flow drop formation under gravity. A list of some physical properties is shown in Table 7.1:

Table 7.1   Some properties of human blood.

Property	Data
Specific gravity	Adult males 1.058–1.066
	Adult females 1.050–1.066
	Will vary with time of day and health of person
Viscosity	3.5–5.4 (average 4.5) poise
Osmolarity	300–310 mOsm dm^{-3}
pH	735–7.45
Sodium	135–145 mEq dm^{-3}
Protein	6.0–8.4 g dm^{-3}
Haematocrit	Normal male range 40–52%
	Normal female range 36–48%
Haemoglobin	Adult male 13–18 g dm^{-3}
	Adult female 12–16 g dm^{-3}

As was noted in Section 7.3, blood is a mixture of cells, proteins and electrolytes and this affects its fluid dynamic properties. More specifically, blood can be described as a fluidized suspension of elastic cells. The red cells behave as elastic bodies suspended in plasma. This means that blood responds to changes in its environment. In particular, the flow properties of blood are dependent on shear force. Shear force can be defined as a force that impedes the flow of a fluid. This could be a solid (such as the wall of a blood vessel) or a liquid (blood mixing with blood or other fluids). The influence shear force has on blood is important. Viscosity decreases as shear force increases in a non-linear relationship. In physiological terms, a lowered viscosity when shear force is raised means that less force is required to pump blood through narrow capillaries. This allows the circulatory system to function effectively.

The variable viscosity of blood is in marked contrast to a fluid such as water, where viscosity remains constant with change in shear force. Fluids with constant viscosity are described as Newtonian fluids. Because of its behaviour, blood is often referred to as a non-Newtonian fluid.

The non-Newtonian characteristics of blood also extend to the way blood droplets hold together in flight. Newtonian fluid drops are prone to break up into smaller droplets during flight. However, the viscoelastic and colligative properties of blood means that blood drops do not disperse in flight and the drop produces a single stain (dependent on the contact surface) when it lands.

Self-assessed questions

7.5 (a) What is the major difference between Newtonian and non-Newtonian fluids?

(b) To which class in (a) does blood belong?

(c) What physiological benefit results from blood's viscosity properties?

7.6 Give two reasons why blood droplets do not break up in flight

7.5 Causes of bleeding

Blood distribution at the scenes of crime is a result of a variety of causes. There are three reasons why blood may be present at the scene of a crime:

- injury to a person;

- diseases which cause blood to be released from the body;

- post mortem tissue degradation.

In addition blood may be present at the scene because there has been an attempt to cover up the real events by distributing blood over the scene.

Injuries.   There are many types of injuries that can result in blood being left at the scene. Most commonly, these are abrasions (such as a graze), lacerations (where the skin has been split), cuts (made with a sharp instrument), stabs (made with a sharp instrument) and gunshot wounds. Of these, lacerations and cuts can cause significant blood loss, whilst the blood loss from gunshots and stab wounds can be variable.

Disease states.   There are a variety of medical conditions that can result in blood being left at scenes. These include surface sores and ulcerated skin resulting from a variety of causes (e.g. diabetes), or the latter stages of many cancers, where tumour growth has weakened blood vessel walls, causing a rupture. Haematemesis (vomiting of blood) due to liver disease is also a possible source. Blood spread from these events will produce essentially the same patterns as those formed by deliberate actions. It is always useful to check for medical causes if investigating a crime scene where blood is present.

Post mortem.   Blood is lost *post mortem* as cell breakdown autolysis weakens the walls of blood vessels, which then rupture. Typically the thin walled vessels near the surface, such as those of the bodily cavities are susceptible to this type of blood loss. Another type of loss comes as blood is forced out of the body by the gases produced in the putrefaction process; again most commonly from bodily cavities.

Self-assessed questions

7.7   (a) Name three common types of injuries resulting in blood loss.
           (b) State two causes, other than injury, which can result in blood being present at the scene of crime.

7.6 Blood dynamics

Interpretation of the complex patterns present at the scene of a crime is based upon our understanding of the way blood drops form, their characteristics in flight and the likely pattern that they form when they come into contact with a surface. The study of single drops has allowed us to interpret most of the patterns that arise from more complex patterns, such as those resulting when an object impacts upon blood.

   There are two forces holding blood in a single pool. These are surface tension and cohesion. Surface tension arises from the fact that at the surface of a liquid there is more inward force than in the middle of the fluid. The surface tension in blood varies as the composition of blood varies. Cohesion is the way in which molecules within a substance are attracted to each other. In blood, this force is strong. These forces also act to hold a single droplet together, stopping further break up.

Blood drops can form due to the effect of a force upon the fluid. The fluid within blood separates into drops when the forces holding the source of blood in a single pool are less than the forces causing them to separate. This force could be gravitational (blood drips passively from a wound) or the result of movement of something interacting with the source of blood (e.g. a hammer hitting a blood-filled cut). A force within the blood source (e.g. flicking blood off a cut finger) or a mixture of the above may cause blood drops to form.

The effects of cohesion and surface tension means that blood drops are *spherical* in shape and not tear shaped drops (as seen in cartoons). This means that the droplets coming into contact with a target surface will interact as though they are spheres and the pattern that results can be interpreted as such. A record of these interactions will be left as a spatter pattern on the target surface.

Self-assessed questions

7.8 (a) State the two major forces holding blood in a single pool.
   (b) State three forces that can cause blood pools to separate
   (c) What shape are blood droplets in flight?

7.7 Drop-surface impact and droplet pattern

We can understand spatter pattern by examining the effect of angle of impact for a drop-surface contact. We will consider two angles of blood impacting with a surface, perpendicular to the surface and at an angle to the surface.

Perpendicular droplet-surface contact (see Figure 7.1) means that the maximum area of contact is equivalent to the area of the circle at its midpoint. The resultant spatter should be:

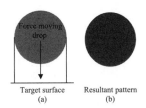

Target surface   Resultant pattern
     (a)   (b)

Figure 7.1 Blood dropping at 90° to target surface. (a) Note that the spherical drop will result in (b) a circular pattern.

- circular in shape;
- there may be distortion around the circumference;
- the minimum surface area will have the same diameter as the drop.

   The blood droplet is still a fluid. Depending on the speed at which the droplet impacts with the surface, there may be movement of the droplet outwards from this first area of contact. The type of recipient surface may also have an effect on this. Outward movement will be more marked as impact velocity increases and/or surface texture becomes rougher.

   Figure 7.2 demonstrates this by means of experiments looking at the effect of height between drop release and target surface (where the velocity increases due to acceleration by gravity). A greater drop diameter and greater spread of blood outside the droplet is seen with increasing drop height. Note also that distortion at the edges also increases as the drop height increases. This type of distortion is described in some texts as 'scallops'.

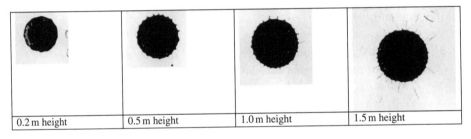

| 0.2 m height | 0.5 m height | 1.0 m height | 1.5 m height |

Figure 7.2   Blood dropped from a plastic pipette onto paper at various heights.

   The pattern that results from impact of a drop with a surface is different where the angle between direction of the blood drop and surface is other than 90° to the target surface (see Figure 7.3). The angle of the ellipse will relate to the angle of impact between blood drop and surface in a predictable way and is given by the following equation:

$$\sin \theta = \frac{width}{length}$$

where θ is the angle of impact (as shown in Figure 7.4). This equation converts into:

$$\theta = \arcsin \left(\frac{width}{length} \right)$$

   The pattern that results from blood impacting with a surface will not be a perfect circle or ellipse. One of the reasons for this is that blood is a liquid that does not solidify on contact with the surface. The initial impact with the target surface will leave a spatter,

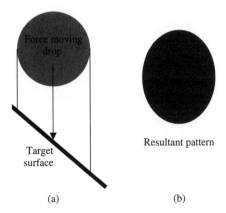

Figure 7.3   Blood dropping at an oblique angle to the target surface. (a) Note that the spherical drop will contact the surface leaving (b) an elliptical pattern.

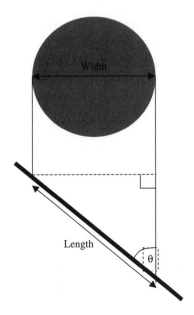

Figure 7.4   Relationship between width and length of blood drop and angle of drop-surface impact. θ is the angle of impact.

but since the blood is a liquid it will continue in motion. There will almost certainly be some radial spread of blood broadening the initial impact and some droplets of blood will be cast off from the initial contact. Cast-off will be in the direction of travel if the blood drop is contacting the surface at an oblique angle. This leaves an effect known as a *leading edge*. A diagrammatic representation of this process is shown in Figure 7.5.

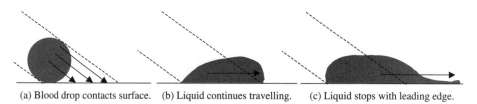

(a) Blood drop contacts surface.   (b) Liquid continues travelling.   (c) Liquid stops with leading edge.

Figure 7.5   Blood landing on a surface continues in motion leaving a leading edge. The dotted lines show the area that would be made by a perfect elliptical pattern.

Origin of drop

Figure 7.6   Blood leading edge used to determine direction that droplet travelled in.

There are various leading edge patterns that are formed but the main point is that the blood continues travelling in a straight line from the origin of path of flight. This means that the leading edge will point directly away from the site of drop origin. An arrow drawn back from the leading edge through the middle of the spatter pattern will go through the origin of the blood drop. This is shown in Figure 7.6.

Self-assessed questions

7.9   (a) State two reasons why blood drops may spread on impact.
      (b) A blood drop is measured to have length 2 mm and width 1 mm.
         (i) Calculate the angle of impact between drop and surface.
        (ii) Explain why leading edges form in blood drops.

7.8 Determination of area of origin of spatter

When blood drops leave a site (whether by impact or other means) droplets will travel in a straight line away from the point of origin, although the trajectory may be altered by the effects of gravity or wind. Each droplet in the resulting pattern will leave a leading edge that can be used to trace back to the area of origin. It is unlikely the area of origin will be a single point due to the fact that the blood source may be:

- moving (as in avoiding a blow from a weapon);
- spread over a large surface;

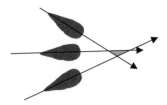

Figure 7.7 Calculating area of origin from blood distribution. This figure shows that the area of origin lies perpendicularly above the shaded area.

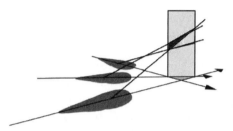

Figure 7.8 Calculating area of origin from blood distribution. This figure shows that the area of origin calculated from combining the two-dimensional region below the area combined with use of angle of impact. Note the different shading for the actual area.

or the force causing blood spatter is spread over a large area (such as a blow from a baseball bat). In simple cases where there is a single impact resulting in spatter, the blood will spatter radially from the site of impact. Figure 7.7 shows how the area perpendicularly below the area of origin can be worked out from using the shape of individual droplets.

The pattern shown in Figure 7.7 will not give the precise area of origin, as the lines have only been drawn in two dimensions. The precise three-dimensional area of origin can be calculated if we combine the two dimensional pattern with the calculation of angle of impact (see Figure 7.8). This method is often achieved by 'stringing' (see Section 7.13). Combination of determining area of origin with digital scene reconstruction can give high impact courtroom presentations.

Self-assessed questions

7.10 (a) Explain why a blood pattern rarely originates from a single point origin.
(b) What two features of a droplet can give an idea of the point of origin of that droplet?

7.9 Cast-off patterns

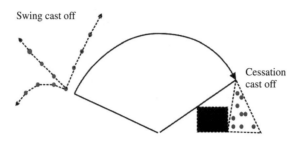

Figure 7.9   Actions resulting in swing and cessation cast off.

These patterns are caused by blood being thrown off an object (which could be part of the body). The result is characteristic patterns both on the object and the recipient surface. Cast off results when sufficient force is given to an object to overcome surface tension and internal cohesion of the blood source to form drops. There are two types of cast off, swing cast off and cessation cast off.

Swing cast off results from swinging an object such as an arm or weapon covered in blood. The droplets are spherical until they make contact with the recipient surface. The direction of the droplet will be a vector of the force applied and gravity. The resultant pattern gives classic 'in-line' staining.

Cessation cast-off results when a bloody object is stopped suddenly. Blood is forced off the object onto the recipient surface. Superficially the pattern resembles impact spatter but leaves a conical spatter pattern.

Both methods of causing cast off are shown in Figure 7.9.

Self-assessed questions

7.11   Name two actions that result in cast off patterns.

7.12   (a) State the pattern that normally arises from swing cast-off.
        (b) Describe the common pattern caused by cessation cast-off.

7.10 Arterial damage patterns

When an artery is breached, varying amounts of blood will be projected from the wound depending upon the location of the artery and the extent of the wound. This will have an effect on the size and shape of the pattern formed. Very large volumes (resulting in gush or spurt patterns) escape from major arteries, whilst smaller spray-type patterns result from either smaller breaches of major arteries or a breach of minor arteries (such as craniofacial arteries).

Arterial damage stains can have characteristic features resulting from the beating of the heart, depending upon the orientation of the wound to the contact surface and whether the victim is moving or stationary (see Figures 7.10–7.12). If the victim is stationary, the blood droplets can fall evenly around the victim as arterial 'rain' (if the wound is facing upwards). Arterial 'fountain' stains may be present if an upward facing wound is in close proximity to a vertical surface. If a victim is stationary and blood is projected onto a vertical surface, an arterial 'gush' is seen. This results from the column

Figure 7.10 Arterial spurt. Note the 'V or W' shape of the overall pattern. Also note the 'runs' caused by the volume of blood shed.

Figure 7.11 Arterial spurt. Note the directionality of the individual stains in the overall pattern.

Figure 7.12   Arterial rain.

of blood escaping from the artery breaking up into droplets which hit the target surface together. These patterns form a dense central disc surrounded by satellite spatters.

Movement of the victim can result in an arterial 'spurt' with characteristic 'S', 'V' or 'W' shaped patterns formed as the pressure fluctuates. Individual stains within the pattern will align with the shape of the overall pattern. They will also be aligned parallel to the direction of travel. This can sometimes result in confusion of arterial damage with cast off patterns. They can be differentiated because a cast off pattern will have individual stains pointing in opposite directions on different arms of the stain. With arterial damage, all stains in the overall pattern will point in the same direction. Additional characteristic features are uniformity in size of, and spacing between, individual stains within the pattern. Also, because of the amount of blood being expelled, there can be evidence of 'runs' from the parent stain if it has been deposited on a vertical surface. Occasionally, spurt or gush patterns may be found close to a small group of randomly arranged spatters that could be mistaken for impact spatter. This is indicative of arterial 'breach' and represents the site at which the injury to the artery occurred. Breach can only be identified and located after other arterial damage patterns have been characterized.

In all cases of suspicious sudden death, a pathologist would attend the scene prior to conducting the post mortem. However, an autopsy report may not mention arterial damage. If analysis of the scene causes you to suspect arterial damage, it is best to confirm this with the pathologist. There have been cases where breach of small arteries (e.g. temporal arteries) have not been recorded during an autopsy, only to be confirmed upon performing a second autopsy after arterial damage patterns had been noted at the scene. Communication with the pathologist in these instances will often help them with their investigations as well.

Self-assessed questions

7.13   Why do arterial damage stains have characteristic S, V or W shapes?

7.14   How are these patterns differentiated from cast off patterns?

7.15   With what other pattern might arterial rain be associated and under what conditions?

7.11 Non-spatter patterns

Any blood stain arising from an event that did not produce spatter is, by definition a non-spatter pattern. These are divided into three groups (transfer patterns, volume blood stains and physiologically altered bloodstains – PABS). Although spatter patterns are not needed for identification of non-spatter patterns, there may be spatter included in the final pattern. These 'complex' patterns (see Section 7.12) provide information about the sequence of events at the scene that is important in corroborating witness or suspect statements when reconstructing events.

7.11.1 Transfer patterns

These patterns involve deposition of blood on a surface as a result of contact with a bloodied item (e.g. a weapon, clothing or parts of the assailant's body or hair). This can be simple direct transfer (see Figure 7.13 contact without movement, e.g. when a weapon is put down), contact of a moving surface against a stationary surface or contact between two surfaces in motion (see Figure 7.14). Patterns can also be produced by an object blocking the deposition of blood on a surface.

7.11.2 Blockage patterns

Technically, these types of pattern could be included in the impact spatter group, as they are generally produced when impact spatter is prevented from landing on a surface by the presence of an object blocking the path of flight. For example, ornaments, crockery, pictures all produce blockage patterns. They are sometimes referred to as 'voids' although care should be used when using this word in reports to indicate

Figure 7.13 Transfer pattern. Bloodied hammer placed on carpet. Note that in certain cases it is possible to determine the type of implement used from the shape of the stain.

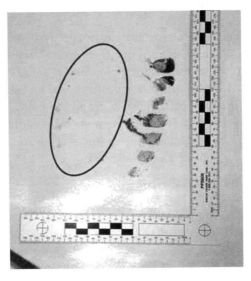

Figure 7.14 Transfer pattern. Bloodied shoeprint (partial). Note that it may be possible to use enhancement techniques to develop more detail in the circled area.

that it is a void in the overall pattern. The term void on its own does not differentiate between a void produced by blockage and an absence of spatter. Voids can sometimes be present in pools of blood if an item has prevented blood from covering a surface as it flows. Subsequent removal of the object will leave a 'void' in the pool.

In both cases, blockage patterns give important information about the sequence of events at a scene. For example, assailant and victim can sometimes be moving through a scene and a blockage pattern resulting from an event at one position can be covered in spatter from a later event occurring at a different position. In these cases, it is possible to distinguish the order of events, because the blockage pattern will contain fewer spatters, which will show directionality. If an item is removed from a blood pool, leaving an impression of its shape behind, it is sometimes possible to identify the item from this impression.

7.11.3 Simple direct transfer

This involves direct contact of surfaces between which blood is transferred. The types of surface involved can have an effect on the transfer pattern. For example, if blood is absorbed on contact with a surface such as unfinished wood or fabrics, the original pattern can be distorted. However, even if this does happen, it is usually possible to discern the original shape of the object. This can be important in determining the size, shape and type of weapon used, especially if such a weapon is recovered in the possession of a suspect.

Bloodied fabric (or fabric that has contacted a bloody surface) can often leave a discernible pattern. Again, this is important in matching a suspect (or their clothing) to a scene. It can also be important in establishing a timeline of events at the scene if such patterns occur in conjunction with other events resulting in blood spatter (complex patterns).

Physiologically altered bloodstains (PABS) also need to be considered when examining transfer patterns. It is important to distinguish between contact with fresh blood, clotting blood, dried (or partially dried) blood and diluted blood (e.g. from attempts to clean up a scene) because this will again provide important information about the timeline and sequence of events.

7.11.4 Moving transfer

With moving transfer, identification of the type of pattern is dependent upon whether the bloodied item was moving or stationary. A 'wipe' pattern is formed when a non-bloodied surface moves through a stationary bloodstained surface. The direction of movement can be determined because the depth of blood increases as it is deposited along the path of movement. A 'damming' effect is also noted, resulting in a concentration of blood at the point of lift-off.

When the bloodied surface is moving and the non-bloodied surface is stationary, a 'swipe' pattern (see Figure 7.15) is seen. These are characterized by a decrease in the amount of blood as it is moved across the surface. A 'feathering' effect is also noted at the point of lift-off, making it possible to determine the direction of movement. Smudges result from movement of two bloodied surfaces coming into contact, for example if there has been an attempt to clean weapons or surfaces at the scene.

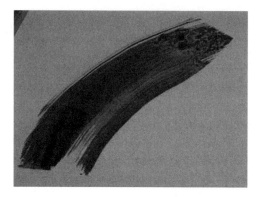

Figure 7.15   Transfer pattern. Swipe blood transfer from a moving source onto an unstained surface.

Hair produces distinctive wipe, swipe or direct transfer patterns. The presence of natural oils on hair means that blood does not adhere evenly to the whole length of the hair. This causes a 'beading' effect on the stain deposited on a surface. It is also possible that the impression of individual strands or locks of hair can be seen in the overall pattern.

Self-assessed questions

7.16   How are wipe and swipe patterns produced and how do we differentiate between them?

7.12 Physiologically altered blood stains (PABS)

These are patterns resulting from effects that cause changes to the blood before it is distributed by other events. These physiological changes may be important in interpreting the subsequent events resulting in pattern formation. They can provide information for scene reconstruction, elapsed time since blood was shed and the sequence of events that took place.

There are four possible changes to blood after shedding:

- drying;
- coagulation;
- settling of cells;
- admixture of blood with other fluids or materials.

The speed at which blood dries is dependent upon the volume of blood present in the stain, air temperature, humidity and the presence of air currents at the site. Small volume stains in warm arid air dry very quickly. It is possible that evidence of gunshot wounds (high velocity spatter) can be lost completely in very warm environments, because the mist-like droplets formed can dry completely before they make contact with the target surface. Alternatively, large volume stains may still be wet for several days after bloodshed if it is cold and there is little air movement. In cool and still air, pools of blood crust over but remain wet underneath. Pooled 'dry' blood on, for example, carpets should be handled carefully, as presence of wet blood that has seeped underneath can result in transfer during scene investigation (this is known as 'investigative transfer'). It has been known for blood to flow underneath the carpet to areas that appear blood free on the surface, only for the stain to become apparent when someone treads on the affected area. Dried spots can 'skeletonize' (loss of central material whilst the outer ring remains intacts, see Figure 7.16). All of these changes will need to be carefully documented in addition to the environmental conditions at the scene, in order to assist with reconstruction of the timeline of events.

Coagulation of blood commences immediately after injury. The process of coagulation provides a plug to seal the wound site and prevent blood loss. The clotting process follows three stages and can give some indication of the timing of events, if sufficient blood is shed and/or conditions permit clotting before drying.

Figure 7.16   PABS dry. Dried blood stain. Note 'skeletonization' (arrowed).

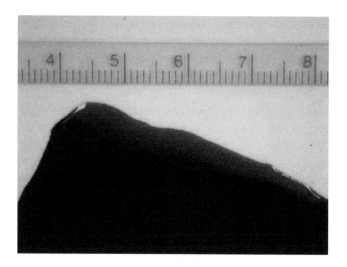

Figure 7.17 PABS clot. Clotting blood in which the clotted material is retracting to leave clearer serum behind.

Clotting is initiated within two to ten minutes of a wound being inflicted, after which the clot will 'firm' (between 10 and 60 minutes after injury). Between one and five hours after injury there will be evidence of clot retraction (see Figure 7.17) and visible separation of clot material and serum. These three stages can be differentiated by the characteristics of the bloodstain.

During the initiation phase, the blood is still fluid, although there may be some evidence of 'beading' if an implement (e.g. scalpel) is drawn through the stain, as parts of the stain have clotted, whilst others have not. The 'firming' stage begins once the initiation process has spread throughout the entire sample. The blood appears 'gelled' and can be difficult to cut. Drawing a scalpel through a firming stain can cause it to break up into smaller clumps (although some red cells and plasma can be left behind). As stains firm on fabric, they take on a characteristic appearance of a dark irregular clump in the centre of a lighter pink halo. The closer the colouration of the halo to that of the fabric is an indication of how firmed the clot is (although determining this is obviously dependent upon the colour of the fabric).

Clot retraction occurs (see Figure 7.17) when the mass containing all of the red cells begins to shrink. This results in the extrusion of a light, straw-coloured serum. At this point, blood will behave both as a solid and a Newtonian liquid if it is redistributed. Because the clot is very difficult to cut, events leading to break-up and redistribution of the clotted material provide information not just about timing of events, but also the sequence of events, as some actions must have taken place at least an hour after the initial events in order for the firming process to have occurred.

Although the duration of each phase is known, only a rough guide to timing of events at a scene can be made. This is because the rate of initiation and firming is dependent upon the type of wound inflicted. Different injuries have different clotting times. For example, compression or tearing of the skin exposes more of the factors responsible for clot initiation, therefore accelerating clot formation. Wounds resulting in less tissue damage (clean cuts, stab wounds to arteries, etc.) result in longer clotting times. The nature of the wounds on the victim should be established before any attempt is made to establish a timeline from the degree of clotting seen.

Settling can occur because erythrocytes are heavier than plasma and once blood is no longer being pumped around the body they will settle out (as seen with 'livor mortis' in corpses). Settling is a relatively slow process (there is little settling observed 60 minutes post-phlebotomy) and it is not usually seen before drying or clotting of shed blood. However, it can be seen if blood is prevented from clotting (e.g. if anticoagulants are present or clotting factors are absent) or drying (e.g. in cold, damp conditions).

Blood can become mixed with a variety of different substances once it has been shed. This can range from other biological fluids (see Figure 7.18, saliva, semen or vaginal secretions, urine, etc.) to non-biological fluids (water and detergents/bleach used to clean up evidence, for example). It may also be mixed with biological solids (bodily tissues, bone fragments, vomit, faeces) or other materials (soil, dust, etc.) present at the scene. Blood can interact with other materials in one of three ways. Intermingling without dilution (often seen with viscous diluents such as semen), intermingling with dilution but without alteration (admixture with watery biological fluids such as sweat and tears does not cause rupture of red cells) or dilution with alteration (red cells are ruptured – haemolyzed – by diluents with a lower concentration than blood).

Figure 7.18 PABS mix. Blood mixed with saliva. Note diluted appearance of some stains. Also note 'beading' effect (arrowed).

It is possible to differentiate between the types of interactions with other fluids using a good magnifier and oblique lighting. Hand-held magnifiers (or a dissecting microscope if the sample can be transported to the laboratory) may show clumps of red cells among strands of mucus if it is mixed with a viscous biological fluid. Diluted blood will have an even, pink or beige appearance (as compared with red, rust or brown coloured stains of undiluted blood) if cells haven't haemolyzed. Often it will have a pale centre and a darker outer edge if cells have lyzed. Blood diluted with watery fluids can be investigated using oblique lighting once the stain is dry. If the contact surface is clearly visible through the stain, this is evidence that the red cells have lyzed. Presence of unlyzed cells will give the stain a grainy opaque appearance.

Self-assessed questions

7.17 Why is it important to note the environmental conditions when examining bloodstain pattern evidence?

7.18 Under what conditions may settling of blood be observed?

7.19 How are diluted bloodstains examined and why?

7.13 Volume blood stains

The definition of a 'volume' stain is somewhat vague. It is generally accepted that it is a stain arising from more than a few drops of blood. Its significance is largely dependent upon the individual factors associated with each case, but an important application of identifying volume stains is an estimation of the amount of blood that has contributed to the stain. This is especially true if a stain is found with no body present at the scene. To be able to tell investigators the amount of blood present is to give them an idea about whether the stain originated from a living or dead body and allow them to direct resources accordingly.

Methods for estimation are available, but all have drawbacks and the results obtained should be treated with caution. The simplest method is the use of plane geometry. Describing the stain as a combination of geometric shapes, coupled with measurement of the sizes of each shape will result in the calculation of the overall surface area. To calculate the volume, the depth of the stain is assumed to be 1 cm (it can be difficult getting an accurate measure of depth, as you cannot determine what effect clotting or drying has had on the sample, or the effect of absorbent surfaces). The obvious disadvantage of this method is that, without an accurate measure of depth, the estimated volume can be wildly inaccurate. For example, if the actual depth of the stain was 0.5 cm, the volume estimate is

100% greater than the actual volume (if the depth is assumed to be 1 cm). If the blood is still liquid, depth can be measured with a stick (but remember to correct for the meniscus formed by surface tension). When reporting the amount of blood, the *minimum volume* present should be stated. As long as the depth is 1 cm or greater, minimum volume statements can be based on estimating the surface area alone.

Another drawback of plane geometry is the need to carry formulae to calculate the surface area for each type of basic geometric shape used. To avoid this, a grid overlay can be used (if the stain is dry). Marking clear plastic sheeting with a 1 cm^2 grid allows the surface area to be calculated from the number of squares covered. Whilst this is more rapid than plane geometry, it has the same disadvantage when calculating volume, in that the depth is assumed to be 1 cm.

A photograph of the stain can be taken, along with a suitable scale placed at right angles to the stain. Printing a photograph and cutting out the shape of the stain, along with a 1 cm square of the scale used, will allow the area to be calculated from the respective weights of the 1 cm square and stain. Again, errors are incurred because the depth is assumed to be 1 cm and inaccuracies in cutting precisely the 1 cm square and the stain will also be introduced. Also, the depth and other characteristics of the stain cannot be determined from the photograph.

A measure of the dry weight of the stain is probably more accurate than any of the above (especially for blood on absorbent surfaces), but is also the most time consuming. A sheet of greaseproof paper (or plastic) is placed under the stained material. This is then placed on top of the same (unstained) material and the shape of the stain is cut out, leaving a copy of the shape of the stain on the unstained material. Care must be taken not to dislodge any dried blood flecks. Both stained and unstained material are then dried thoroughly and weighed, to give an estimate of the dry weight of the blood. Comparison with a standard curve of blood dry weight gives an estimate of the volume of the blood in the stain. The main limitation of this technique (apart from being time consuming) is the variability of dry weight of blood with haematocrit. Drug addiction, alcoholism, certain diseases or other medical conditions can cause large differences in red cell count, and therefore dry weight, compared to blood used for constructing standard curves. Because of this, dry weight determinations should only be relied upon for minimum volume estimates if the volume is 500 cm^3 or more.

Self-assessed questions

7.20   What methods are available for estimation of volume bloodstains?

7.21   What are the limitations associated with the methods used?

7.14 Composite patterns

Violent crimes involving bloodshed do not always leave discrete patterns that are easily interpreted. Quite often, there are multiple events resulting in bloodshed, which can be from different sources (see previous). With an ongoing struggle, the victim and the attacker can be moving, as can blood-soaked weapons, resulting in a variety of patterns at a scene, some of which can overlap. For example, defensive gestures can produce cessation cast-off, moving transfers and direct transfers (usually bloodied footwear impressions). A volume bloodstain could show signs of the struggle between victim and assailant, resulting in a volume and wipe pattern. If a bleeding victim is stationary for some time, blood can drip into a blood pool, resulting in secondary (satellite) spatter. Arterial damage patterns can have elements of volume stains and satellite spatter. Blood that has clotted and then been disturbed will produce a distinctive spatter pattern and can provide important information about the timing of events.

Recording of composite events should include details of the actions that form the composite pattern. This can be important in differentiating between the events and also in establishing the timing of the events. For example, composites produced during a struggle will have different elements (e.g. cessation cast-off produced by defensive gestures) to composites produced by moving an unconscious or dead person.

The identification and characterization of such complex patterns requires the presence of an expert bloodstain pattern analyst. They should be called as soon as possible to assist with investigation of the scene, to minimize the problems that may arise from, for example, investigative transfer.

Self-assessed questions

7.22   Why is it important to document composite bloodstain patterns?

7.15 Investigative transfer and contamination issues

Scenes involving bloodshed are inevitably messy and it is possible that, even with the most careful approach to scene examination, first responders or investigators at a scene will unintentionally create additional bloodstains. Transfer patterns created by individuals present at the scene after the time the crime was committed but before the investigation commences (i.e. the person discovering the scene and the first responding personnel) are called contamination and can be difficult to distinguish unless detailed accounts are taken from these people and the stains can be eliminated from any reconstruction of events. Transfer patterns created after the investigation has commenced are termed investigative transfer. In both cases, these are most often footwear impressions, especially if a large volume of blood has been shed on carpeted floors. As previously mentioned, there have been cases where blood has seeped unseen underneath the carpet only to be drawn to the surface by someone treading on what was thought to be a clean area. Subsequent transfer from now bloodied footwear to other locations in the scene is then possible. Transfer from protective gloves is also known to have occurred, especially from medical personnel treating an injured victim. Occasionally, fabric impressions in blood pools near the body can result from contamination or investigative transfer. In all cases it is important to document when a stain was created and how, because to ignore it could call the entire report into question. A better alternative is to educate all first responding and scenes of crime personnel about the importance of avoiding contamination and investigative transfer whenever possible.

Self-assessed questions

7.23   Why is it important to document investigative transfer?

7.16 Recording traces

Bloodstain patterns are often found on immovable objects and surfaces at a scene. Also, it is often impossible to revisit them once a scene has been cleared. For this reason, good documentation of the precise location and types of pattern found at a scene are of importance. Attention should be paid to the following points when documenting a scene:

- Any records should be completed in a format that allows third parties to reconstruct the scene in its entirety. Detail is important, so don't be concerned about taking too many photographs, notes, and so on.

- Include detail about stains resulting from investigative transfer and contamination. If you ignore these, your report could be disputed.

- More than one medium should be used to document the scene. Video and photography, as well as detailed diagrams and notes are preferred. Recently, LIDAR (LIght Detection And Ranging) has been used. A commercial package is available from Delfttech BV that can document a scene using LIDAR without the need to physically interact with the scene. The data is combined with photography and fed directly to programs that can be used for stringing (see below) and computer aided design (CAD) programs for scene reconstruction.

- The size and shape of the whole spatter pattern should be noted. This helps in determining the events that produced the pattern and is needed for effective presentation of your findings. The sizes and distribution of individual stains within the pattern should also be noted.

- Photography of the whole stain should place it in context with other items in the scene. A size marker should be clearly visible in these photographs so that accurate scaling from transparencies can be used to effectively reconstruct the scene if required. Mid-range and close-up (macro) photography should also be used, especially for individual blood stains in the overall pattern that are to be used for stringing. Adhesive 'ruler tape' printed with both metric and imperial size markers is available for this purpose (see Figure 7.19).

- Any articles that can be removed from the scene (e.g. clothing, bedding) should be packaged after their position in the scene has been documented using the methods above. Care needs to be taken to avoid disruption of the spatter pattern or 'investigative transfer' of blood to non-bloodied areas of the item.

Once measurements of the spatter patterns have been completed, 'stringing' can be used to determine the area of origin of the blood contributing to the stain (see Figure 7.8). Stringing involves the use of poles and string to determine the area of origin manually. This is a time consuming and painstaking process, but is often necessary to reconstruct the events that have taken place. Recently, several computer

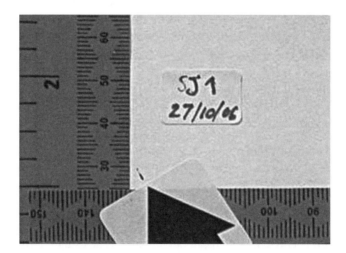

Figure 7.19 Documenting traces. Adhesive ruler tape provides reference to vertical and horizontal axes. Direction of flight indicated by arrow. Unique identifier for stain and date recorded should also be present.

programs (such as 'Backtrack' and 'Haemospat') have become available which can simplify this procedure. LIDAR apparatus records a 360° representation of the crime scene without having to take physical measurements by hand. The stringing programs automatically 'string' the blood spatters, meaning that physical stringing is no longer required, providing a time saving benefit as well as improving health and safety since it minimizes interaction with a scene contaminated with blood. Data from stringing and LIDAR can be fed into CAD software programs to provide 3-D representations of the area of origin and helps with presentation of evidence in court.

Self-assessed questions

7.24   What is 'stringing'? What advantages do automated stringing methods have over manual methods?

7.17 Summary

Blood is a non-Newtonian fluid. Blood droplets are spherical and impacting with a surface as a sphere. This allows the angle with which the droplet impacts with the surface to be calculated. This can be used to determine the area of origin for impact spatter patterns. Blood can leave characteristic patterns that allow us to determine the cause and sequence of events of deposition onto a surface. The recording of such patterns requires careful image processing and may require the bloodstain image to be visually enhanced.

Suggested further reading

An online tutorial introducing bloodstain pattern analysis can be found at: http://www.bloodspatter.com/BPATutorial.htm

Bevel, T. and Gardner, R.M. (2008) *Bloodstain pattern analysis with an introduction to crime scene reconstruction. Practical Aspects of Criminal and Forensic Investigations*, 3rd edn, CRC Press Inc.

International Association of Bloodstain Pattern Analysts (www.iabpa.org).

James, S.H. and Eckert, W.G. (1998) Interpretation of bloodstain evidence at crime scenes. *Practical Aspects of Criminal & Forensic Investigation*, CRC Press Inc.

Scientific working group on bloodstain pattern analysis (SWGSTAIN) (www.swgstain.org).

Wonder, A. (2001) *Blood Dynamics*. Academic Press.

8
Physical Evidence

Craig Williams

8.1 Introduction

Articles left at a crime scene can be either macroscopic or microscopic, the latter often being termed trace or contact evidence. This chapter will explore both types of physical evidence. The range of physical evidence is large and it is worthwhile listing them. The major types of items recovered at the scene include tool marks, clothing, fibres, footwear impressions, firearms, explosives and their residues, glass fragments, paint flakes, soil, drugs and IT equipment. However, since any object found at a crime scene is capable of being of evidential value this list is by no means exhaustive.

The subsequent analysis of items of physical evidence recovered from scenes of crime is covered in other texts, but an appreciation of how such items are to be analyzed will govern the appropriate collection methods. Each of these types of physical evidence will be covered separately in this chapter.

8.2 Tool marks

A tool mark is an impression or gouge left in an object by cutting, drilling or levering, (often a door or window frame) by a tool because the metal of the tool is harder than the item being cut. Most tools have characteristic nicks or dents in their working surface caused during normal use, these are called striations. New tools will also have random striations produced during their manufacture.

Crime Scene Management: Scene Specific Methods   Edited by Raul Sutton and Keith Trueman
© 2009 John Wiley & Sons, Ltd

Damage on the tip of a wood chisel used   Test striations left on lead by the chisel
during a break-in

Figure 8.1 Comparison of tool mark with its impression. (a) damage on the tip of a wood chisel used during a break-in; (b) test striations left on lead by the chisel.

These striations can be microscopic and will thus leave microscopic ridges and valleys. Most marks allow the examiner to identify the type of tool used and its size but to identify a particular tool the microscopic ridges and valleys, together with any larger 'nicks', need to be matched. Figure 8.1 shows an example of both larger nicks and the microscopic striations used in identification.

Whenever possible, the whole object containing tool marks should be submitted to the laboratory instead of just removing the area containing the mark. If this is not possible, take a scaled photograph and sketch the area containing the mark prior to using a casting material to replicate the damage. Although the photograph will not be sufficient to allow the laboratory to perform a tool mark comparison with the tool, it will assist in determining how the mark was made so that test marks can be more easily made. It is important that oblique lighting is used to make the individualizing features of the tool mark cast shadows so they can easily be seen and photographed.

A comparison microscope is often used when studying tool marks. It must be remembered that it can be very difficult in laboratory conditions to replicate a tool mark from a crime scene. The usual method used to prepare a series of standards is to apply the suspect tool at various angles and pressures onto a piece of lead. If practical, the object bearing the tool mark should be submitted for laboratory examination. If the object cannot be moved then a cast of the mark using dental plaster, or a proprietary silicone moulding material such as SILMARK, should be made, after comprehensive photographs have been taken (see Figure 8.2 for methodology). Poor casts are useless for comparison purposes and remember that some marks will be damaged if improper methods are used.

If a tool and tool mark are both recovered from the same crime scene they must be kept apart and packaged separately, to maintain the integrity of the evidence. It is important that the tool is handled in such a way that the working surface is protected from further damage in order to make the comparison with the scene

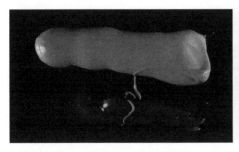

(a) 'SILMARK' is a two-part compound....

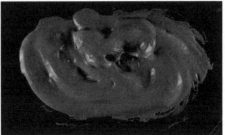

(b) .....which is mixed thoroughly,.....

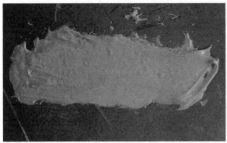

(c) ....spread evenly and smoothly over the striations

(d) .....and when set can be lifted to reveal impressions of the marks

Figure 8.2 The use of silicone resin to capture tool marks left on a recipient surface. (a) 'SILMARK' is a two-part compound; (b) which is mixed thoroughly; (c) spread evenly and smoothly over the striations and (d) when set can be lifted to reveal impressions of the marks.

marks. Tools are normally packaged in rigid cardboard boxes or clear cylindrical plastic tubes, suitably packed to stop the tool moving about during transit. Finally, when dealing with the suspect tool and its mark it should be borne in mind that other material such as paint or oil may also have been transferred from one to the other. This could add greatly to the evidential value of the tool mark.

Self-assessed questions

8.1 The most famous case where tool mark evidence was used is the Lindbergh case of 1932 in the United States. Do your own literature search and answer the following. What types of tool marks were left on what object in this case?

8.2 Why was the tool mark matching evidence of such high evidential value?

8.3 Clothing

The damage to articles of clothing can often give a clue to the type of crime that has been committed. The damage is often examined by eye or with the aid of a hand lens. Things to be considered are the position of the fabric damage, whether the damage has neat or frayed cuts, and the shape of the cut. These observations can make it possible to deduce if a stabbing assault was by knife, scissors or screwdriver and so on. However it must be noted that the clothing article should be examined prior to any cleaning as this will make the examination of a cut or tear much more difficult. Any suspect clothing must also be carefully packaged to avoid any possibility of a rip or tear being aggravated. If articles of clothing are wet or blood stained they should be air-dried before packing. Once dry, clothing should be carefully interleaved (this is where the article of clothing is sandwiched between two sheets of brown paper and then folded) with the minimum of disturbance, thus minimizing the chance of any trace evidence being shaken off the article or transferred from between different areas on the article of clothing. Once interleaved, the clothing should be folded and sealed in brown paper bags with tamper evident seals. The bag size should be such that the clothing fits snugly into it to minimize movement during transit. If the clothing is stained with DNA-rich materials then it is imperative that the stain is analyzed for its DNA content as quickly as possible. The reader should refer to the chapter on DNA evidence.

Self-assessed questions

8.3   One of the most famous cases where an article of clothing played an important part was that of former US president Bill Clinton:

(a) Do your own literature search to identify the article of clothing;

(b) Describe the evidence obtained in this case.

8.4 Fibres

The number of different fibres in our modern world is enormous. Not only do we have natural and synthetic fibres but there are a large number of colours and finishes available. However the evidential value of fibres is not great due to the mass production techniques now used. Having said this, fibres are still important physical evidence in helping to secure convictions.

The most common natural fibre is cotton followed by wool, then cashmere and mohair. The evidential value of cotton is very low unless it is dyed an unusual colour, while the evidential value of mohair is much greater due to its relative scarcity.

Man-made fibres were introduced in the 1930s and large-scale production began in the 1950s and continues today. They are all polymer based and can be identified by a number of microscopic and chemical means.

One of the most conclusive ways of identifying if a control fibre sample matches a suspect fibre is by physical fit. If a torn shred of textile material left, say, on a broken window exactly matches the tear in a suspect's clothing then the evidential value is very high. However, very often, only strands of material are left behind. When this is the case, the method of fibre removal is very important as the method should remove the target fibres while leaving behind as much unwanted fibre as possible. It is important to record the location of each of the fibres. Various methods have been employed with varying success. These include portable narrow nozzle vacuum cleaners with appropriate collection systems, hand removal of obvious fibres with a hand lens and tweezers or fibre tape lifting.

The most commonly used method in the United Kingdom is tape lifting, where sticky tape is pressed against the surface in question so that the fibres adhere; the tape is then lifted off. The tape is then stuck to a clear plastic sheet, securing the fibres and ensuring there is no contamination and if gathered at the scene labelled and secured in the same way as a fingerprint lift. The fibres can then be examined by eye. If required, any of the fibres can subsequently be removed from the tape/plastic film sandwich for further tests by using a suitable solvent to loosen the fibre from the tape's adhesive. It is also important when using trace fibre evidence that control samples are taken. So if we have a crime scene with fibre evidence and a suspect then control fibres from the suspect's clothing or other suitable source are taken to see if they match those at the crime scene.

The first step in identifying a fibre is light microscopy examination of the diameter and shape of its cross section, together with determination of its colour. Other features to be examined are the presence or absence of delustrant and any striations along the fibre's length.

Self-assessed questions

8.4   Perform your own literature search for the case of Wayne Williams convicted in the United States in 1982. Briefly describe the type of fibre evidence that was used in this conviction.

One of the most useful methods of determining the diameter and cross sectional shape of a fibre is scanning electron microscopy, which, if linked to an EDX unit, can also provide elemental composition data. However if SEM/EDX is not available the diameter and cross sectional shape can be determined using light microscopy at 100x–400x magnification (Figure 8.3).

The colour of a fibre is usually determined using a micro-spectrophotometer (see Figure 8.4), where very small fragments of fibre can be examined in a non-destructive manner and the absorption spectrum of the fibre determined.

Very often similarly coloured fibres give quite different absorption spectra because dye manufacturers often use different dye mixtures to produce similar

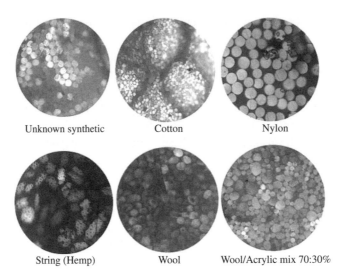

Figure 8.3 Micrographs of cross-sections through several different fibre types at 100x magnification.

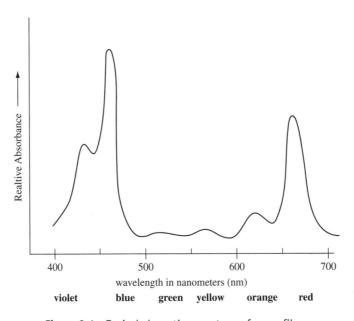

Figure 8.4 Typical absorption spectrum of green fibre.

shades. More recently, micro-infrared spectrometers have become available and it is possible to get compositional information from very small fibre fragments.

Another important property of man made fibres is that of birefringence. This feature is a result of the manufacturing process whereby the polymer molecules all become aligned in the same direction. Therefore if light is passed through a fibre it emerges polarized, perpendicular and parallel to the length of the fibre. The two planes of light will have different refractive indices and birefringence is the numerical difference value between the two refractive indices. This numerical value is a characteristic of the fibre and can be compared to a reference table of known fibres and their birefringence value. Therefore the forensic scientist can quickly identify the colour and chemical nature of a small fibre typically only 1 mm long.

Self-assessed questions

8.5 Why is the use of EDX alone not a satisfactory method for determining the identity of a man made fibre?

8.5 Footwear impressions

Every crime scene has the potential to reveal footwear impressions if you consider that the offender must have been in contact with the floor or other surfaces and these impressions are most likely to be left at the scene. However, they are also the most likely to be arbitrarily destroyed. Footwear impressions (see Figure 8.5) that

Figure 8.5   Footwear impression left at the scene of a crime.

are found at crime scenes may be from materials transferred from outside, an imprint in dust on a hard floor or an imprint found in blood.

The first thing to do on finding an impression is to photograph it with an appropriate scale. This has already been discussed earlier and the reader should refer to the scene photography chapter for further details.

If the impression is on an item that can be removed from the crime scene then this should be done, again appropriately packaged to ensure sample integrity. If the imprint cannot be moved, but is on a hard surface, then an impression of the print can be taken, similar to lifting a fingerprint. If possible, an impression of the whole print should be taken, but if this is not possible, where, for example part of the print is on a hard surface and part on a fabric, then an electrostatic lifting technique can be used. The reader is directed to Milne's 1998 article on electrostatic lifting of marks at crime scenes for a full explanation of this recent development.

If the footwear impression is outside in soft earth then the usual procedure after photography is to make a plaster cast of the impression. It is important to allow the plaster to fully harden before being moved and this may necessitate the loose covering of the plaster *in situ* with polythene in case of rain.

If the impression is in mud or snow and the weight of the plaster would deform the impression it may be advisable to spray the impression with an aerosol wax several times, allow this to harden and then pour the plaster into the impression and then allow it to set fully before removal. If the footwear impression is in blood (see Figure 8.6) again the first action is to photograph it. If the impression is very faint then a number of chemical agents can be used to enhance the impression (see chapter on DNA-rich materials for more information). All these enhancers appear to have no adverse affects on subsequent STR DNA typing.

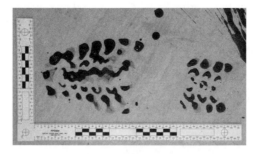

Figure 8.6   Footwear impression left a perpetrator at scene of crime in blood.

Once the impression or cast arrives at the forensic laboratory it can be identified as a certain shoe size and the manufacturer can normally be identified from the sole pattern. This initial identification is currently done using a computerized system such as SICAR (Shoeprint Image Capture And Retrieval). This system not only carries the sole patterns for many manufacturers, but it also contains sole impressions from the shoes of suspects in custody and impressions left at other crime scenes. However when matching a suspect's shoe with the imprint this is not enough and further evidential value is required. This is normally found in the individual wear damage to the sole, such as worn out sections of the sole pattern, cuts or tears, and so on.

Self-assessed questions

8.6 What type of enhancers can be used for very faint impressions in blood?

8.6 Glass fragments

Many crime scenes, which involve a 'break in' through a window, will have glass fragments, as do many road traffic hit-and-run crime scenes. Therefore the identification of glass fragments is important to forensic science.

Glass is a hard, but generally brittle, amorphous solid made by reacting sand with a number of alkali or alkaline earth metal oxides. The most common form of glass is soda-lime glass, made by reacting sodium carbonate and calcium oxide with sand. It is widely used in windows and bottles.

There are a number of specialized glasses and special treatments available, including lead crystal and heat resistant glass (e.g. Pyrex). In the former, lead oxide is added to the glass melt and in the latter, boron oxide is added. Special treatments include the rapid heating and cooling of glass to induce a large amount of strain and when this glass breaks it tends to fragment into cubes rather then shatter into long shards. This material is known as 'toughened' glass and is used in the side and back windows of motor vehicles. Another form of special treatment involves sandwiching a layer of plastic between two layers of ordinary glass. This is termed laminated glass and as it is less likely to shatter on impact has led to its use in vehicle windscreens.

During glass collection it is important that Mylar gloves are worn to protect the collectors' hands from cuts.

The shoes and clothing of suspects or other objects contaminated with glass should be dried if wet then wrapped in paper, sealed in a tamper evident bag and submitted to the laboratory for examination. If possible, all glass found at hit-and-run scenes should be recovered. Remember that the search should not be limited to the point of impact, because headlight glass may become dislodged at some distance away as the car leaves the crime scene. Glass from different locations should be carefully marked and packaged in different containers. Ideally, *all* glass should be collected because more than one type may be present. In addition, if just a few representative samples are saved, individual pieces that could be physically matched with glass remaining in the headlight shell of the suspected vehicle may be overlooked.

Any *small* glass fragments should be placed in paper bundles, and then in coin envelopes, pillboxes, or film cans which can be marked and completely sealed.

Any *large* glass fragments should be placed in cardboard boxes. Separate the individual pieces with cotton wool or tissue paper to prevent breakage and damaging the edges during transit. Seal and mark the boxes containing them.

If the broken window is small and can easily be removed, send the whole window or all glass remaining to the laboratory. If the window is large, recover several samples from different areas of the window. If the evidence glass is large enough for physically matching the broken edges, or for comparing the fracture lines, surface abrasions or contamination, then take as much of the broken window as necessary. For car headlights all glass remaining in the headlamp should be recovered. If it is suspected that a new glass has been installed, this should be removed and a careful examination made for small chips remaining in the headlamp from the previous lens. In such cases, also submit the new lens to the laboratory.

When bottles or other glass objects are broken, recover all remaining glass.

If the glass fragments found are large then certain physical characteristics can be directly observed, such as curvature (for bottle fragments or vehicle lights), colour, thickness and so on. Physical fit may also be possible and, if so, has enormous evidential value. Unfortunately most fragments found on suspects are microscopic and physical fit is not an option. When this is the case, the two most widely used methods to identify the type of glass found are determination of density and refractive index: both are readily observed and the methods employed are non-destructive.

The flotation method is used to measure the density of glass. Here the fragment is placed in a suitable container, such as a measuring cylinder, and bromobenzene (density $1.50\,\mathrm{g\,cm^{-1}}$) is added. The glass will sink (typical density for glass is around $2.5\,\mathrm{g\,cm^{-1}}$), then bromoform (density $2.89\,\mathrm{g\,cm^{-1}}$) is slowly added and when the glass becomes suspended in the solution the ratio of bromobenzene/bromoform is noted and the liquid density calculated. As the glass is now suspended in that solution it too has that density. The glass control is also subjected to the same procedure and if it floats at the same ratio then the control and suspect glass fragment have the same densities.

A further confirmatory test is to determine the refractive index of the suspected fragment (this is the ratio of the speed of light in a vacuum to the speed of light in the suspect glass and it has the symbol n) and a control. This is done using the immersion method. Here the glass is immersed in a transparent, colourless, high boiling-point liquid, such as silicone oil, whose refractive index is varied by adjusting the liquid's temperature. The instrument used to carry out this test is a hot stage microscope. As the temperature increases, the refractive index of the oil changes while that of the glass remains constant. The 'match point' is reached once the Becke line (the bright halo surrounding the glass fragment) has disappeared and there is minimum contrast between the oil and glass. The refractive index of the glass and oil are now very similar. A calibration graph is consulted and the refractive index of the glass determined.

There is an automated system for refractive index determination known as the GRIM 3 supplied by Foster and Freeman in the United Kingdom, which uses a PC driven hot stage and image analysis software to determine match point. The chemical composition of glass fragments can be determined using SEM/EDX analysis. To distinguish between toughened and non-toughened glass you measure the refractive index as normal then slowly heat and then cool the glass fragment to anneal it. The change in refractive index before and after annealing for toughened glass is significantly greater then non-toughened glass.

Self-assessed questions

8.7   List the different types of glass that can be found and identify which is the most common.

8.7 Glass fragmentation

When glass is hit by a small fast-moving object it fractures to produce a circular hole with cracks both encircling and radiating outwards from the hole. The cracks encircling the hole are known as concentric fractures, while the ones radiating from the hole are termed radial fractures (Figure 8.7).

The hole is narrowest on the impact side and so it is relatively easy to determine the direction the object was travelling. The case is not so simple with slow moving or large objects; here the hole formed will be irregular or the pane may be completely broken in pieces. In this instance information may be obtained from examination of the concentric and radial fractures. As glass is hit by an object, it initially bends away from that object until it reaches a point where it shatters. During this bending, stress marks, known as Walner Lines, are formed within the glass. If glass fragments still housed in the window frame are examined edge on, using a low power microscope or a magnifying glass, it is possible to see these stress marks (Figure 8.8).

As can be seen from the photo, such stress marks take the form of J-shaped curves with one end of the 'J' perpendicular to one glass surface and the other nearly parallel. If the fracture is radial then the perpendicular section of the stress mark is on the reverse side of the impact direction. For concentric fractures the perpendicular section is on the side of impact. Unfortunately toughened glass does not form radial and concentric fractures and impact direction information cannot be gathered.

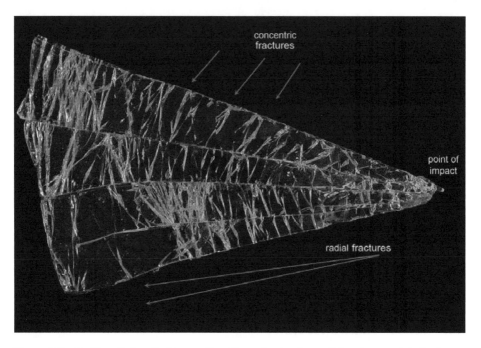

Figure 8.7 Section of glass that has suffered impacts showing radial and concentric fractures. Note that the concentric fractures butt up against but do not cross the radial fractures, indicating that the former occurred after the latter.

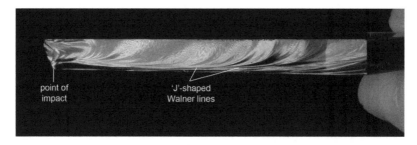

Figure 8.8 Picture of glass showing the direction of stress lines in cross section caused by impact of object shattering the glass.

If a sheet of glass has received several high-speed impacts but remains intact then it is possible to determine the sequence of impacts. This is because a new fracture always terminates at an existing fracture. Figure 8.9 below shows a sheet of glass that has received three impacts and by observing the radial fractures we can see the sequence.

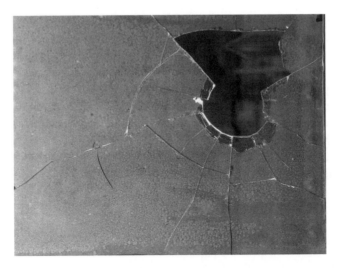

Figure 8.9 The order of impact of bullets in a pane of glass can be worked out from the shatter lines. New lines caused by later impact will not cross existing fractures.

It is important to gather as many glass samples as possible from a crime scene so that either a physical fit or a compositional analysis can be made to any fragments found on a suspect. The glass from a crime scene must be handled and stored very carefully to avoid further fragmentation. As no two panes of glass fragment in the same way any physical fit has very strong evidential value.

Self-assessed questions

8.8 (a) Will a fracture line always terminate at an existing fracture line?

(b) What are the characteristics of a hole made in glass from a bullet?

8.8 Soils

Soils are a complex mixture of minerals, organic material, vegetation and, depending upon locality, man-made materials such as brick dust, concrete and tarmac. The usefulness of soil in forensic science is its prevalence and transferability to a suspect's shoes, clothing or even weapons used at a crime scene. Luckily, although prevalent soil does vary significantly from location to location, if the soil type can be determined it is possible to either match the soil on a suspect to a crime scene or, if the crime scene is unknown, then it can help in determining the scene location. There are a number of tests used to identify and match soil samples. The first test is colour comparison. There are around 1100 different soil colours and, as soil colour varies with moisture content, it is vital that both sample and reference soils are dried in identical conditions. If the soil sample is ingrained into a fabric then it is best to smear the reference sample onto an identical fabric, if possible, before making the colour comparison. After colour comparisons the soil can be examined with a low powered microscope to show animal, plant and man made debris. A high powered microscope will reveal the mineral and rock fragments within the soil. There are a large number of minerals and different rock-types which can be present in soils and it is their presence or absence which makes soils so variable from location to location. There are a number of other techniques used in soil analysis and these include soil density measurements, particle size determination, thermal analysis and X-ray diffraction. The reader should refer to Ken Pye's book on soils (reference at end of chapter).

8.9 Firearms

Figure 8.10 shows the key features that can individualize a weapon or the ammunition that has been used by two types of firearms, a 9 mm semi-automatic weapon and a revolver. The barrel is drilled out from a solid rod of steel in the manufacture of a firearm. This drilling process leaves microscopic striations on the inner surface of the barrel. Furthermore, the manufacturing process introduces spiral grooves, typically 1 mm deep, known as 'rifling' (see Figure 8.11). This rifling is to impart spin to the bullet as it travels along the barrel. Once the bullet has left the gun the spin ensures that the bullet will travel on a straight and accurate course. The non-grooved sections of the barrel represent the original bore and are called 'lands'.

Note here that shotguns are 'firearms' but are not rifled and are termed 'smooth-bore' weapons. Different manufacturers use different rifling methods and these produce different numbers of lands. In addition, the spiralling, known as 'twist', can be clockwise or anticlockwise.

The calibre of a firearm is the diameter of the gun barrel measured between opposite lands and is quoted in mm (i.e. 9 mm) or hundredths of an inch (i.e. 38, often just termed '38'). Cartridges normally have the calibre stamped on them, together with other coded information such as the cartridge length. It would be expected that guns of the same calibre from the same manufacturer would have identical characteristics, but luckily for the forensic examiner this is not so. During a gun barrel's manufacture very small fine lines or striations are formed and these are randomly generated. This means that identical-type guns produced by any manufacturer will be different even if made in succession. When a bullet is fired its outer surface is impressed with both the rifling marks and more importantly the

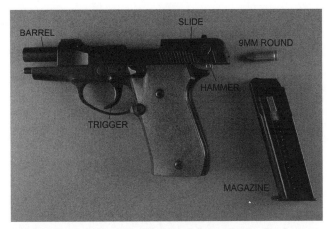

(a) 9 mm semi-automatic pistol in unloaded state, showing key features

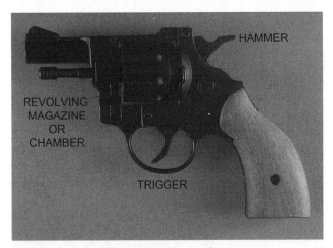

(b) Revolver, showing key features

Figure 8.10 Handgun key features (a) pistol (b) revolver. (a) 9 mm semi-automatic pistol in unloaded state, showing key features. (b) revolver, showing key features.

striations (see Figure 8.12). This links the bullet to one particular firearm. If bullets are retrieved from a crime scene then they can be compared to a suspect weapon. However, as it is impractical to saw the gun barrel along its length another way to make the comparison has to be found. The normal practice is to load the suspect weapon with identical ammunition and discharge the gun into a box of ballistic gel, wax, cotton waste or water. The bullet is then retrieved and an examination begins. Initially the number of grooves and lands are checked, together with the direction of twist. If the number of lands, grooves and twist match then further

Figure 8.11 Cross-section of a typical firearm barrel showing the arrangement of lands and grooves that form rifling.

Figure 8.12 Composite photo of two 9 mm bullets under a comparison microscope. The matching of the striations should be carried out by an expert.

investigation into the striation pattern is undertaken using a comparison microscope.

The matching of striations is not infallible and there are a number of factors that can make matching difficult. These include corrosion on the inside of the barrel (this is especially a problem with weapons discarded into water), deliberate damage to the barrel to avoid forensic matching, barrel wear due to excessive use, changing the barrel used in the offence or damage to the bullet on impact. These factors should be taken into account when declaring a match or not. Other forensic evidence may also be obtained from recovered bullets such as paint, cement, blood, bone, fibres or hair. This evidence can be examined using appropriate analytical techniques.

If spent cartridge cases are recovered from a crime scene consideration must be given to their examination for all types of forensic evidence, not just ballistic. For example, spent cartridges have the potential to retain DNA and latent fingerprints. Therefore consideration must be given to recover these types of material before any other analysis is made that might obliterate such evidence. From the cartridge case design it is possible to deduce if it is from a handgun, rifle or shotgun and what calibre, shape and type of weapon was used to fire the cartridge. Marks on the cartridge case can also indicate if the weapon was self-loading, as such weapons create marks during the extraction or ejection of the spent cartridge case (Figure 8.13).

When a cartridge is fired the shape of the firing pin will be impressed into the soft metal of the primer. As the bullet moves down the barrel the cartridge is forced back against the breechblock, when it becomes embossed with the markings of the firing and loading mechanism. These various marks may be individual enough to be matched to a single firearm. Again a comparison microscope is used for the visible examination (Figure 8.14).

A shotgun has a smooth, non-rifled barrel and consequently the lead shot that passes through the barrel will not gain any characteristic markings. However, the gauge of the shotgun can be determined by the diameter of the lead shot, or the 'wad' (which is packing inside the actual cartridge) left at a crime scene. The wad may also indicate who the manufacturer was, and if the wad is turned inside out this indicates that the shotgun had a sawn off barrel. In instances where a sawn off shotgun is used it may be possible that the wad will have characteristic marks left by metal burrs that have formed in the barrel during the sawing off process.

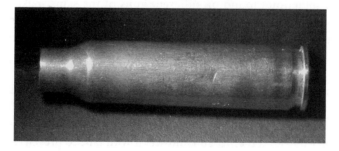

Figure 8.13 5.56 mm rifle cartridge case showing distinct scratches caused after leaving the ejector port of the weapon.

Figure 8.14 Firing-pin impression and breech-face scratches on a 9 mm cartridge case.

8.10 Scene recovery of firearms

It is important to remember that you should never submit a loaded gun for laboratory forensic analysis. However, unfired cartridges may be left in the magazine of a weapon, provided the magazine is removed from the gun. A firearm with the cartridge in the chamber should never be shipped by any method, even if the weapon is not cocked or on safety.

Do not clean the bore, chamber, or cylinder before submitting a firearm, and never pick up a weapon by placing a pencil or other object in the end of the barrel.

It is important to record serial number, make, model and calibre of the weapon, and mark it in some inconspicuous manner that does not detract from its value before sending it to the FSP. Marking firearms is important since duplicate serial numbers are sometimes found on different guns of the same make and general type. Make sure that you do not confuse model numbers or patent numbers with serial numbers. It is also useful to remember that, in many cases, obliterated serial numbers can be restored if very little metal has been removed in erasing the number.

Recovered weapons should be placed in a strong cardboard or wooden box, well packed and tied in place to prevent the weapon shifting in transit. If during your initial checking of the weapon you find that blood or any other material is present place clean paper around the weapon and seal it with tape to prevent movement of the gun and loss of the sample during shipment. The weapon must be handled carefully so any latent fingerprints or DNA are not destroyed.

It is important to submit all evidence bullets recovered for forensic analysis. A conclusive identification may be possible on only one of several bullets recovered, even when they all appear to be in good condition. If bullets are found at the scene, do not mark the bullets themselves. Instead you should wrap them in paper and seal them separately in labelled rigid containers. If bullets are recovered from a body they should be air dried and wrapped in paper, as washing them may destroy trace evidence.

If cartridge cases are recovered they should be sealed in separate labelled rigid container. It is important to note that fired shotgun shells may be marked either on the inside or outside of the paper or plastic portion of the shell. To determine if a shot, shell or cartridge case originated from a specific weapon, submit the weapon and all recovered unfired ammunition. Again, as in the case with bullets, submit all evidence cartridge cases or shotgun shells recovered to the forensic analyst. It is possible that some cartridge cases contain more identifying detail than others. It is important that you wrap each in paper to prevent damaging the breech lock, firing pin, or other markings by contact with other cartridge cases. Place the wrapped cases in labelled and sealed rigid container.

You should always attempt to recover unused ammunition for comparison purposes when firearms are obtained as evidence. Unfired ammunition should not be marked but the box with the ammunition may be marked. Any clothing or other material showing evidence of gun powder residue or shot holes should be carefully interleaved and folded as little as possible to prevent dislodging powder particles and sent to the forensic science service. It is important that each item is packed separately.

Self-assessed questions

8.9 (a) What type of instrument is most useful for comparing bullets?
(b) What characteristics are useful in bullet and cartridge identification?

8.11 Gunshot residues (GSR)

When a firearm is discharged not only is the bullet ejected but also many microscopic particles, called gunshot residue (GSR) or firearms discharge residue (FDR), are blown back towards the person who discharged the weapon. This residue is composed of unburnt or partially burnt combustion products from the primer and propellant, together with material derived from the cartridge case, projectile and barrel. These microscopic particles adhere to the hand of the shooter and their clothing. GSR has a very characteristic chemical make up, normally containing lead, barium and antimony, all derived from the primer, but note that some 0.22 calibre ammunition uses primers which do not contain these elements. Due to the transient nature of GSR on the hands it is important to swab any suspect quickly, preferably within three hours of the discharge of the firearm, (in the case of live suspects). If more than six hours have passed, or if the subject has washed their hands, it is unlikely that meaningful results will be obtained. GSR that becomes ingrained into clothing remains there much longer. If a body is to be sampled, GSR collection should be performed prior to moving the body whenever possible.

A number of methods have been developed to identify GSR, which include graphite furnace atomic absorption spectroscopy (GFAAS), neutron activation analysis (NAA) and scanning electron microscopy with microanalysis (SEM-EDX). By far the most popular and useful method is SEM-EDX, because you not only get chemical information but you can also image the microscopic particles and determine their morphology. This information can greatly help in determining what type of primer was used and this in turn can help identify the cartridges used (Figure 8.15).

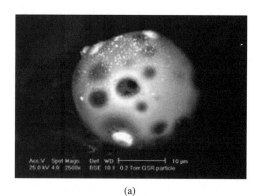

(a)

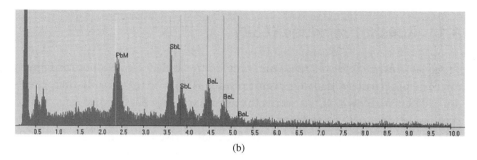

(b)

Figure 8.15 SEM-EDX (a) photomicrograph and (b) spectrum of gun-shot residue showing characteristic elemental composition.

There are two main methods to gather GSR from the hands. One is swabbing with cotton swabs dampened with 5% nitric acid. Here, one swab is run over the suspect's thumb and forefinger and a second swab is run over their palm. The process is repeated on the other hand giving a total of four swabs. Two blanks (cotton swabs just dampened with 5% nitric acid) are also prepared at the same time. It should be noted that swabs of the suspect's face and hair are also taken. All swabs are sealed in tamper evident tubes and sent for GFAAS or NAA analysis.

The other method is specifically for SEM-EDX analysis. Here electrically conducting double-sided carbon adhesive tape is attached to a small aluminium stub. The stub is then pressed along the suspect's thumb and forefinger and a second stub is pressed along the palm, with the process repeated for the other hand. The aluminium stubs fit directly into the SEM-EDX without further sample treatment. As stated earlier, GSR has a limited life span on the hands and so methods for GSR removal from clothes should also be mentioned. These include the use of sticky tape or specialist micro vacuum cleaners. If GSR is found on the clothing it *only* indicates that that person was close to the firearm when it was discharged, it does not prove that the wearer pulled the trigger. However the density and position of the FDR on the sleeve may provide strong evidence that the shooter wore the garment.

Self-assessed questions

8.10   (a) What elements are found in GSR?
(b) Why is SEM/EDX such a good tool for examining GSR?

8.12 Drugs of abuse (DOA)

The clinical definition of a drug is 'a natural or synthetic substance that is used to produce physiological or psychological effects on humans or other higher order animals'. Drugs are widely used in society both legally and illegally; there is evidence that man has used drugs since prehistoric times. However, it is only since the 1960s that the illegal misuse of drugs became widespread. In 1971 the Misuse of Drugs Act was passed in the United Kingdom and the act attempts to prevent the illegal use of specific substances. This was modified in 1985 and again in 2001 with the introduction of the Misuse of Drug Regulations.

The continual misuse of any drug will lead to one or both of psychological or physical dependence (see Table 8.1). In the UK drugs are classified into one of three groups A, B or C (see Table 8.2). Category A drugs are those that are considered most harmful while category C are those that do the least harm. The severity of any prison sentence reflects what category of drug was involved in the criminal case as well as the amount of drug and its intended usage.

Table 8.1 The typical dependency of common drugs of abuse.

Drug	Psychological dependence	Physical dependence
Herion	High	Yes
Morphine	High	Yes
Codeine	Low	Yes
Alcohol	High	Yes
Diaxepam	Moderate	Yes
Chlordiazepoxide	Moderate	Yes
Amphetamines	High	Unknown
Caffeine	Low	No
Cocaine	High	No
Nicotine	High	Yes
LSD	Low	No
Marijuana	Low	No

Table 8.2 A summary of drug categories with common DOA and indicative maximum sentences.

Drug category	Examples	Maximum prison sentences	
		Possession	Supplying
Class A	LSD, Cocaine, heroin	7 years	Life imprisonment
Class B	Barbiturates amphetamine powder	5 years	14 years
Class C	Cannabis, benzodiazepines	2 years	5 years

The mode of action of drugs can broadly be categorized into three types of effect: depressants, hallucinogens and stimulants. Some drugs may exhibit effects in more than one category. Depressants include barbiturates, alcohol, heroin and benzodiazepines; hallucinogens include cannabis (in high doses), LSD and ecstasy, while stimulants include cocaine and amphetamines.

8.13 The crime scene characteristics of various DOA's

Amphetamines (street names: 'speed' or 'uppers') can be taken by swallowing (if in tablet form), snorting (if in powder form), injecting it (as a solution) or, if the amphetamine is methamphetamine, then by smoking it. Methamphetamine is usually in the form of large clear crystals commonly called 'rocks' and when the crystals are broken up for smoking the drug is usually called 'ice'.

3,4 methylenedioxymethamphetamine (MDMA; street names: 'Ecstasy', 'Adam', 'hug drug', 'M&M', 'XTC', 'E', 'doves' and 'disco biscuits') is usually in capsule or tablet form for swallowing. However it can be smoked or, if in powder form, snorted. Ecstasy is widely used in nightclubs and 'raves', together with other so-called club drugs. These include gamma hydroxybutyrate (GHB) and Rohypnol, the so-called 'date-rape' drug (street name: 'roofies'). Both these substances are odourless, colourless and tasteless and can therefore be easily slipped into a drink.

Cocaine (street names: 'coke', 'snow' and 'Charlie') is usually found in the form of cocaine hydrochloride, which is a white, crystalline powder. It can be taken by inhaling the powder through the nose or by swallowing and, if dissolved, it may be injected. One form of cocaine that is becoming increasingly popular is 'crack'-cocaine (street names: 'stone' or 'rock'). Here ordinary cocaine hydrochloride is mixed with equal parts of baking powder (sodium bicarbonate) in water, and then heated in a pot, then dried and broken into small pieces. These pieces may then be mixed with tobacco and smoked, normally in a glass pipe.

Heroin (street names 'H', 'horse', 'junk' and 'smack') is from opium and is derived from the dried juice extruded from the opium poppy seed head when cut. Opium is normally brown in colour and contains from 4 to 21% morphine. To create heroin, the morphine must be reacted with acetic anhydride or acetyl chloride which produces diacetylmorphine (also called diamorphine), which is very soluble in water. On the street, heroin is frequently diluted with other materials including quinine (which, like diamorphine, is very bitter), caffeine, sugars, starch, lactose and even milk powder. The percentage of diamorphine in street heroin normally ranges from 35 to 40% and its colour ranges from white to brown. The preferred method of administration is by injection and frequently the addict will dissolve it in a small quantity of water in a spoon. Heating the spoon over a candle can speed up the process. The resulting solution is then drawn into a syringe and injected, normally into the arm. Heroin can also be inhaled or smoked.

Lysergic acid diethylamide (LSD) is a very potent hallucinogen and as little as 25 microgrammes can produce effects that can last up to 12 hours. Because of the very small amounts involved, the only way of street administration is by either microdots (which are small brightly coloured tablets) or blotter acids (small squares of adsorbent paper impregnated with the LSD). Another hallucinogen often mixed with LSD is phencyclidine (PCP), which can be prepared following a simple chemical process. It is sold as a powder (street name: 'angel dust'), a capsule or a liquid sprayed on plant leaves. The drug can be smoked, snorted, inhaled or swallowed.

Barbiturates (street name: 'downers') are a group of around 25 chemically related substances that induce relaxation and drowsiness. It is the short acting secobarbital which is favoured by drug abusers. Barbiturates are normally in coloured tablet form and are swallowed. Barbiturate abuse is now quite rare.

Anabolic steroids are synthetic compounds similar to the male hormone testosterone. They were initially thought to promote muscle growth and as a consequence most abusers were amateur or professional athletes. Research has now shown that taking anabolic steroids does little to enhance your sporting performance.

Benzodiazepines (street names: 'moggies' or 'jellies') are legally manufactured for use as anticonvulsants and tranquillisers. They are invariably in tablet or jelly capsule form. When abused they can be dissolved and injected and they are usually tasteless and rapidly metabolized. Flunitrazepam has been slipped into drinks in 'date-rape' cases.

Cannabis is a natural substance obtained from the leaves and flowering tops of the hemp plant and is a mild hallucinogen. It is supplied in three forms: herbal cannabis (street name: 'marijuana'), which is the dried, crushed, leaves mixed with the flowering tops and seeds and which has the lowest concentration of the active drug tetrahydrocannabinol (THC); cannabis resin (street name: 'hashish'), which is the resin from the surface of the plant, supplied as compressed slabs and this is intermediate in its levels of THC; cannabis oil (street name: 'hashish oil' or 'hemp oil') is dark-coloured, tarry oil, which has the highest concentration of THC. Cannabis is usually smoked with or without tobacco but it can also be consumed, normally in cakes.

Self-assessed questions

8.11 (a) What are the classifications given to DOA and which does the most harm?
(b) List the common DOA found in the United Kingdom

8.14 Presumptive tests for drugs

Presumptive tests for drugs of misuse are usually based on a series of reagents reacting with the drug to produce a colour change (see Table 8.3). It is imperative that a blank test (i.e. with no sample present) is also run. These tests are for screening purposes only and any positive result must be backed up by further instrumental chemical analysis done in a qualified laboratory. However they are extremely useful for 'on the spot' tests by scene of crimes officers.

Table 8.3 Some common presumptive tests for drugs of abuse.

Drug	Marquis	Mandelin's	Dillie-Koppanyi	Duquenois-Levine	Van Urk	Scott	Zimmerman
Amphetamines	Orange						
Barbiturates			Violet-blue				
Benzodiazepines							Pink or red-purple
Cannabis				Purple			
Cocaine	Pink/orange	Orange				Blue	
Codeine	Blue	Olive green					
Diamorphine	Purple	Blue-grey					
LSD					Blue-purple		
MDA, MDMA and MDEA	Purple/blue						
Morphine	Mauve	Blue-grey					

The composition of the various reagents used is given below:

(a) Marquis reagent is sulfuric acid containing 2% formaldehyde.

(b) Mandelin's reagent is concentrated sulfuric acid with 0.5% ammonium metavanadate.

(c) Dillie-Koppanyi solution comprises of two separate reagents, methanol with 1% cobalt acetate is added first, followed by methanol with 5% isopropylamine.

(d) The Duquenois-Levine test comprises of three separate reagents: ethanol with 2% vanillin and 1% acetaldehyde is added first, followed by concentrated hydrochloric acid, then chloroform.

(e) Van Urk reagent is ethanol with 1% p-dimethylaminobenzaldehyde and 10% concentrated hydrochloric acid.

(f) The Scott test comprises of three reagents: the first is 2% cobalt thiocyanate dissolved in water and glycerine in a 1 : 1 ratio; the second is concentrated hydrochloric acid and the third reagent is chloroform.

(g) The Zimmerman test comprises of two reagents: the first is methanol with 1% 2,4-dinitrobenzene and the second is 15% potassium hydroxide in water.

It cannot be stressed too much that any positive presumptive test must be confirmed by full laboratory analysis using appropriate analytical methods.

If the crime scene is a clandestine laboratory then this is a specialized area that would need a specialist team to investigate (because of, e.g. the danger explosion when red phosphorus is used in MDMA synthesis). The reader should consult Cole (2004) on this subject.

It is important in the handling of DOA to take effective safety measures: a facemask will help avoid the accidental inhalation of any powdered drugs; wear protective gloves if hypodermic syringes are to be handled. Each sample of solid material recovered should be placed in a paper container, which can be sealed and marked. Some drugs, such as cannabis, can be in the form of oil or others, such as barbiturates, in the form of a solution. These should be placed in small sealable plastic vials. Any prescription drugs should be left in their original containers and placed in tamper evident bags.

8.15 Amateur explosives

Commercial explosives found at a crime scene require specialist handling and are beyond the scope of this book. However a number of 'home made' explosives can be created from household materials and these need to be described as they may be found during household searches. One of the most common types of these explosives is the weed-killer bomb. This is made from sodium or potassium chlorate (weed killer) and sugar. All chlorate weed killers now contain a flame retardant but this is only present to stop the weed killer self-detonating and cannot extinguish the detonation of a chlorate/sugar mixture. The explosive power of the mixture is greatly enhanced by using finely ground sugar and icing sugar is ideal. Another common home-made bomb is the 'fertilizer bomb'. Here mixtures of finely powdered ammonium nitrate are mixed with substances such as sulphur, fuel oil or sugar. If glycerine and potassium permanganate are mixed together you get a self-igniting explosive mixture and the time from mixing to detonation is determined by the temperature of the glycerine: the cooler it is, the longer the time to detonation. The mixing of concentrated household ammonia with tincture of iodine produces nitrogen tri-iodide. This is very much a touch-sensitive explosive, commonly used as a detonator for a fertilizer or weed-killer bomb.

Another home made explosive that is currently gaining popularity is triacetone triperoxide (TATP). This is made by reacting acetone (or nail varnish remover) with hydrogen peroxide (hair bleach) in the presence of an acid catalyst (such as battery acid). For the reaction to proceed the hydrogen peroxide content in hair bleach has to be increased, normally by gently boiling the bleach solution.

All these mixtures, when packed into metal pipes and then sealed, will produce a powerful bomb and if metal nails are included in the construction, the subsequent loss of life can be very high. If any of the above mixtures are found in quantity during a household search then suspicion of terrorist activities should be made. However, 'amateur' experimenters (mainly schoolchildren) should not be ruled out.

8.16 Summary

- At any crime scene trace evidence will be found but not all evidence has equal evidential value.

- Great care must be taken when examining a crime scene so as not to accidentally obliterate trace evidence.

- All trace evidence should be photographed *in situ* before being moved.

- All trace evidence should be fully catalogued, labelled and placed in appropriate tamper evident packaging.

- Some evidence will need specialist handling, such as explosives and firearms.

- Although presumptive tests are very useful at a crime scene, a full laboratory analysis should be performed in order to present in court.

End of chapter questions

8.12 What type of trace evidence would you look for in a typical house burglary? Detail how the trace evidence would be preserved for further analysis.

8.13 In a suspected clandestine drugs laboratory what presumptive tests would you carry out?

8.14 What analytical methods are widely used in forensic laboratories for drug testing?

8.15 What methods would you employ for preserving biological trace evidence?

8.16 How would you handle and package a firearm found at a crime scene?

Suggested further reading

Bodziak, W. (2000) *Footwear Impression Evidence: Detection, Recovery and Examination*, 2nd edn, CRC Press.

Caddy, B. (2001) *Forensic Examination of Glass and Paint: Analysis and Interpretation*, Taylor and Francis, London & New York.

Cole, M. (2004) *The Analysis of Controlled Substances*, Wiley.

McDonald, P. (1993) *Tire Imprint Evidence*, CRC Press.

Milne, R. (1998) Electrostatic lifting of marks at crime scene and the development of pathfinder. *Science & Justice*, **38**, 135.

Pye, K. (2007) *Geological and Soil Evidence: Forensic Application*, CRC Press.

Saferstien, R. (ed.) (2002) *Forensic Science Handbook Volumes 1 & 2*, Prentice Hall.

PART III

Specialised Scenes and Report Writing

9
The Examination of Fire Scenes

Chris J. Perry

9.1 Introduction

Fire adds extra dimensions to a forensic investigation, in that it changes the scene, and its examination, in a number of important ways. The changes resulting from the fire itself must be well understood if a meaningful investigation is to be conducted. It should always be remembered that every fire scene is a *potential* crime scene, until the evidence within that scene is properly evaluated.

The scene of any fire, regardless of cause, should be carefully preserved until it has been fully investigated. Fires are often the result of industrial or domestic accidents and not just the activities of arsonists. It is therefore essential to understand the cause, or causes, of any fire. The need for fire investigators to establish cause, and to inform the subsequent development of safer practices for the future, is something that does not usually apply to other crime scene investigations. Nevertheless, once a clear case of arson or related criminal use of flammable materials is established, the investigation will follow similar lines to those described in other chapters of this book.

9.2 The nature of fire

The traditional view of fire is often summarized in the fire triangle (Figure 9.1a). This draws attention to three aspects or components, all of which need to be in place for fire to be sustained. Removal of one or more of the three sides of the triangle

Crime Scene Management: Scene Specific Methods   Edited by Raul Sutton and Keith Trueman
© 2009 John Wiley & Sons, Ltd

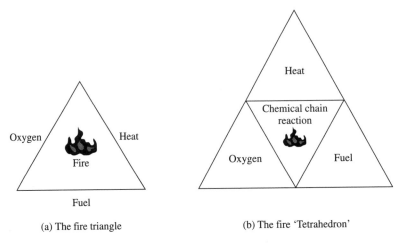

(a) The fire triangle   (b) The fire 'Tetrahedron'

Figure 9.1   (a) the fire triangle. (b) the fire 'tetrahedron'.

prevents the fire from spreading, and results in its termination. More recent thinking, however, acknowledges that it is possible to have all three aspects present (heat, fuel and oxygen) but still not have a recognizable fire. It is only when a sustainable chain reaction is set up that a true fire is established. Anyone who has failed to light a barbecue or bonfire on a damp or very still day will identify with this idea.

For these reasons, the more recent fire tetrahedron (Figure 9.1b) has gained support. Since it is not possible to see all faces of a tetrahedron at the same time, the figure is usually drawn as four triangles, each representing one face of the tetrahedron.

It is helpful to divide the lifetime of a fire into a number of phases. The precise number of phases (or stages) varies, depending on the literature source consulted, and the type of fire under consideration, but the following list gives a realistic view of the sequence of events.

Incipient phase: fuel is being heated by one or more ignition source. In this phase, small amounts of combustible vapour are produced by pyrolysis (literally splitting by fire) or evaporation. Sometimes a *smouldering phase* is identified before the *growth phase*. At some stage, accumulated gases reach their flash point and ignition occurs.

Growth phase: immediately following ignition, the heat output of the fire increases and there is local generation of more vapour and pyrolysis products, which usually appear as smoke. In a building fire these hot gases and smoke will collect at ceiling height. Cooler air is drawn in close to ground level. As the fire builds in intensity the smoke/vapour layer gets thicker until it eventually reaches down to the flames coming up from the ground. At this point a phenomenon known as *flashover* occurs. This is a very rapid increase in intensity of the fire when the built up vapour/air mixture is ignited by contact with rising flames. Flashover is often described by fire-fighters as the point when a room *on* fire becomes a room *full of* fire.

Fully developed phase: following flashover, the fire enters a fully developed, plateau stage where the maximum heat output is observed. So long as there is adequate ventilation and fuel, this stage can exist for a substantial period of time. During this period of intense heat, structural damage and even building collapse may occur.

Decay phase: when one of the components of sustainable fire (see Figure 9.1) becomes limited (usually fuel in an unattended fire), the chain reaction begins to diminish. The ensuing cycle of reduced power output leading in turn to lower temperatures and less pyrolysis or vaporization of any remaining fuel, brings on the final extinction phase.

Extinction phase: the fuel is fully consumed and energy release cannot continue. Flames cease and cooling begins.

All of the above stages are usually seen in the combustion of solid materials, starting with a relatively small heat source, such as in the case of a room fire that has been started accidentally. With more volatile fuels and/or exceptional heat sources (e.g. an explosion), some of the earlier stages are bypassed. A temperature versus time graph is shown in Figure 9.2.

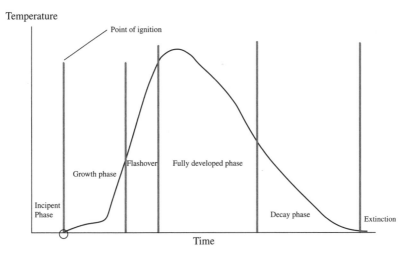

Figure 9.2 Temperature time graph for the progress of a typical room or building fire.

9.3 The oxygen demand of fuels

It is not possible to write chemical equations for 'fire' in the general sense of the word, but if the fire is consuming a specific fuel or mixture of fuels, then equations for combustion can be useful. Some examples are given below for common fuels.

$$\text{Methane}: CH_4 + 2O_2 \rightarrow CO_2 + 2H_2O$$

$$\text{Propane } C_3H_8 + 5O_2 \rightarrow 3CO_2 + 4H_2O$$

$$\text{Ethanol } C_2H_6O + 3O_2 \rightarrow 2CO_2 + 3H_2O$$

$$\text{Polystyrene } C_8H_8 + 10O_2 \rightarrow 8CO_2 + 4H_2O$$

The equations have been written with one molecule of fuel on the left-hand side. This allows a direct comparison of the number of molecules of oxygen required for complete combustion of each type of fuel. As the figures indicate, the quantity of oxygen needed, varies significantly from fuel to fuel. From equations of this type it is possible to estimate the air volume that a kilogram of fuel will consume on complete combustion. Table 9.1 shows the results of such calculations for a range of common fuels. Note that for *poly*styrene, the molecular formula is exactly the same as the styrene molecule itself (C_8H_8 – see Figure 9.3) so the oxygen demand will also be the same in both cases.

In order to estimate oxygen demand we need to make a sensible guess at chemical composition.

For example polystyrene is heavily used in the plastics industry, and may well be a bulk fuel available for combustion in an industrial or domestic fire (either in its

Table 9.1 Approximate theoretical oxygen and air demands of some common fuels.

Fuel	M_r	O_2 per mole	Litres Oxygen per kg fuel	Cubic metres of air per kg fuel
Methane	16	2	3000	14.29
Propane	44	5	2727	12.99
Butane	58	6.5	2690	12.81
Hexane	86	9.5	2651	12.62
Octane	114	12.5	2632	12.53
Acetylene	26	2.5	2308	10.99
Methanol	32	1.5	1125	5.36
Ethanol	46	3	1565	7.45
Styrene	104	10	2308	10.99
Lignin model (wood)	484	28.5	1413	6.73

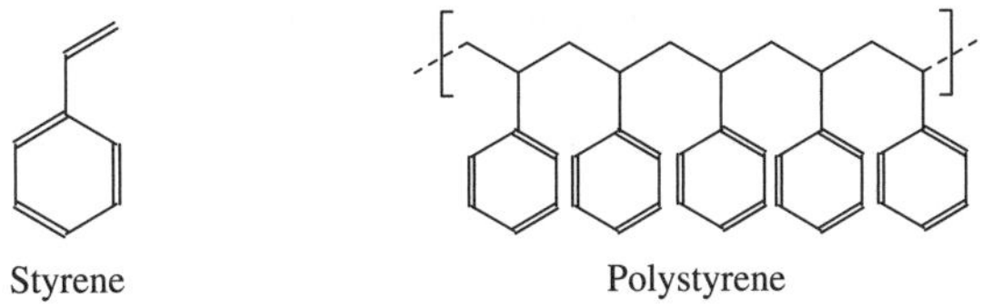

Figure 9.3 The chemical structures of styrene and polystyrene.

expanded or foam form, or as a hard casing material used for televisions and computer monitors, for example).

Table 9.1 tells us that a kilogram of styrene (or polystyrene) depletes the oxygen from about $11\,m^3$ of air at room temperature. A typical lounge has a volume of about $50\,m^3$ so could therefore be completely exhausted of oxygen by as little as $50/11 = 4.55$ kg of polystyrene.

A material like wood (composed mainly of lignin) has a more oxidized structure than polystyrene and so its oxygen demand should be somewhat lower. Lignin is a complex compound that has some features in common with polystyrene. A suitable model for the repeating unit in the structure of softwood lignin is shown in Figure 9.4. Note the increased oxygen content compared to styrene and polystyrene molecules (Figure 9.3). Reference to Table 9.1 shows that lignin has an expected oxygen demand of around 60% of that for polystyrene.

It should be stressed that oxygen demands are useful for estimating the quantity of a fuel that will deplete the air contained in a sealed space, but in real fires there is usually sufficient ventilation to allow near-complete combustion. Often the heat generated by a fire is sufficient to shatter windows, thereby creating new supplies of oxygen. It is the sudden influx of fresh air into an oxygen depleted space that causes the phenomenon of backdraught. The incoming air

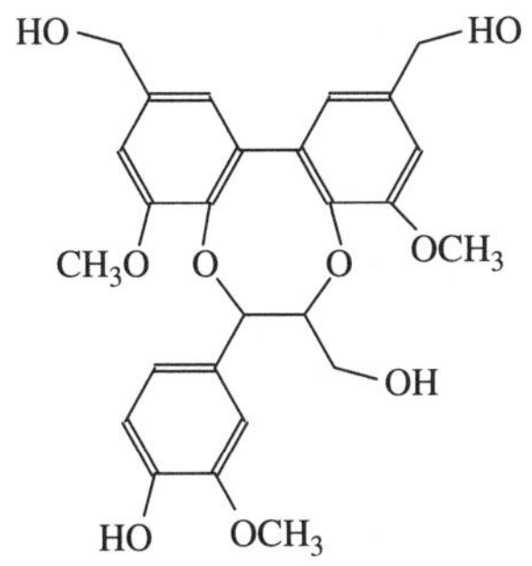

Figure 9.4 'Model' molecule for lignin.

reacts violently with the hot fuel vapours, causing a rapid combustion that gives rise to a dramatic increase in pressure inside the space. Such backdraught explosions can be very dangerous to fire-fighters who are trapped inside a burning building.

Self-assessed questions

9.1 Name the four components that need to be present in order for a fire to maintain itself.

9.2 List five stages that a fire can pass through during its progress.

9.3 Calculate the approximate volumes of air that are required for complete combustion of (i) 1.0 mole of octane; (ii) 0.5 tonne of softwood timber; (iii) 2.0 gallons of ethanol (density of ethanol = 0.789 g/ml and 1 gallon = 4.54 litres).

9.4 Flame and fire classifications

Flames can be divided into four clear categories that are shown in Table 9.2. Such flame classifications are of limited importance to fire investigators but can be helpful in understanding how fires develop from a particular type of ignition source. They can also be useful in the modelling of fire using theoretical and mathematical approaches which we will not discuss further here. More often, fires themselves are classified in the way shown in Table 9.3. The understanding of fire types helps with the decision making processes involved when fire crews prepare to attend a fire. Response times can be reduced, and the strategy for dealing

Table 9.2 Types of flame.

Flame type	Example
Laminar, premixed type	Bunsen Burner – flame shape effectively constant over time. 'Laminar' refers to the layers (rather like inside an onion) found in the flame structure.
Laminar, diffusion type	Candle – like the bunsen flame but not pre-mixed. Fuel and oxidant are mixed by diffusion and convection.
Turbulent, premixed type	Gas boiler – requires engineered conditions to create a stable but turbulent flame.
Turbulent, diffusion type	A pool fire such as a burning chip pan where liquid is burning on a surface or in an open container. Many accidental fires fall into this category

Table 9.3 The classes of fire.

Class of Fire	Type of Fuel	Comments
A	Solid Fuels: coal, wood, paper, straw, hard plastics, cable insulation	Referred to as 'deep seated' fires, which produce flames, but can smoulder for long periods.
B	Liquid fuels or low melting solids: cooking fat, tars, soft plastics, fuel oils	Produce large amounts of flame, and often intense heat (subject to adequate air supply).
C	Gaseous fuels: acetylene, fuel gases (methane, propane, butane), sometimes hydrogen.	Often linked with explosions, and can ignite other fuel types if not extinguished. Important to isolate supply of gas.
D	Metals: Al, Mg, K. Li, Na, U, Fe, Ni	Some metals (e.g. K) cause fire on contact with water. Others (e.g. Fe and Ni) burn when finely divided as powders. Difficult to extinguish, contact burns can be very serious.
E	Electrical components: motors, transformers, white goods, televisions, etc.	Occasional malfunctions cause over-heating, which can initiate local burning. This can spread into other categories of fire if the fuels are available.

with the fire can be more quickly refined, if crews have a clear idea about the nature of a specific fire. For example, some fires (such as Class C ones) carry a much greater risk of explosion than others. Class E fires carry special risks and the method of extinguishing such fires may not be a conventional hose. As can be appreciated, the safety of fire-fighters can be highly dependent on fire classification and the specialist knowledge which is acquired during training. For instance it would be very unsafe to enter a Class E fire without first isolating the electrical supply that started the fire. This may well be a job for the specialist, and fire investigation training includes the safety procedures that must be followed in such an incident.

9.5 Types of evidence specific to fire scenes

Traditionally, the investigation of fire scenes is largely concerned with attempts to determine the cause of the fire and thereby establish whether or not there is malicious intent in the way a fire has been started. Surprisingly, it is only in recent years that the evidence inside a fire scene has been recognized as routinely recoverable and forensically valuable. Before this, the majority view was that fire is too destructive to allow much contact evidence to survive, and that any evidence recovered is usually due to extremely fortunate circumstances that cannot be relied upon in every investigation.

However, the modern view of fire scene investigation is that trace and contact evidence can, and often does survive fires. Recent research has shown that fingerprints and even DNA evidence, can be successfully retrieved from fire scenes under the right conditions, and so should be sought on a regular basis, especially in cases where foul play is suspected. Coupled to this, there is also considerable 'routine' evidence that has long been recovered from the scene, especially in cases where the response has been rapid and the fire may not have reached flashover. Text in magazines, notepads and books will often survive, as will information on the undersides of furniture items or objects that have lain flat on the surface of a table, for example. Occasionally, bar codes or manufacturer's information can survive in this way, as good close contact between surfaces efficiently excludes air; preventing combustion.

Even if a room or building reaches flashover, it is by no means impossible to recover valuable evidence. Cooler areas are found at floor level, especially close to the air supplies for the fire (such as a door), and materials like accelerants can be recovered and successfully analyzed by techniques including gas chromatography/mass spectrometry (GC/MS). Surprisingly, even quite volatile liquids can remain soaked into floorboards, carpets and fabrics under these conditions, and may provide a valuable lead on how the fire may have been started.

Much can be learned from examining the condition of wiring, fuses and components of electrical items recovered from a scene. While the insulation can often be damaged or missing, the continuity of the circuit can be tested. If the circuit for an appliance is closed (in other words it can still draw a current if the circuit is energized) then it is possible that the appliance may have still been running when the fire was started, making it a possible source of ignition. Blown fuses are usually indicative of the appliance failing safe as designed, and are therefore less suspicious. Sometimes an arsonist will deliberately insert a fuse that can allow more current than intended, causing overheating which might not be easily traced. Severe overheating may result in the melting of components other than the fuse and is therefore more suspicious.

Metals and other materials can also melt as a direct result of external heating, giving an indication of the temperatures reached during a fire. Table 9.4 shows some examples of this. On occasions, the heat of a fire can be a positive influence in that copper water piping can melt, allowing a 'sprinkler effect' to reduce the severity of a large fire.

Table 9.4 Melting temperatures of common materials.

Material	Melting Temperature (°C)	Significance
Polypropylene	160–170	Bottles, furniture, etc.
Tin	232	Solders
Lead	328	Roof flashing
Nylon	420	Carpet, fishing line, footwear, plastic gears and bearings
Glass (flow temp)	550–1250 (type-dependent)	Windows, bottles, etc.
Aluminium	660	Some drink cans
Brass	900–940	Ornaments, fittings
Silver	962	Jewellery
Gold	1064	Jewellery
Copper	1083	Water/gas pipes
Iron	1535	Metal fixtures and fittings
Tungsten	3420	Light bulb filaments

9.6 Locating the seat of the fire

Tracking the fire back to its point (or points) of ignition is often called *locating the seat of the fire.* Investigators are trained to interpret the telltale clues found at fire scenes, to home in on the seat of the fire. Additional forensic evidence may be needed to support this initial conclusion, especially when we consider the differences between the location of fire outbreak and the actual ignition source. The material at the seat of the fire has been burning for the longest time of any fuel source in the scene (with the possible exception of fires started by explosions) and this can be exploited in the search for the fire seat.

Smoke patterns can be helpful in leading the trained eye to a fire seat. A classic 'V' pattern on an interior wall (and sometimes on an external wall if the fire started outside the building) often points to the origin of the fire. Adjacent charring patterns and depth of charring can also reinforce original ideas about the location of the fire seat. Objects closer to the fire seat are usually charred more deeply and char depth probes can be used to measure and confirm this effect. With solid items of furniture it is not unusual for one side (nearest the fire seat) to be badly charred or even punctured by fire, while the opposite side can be wiped clean of soot to reveal a near-original surface. These kinds of directional clues can be used systematically to converge on the most probable location of the fire seat. Remember too that fires may have more than one seat, and this can be a complicating factor in an investigation. Sometimes very obvious clues such as witness reports of loud

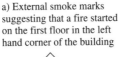

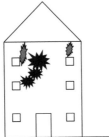

a) External smoke marks suggesting that a fire started on the first floor in the left hand corner of the building

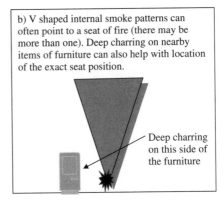

b) V shaped internal smoke patterns can often point to a seat of fire (there may be more than one). Deep charring on nearby items of furniture can also help with location of the exact seat position.

Deep charring on this side of the furniture

Figure 9.5 (a) external and (b) internal smoke and charring patterns can give clues to the location of the origin of a fire.

noises, and a missing roof accompanied by widely scattered debris can lead quickly to an explosion as the likely cause! (Figure 9.5)

Self-assessed questions

9.4 Give examples of where the exclusion of air can protect evidence inside a fire scene.

9.5 It is a waste of time attempting to recover fingerprint or DNA samples from fire scenes, as the organic nature of these materials means almost certain destruction on exposure to high temperatures. Briefly discuss this statement.

9.7 Evidence gathering methods

Apart from gathering any trace evidence from a scene, it also falls within the role of the fire examiner to *excavate* a fire scene. This excavation involves the organized removal of layers of debris that may have fallen down during the blaze, in an attempt to work backwards to the root cause of the fire. During this process, all the normal aspects of good practice in scene preservation and management must apply. Scene mapping and photography, evidence integrity, health and safety considerations and co-operation with the police and other emergency services must all be carefully considered. The goal of scene excavation is to establish the most likely scenario, which has led to the fire being started, and this, of course, will inform the investigators of any need to consider the fire scene as a crime scene. Usually an investigation begins with the premise that a fire scene *is* a crime scene until it is proven otherwise.

A rapid response to a fire is of course the first step in a successful fire investigation. Extinguishing the fire before flashover is a considerable advantage. Crews attending the scene must be as careful as possible to preserve evidence but this must be offset against the need to rapidly extinguish the fire. The techniques and approaches used in scene excavation are varied, but there are a number of key questions that must be answered as part of every investigation. These can be summarized by the following list.

1. Is the scene safe to enter?

2. Have there been any injuries or fatalities?

3. Were there any witnesses?

4. Where and how was the fire started?

5. Is there any evidence that the fire was started deliberately?

6. Is there any evidence that could lead to a conviction for arson?

Questions 4, 5 and 6 are the ones that the scene excavation attempts to address. Questions 1 and 2 must certainly be considered very carefully before excavation starts. Question 3 can be addressed by police and fire investigators while the scene excavation is underway.

Just as with other crime scenes, the gathering of evidence is crucial to the successful outcome of the investigation. In contrast to other investigations, the fire scene will always be markedly different from the way that it was left at the moment a crime was committed. This is one reason why careful, methodical fire excavation procedures are essential to the evidence gathering process. In effect it is inevitable that a fire scene must be disturbed in order to investigate it, and therefore crucial that detailed records of the excavation procedures are kept.

Gathering and preparing evidence from a fire scene is a specialized branch of crime scene investigation, because specialist techniques are sometimes required to correct the changes that the fire has imposed on the evidence. For example fingerprints may be present on bottles or glasses, but a layer of soot has obscured them. Methods now exist (such as washing with dilute alkali or ultrasound bath treatments) to remove the soot to expose the latent fingerprint, which may then be successfully developed (see Chapter 5).

Self-assessed questions

9.6 Describe what is meant by the *seat* of a fire.

9.7 Give three indicators that can be used to estimate the temperatures reached within a fire scene and briefly suggest how these can assist in locating the fire seat

9.8 Methods for ascertaining whether a crime has been committed

At this point it is worth considering the motives for arson. It is important to understand why anyone would want to start a fire deliberately. Some possible motives include:

- mental instability or pyromania (an obsession with fires for their own sake);
- attempted murder;
- attempted destruction of evidence (including a body);
- insurance fraud;
- terrorism and other forms of political extremism;
- personal vendettas;
- children's or adolescents' play that escalates to a major fire.

Whenever a body is found at a fire scene, a pathologist can often determine whether the person was dead or alive at the time the fire was started. This can be valuable information in cases where murder is suspected. Sometimes by demonstrating that a person was dead before the fire took hold it is possible to show that the fire was accidental. Examples of such cases include a person dying in bed while smoking, or collapsing near a naked ignition source (such as a candle) and knocking it over in the fall.

Establishing if a person was dead or alive during a fire involves examination of the trachea, lungs and other organs for evidence of smoke inhalation. If smoke inhalation is the cause of death then murder or suicide has to be considered. Whatever the case, the scene must be preserved (see Chapter 3).

In the majority of cases where fire is started deliberately, there will be some form of accelerant (petrol, shredded paper, straw, oil or plastic, for example) which is used to start the fire. Sometimes though, simulated appliance failure can be used to generate an ignition source in the hope of avoiding detection. Trained search dogs can be very useful in the detection of these accelerants and can quickly find small areas within a scene where accelerants have been applied (Figure 9.6).

If all efforts to show that a fire was deliberately started are unsuccessful, an investigation team will attempt to establish an innocent cause, such as sparks from an open fire, electrical failures and other causes mentioned earlier.

Figure 9.6   An accelerant dog, specially trained to identify the location of accelerants at fire scenes.

Self-assessed questions

9.8   Explain how evidence gathering at fire scenes differs from the examination of most other crime scenes.

9.9   Describe the main questions that scene excavators must address during the excavation period.

9.10 Explain how the existence of a body (or bodies) at a fire scene, can inform a scene investigation, particularly with regard to whether a serious crime or an accident has occurred.

9.11 Explain why a successful search for the ignition source is a key goal in fire scene investigation.

9.9 Health and safety considerations

Health and safety issues are important to the investigation of all crime scenes, but it is generally agreed that fire scenes are especially hazardous to investigate. Apart from the obvious risks of burning or asphyxiation during the fire, one of the major risks after extinguishing the fire, is collapse of the building structure. In countries such as the United Kingdom, where brick and concrete walls are the norm, the major risks are often due to roof or floor collapse. Partial combustion of roof timbers can seriously weaken roofs and this must be properly assessed before allowing investigators onto the scene. Timber walls are much more common in some countries (for example New Zealand, Australia and parts of the United States) and these present an increased danger of wall collapse, even when roofs are relatively undamaged. A comprehensive list of risk factors in scene excavation is not really possible here, but it is important to appreciate that risks must be assessed afresh for each scene. We have already mentioned fires inside buildings but forest or heath fires, for example (accidental or deliberate) present a whole new set of risks such as wind-blown sparks, transfer of fire to property, risks to the general public and livestock. Motorway fires following road traffic accidents, fires following bombings of public areas, tunnel fires such as the 1987 King's Cross tube station disaster, all present their own special health and safety considerations. The examples mentioned here are potentially scenes of crime and so the balance must again be struck between the safety of all people in or around the scene, and the speed of response necessary to preserve sufficient evidence for the investigation.

This is undoubtedly an area where, from time to time, mistakes will be made. It is important therefore that investigators and emergency services work together to minimize the unexpected risks that they are exposed to. This is where feedback from individual investigations serves a valuable role. The sharing of experiences at conferences, and in the published literature can not only protect fire-fighters, investigators and other emergency service workers, but can also help to prevent serious emergencies and accidental deaths in public buildings and places, as well as homes and other residential areas. Sprinkler systems in hotels and the domestic smoke alarm are two examples of where lessons learnt from fire scenes have dramatically improved health and safety in recent years.

Self-assessed questions

9.12   Describe how accurate fire classification can make an important contribution to the response made by fire-fighters.

9.13   Why are health and safety issues crucially important to the work of fire investigators? Give examples of specific circumstances that create safety risks.

9.10 Summary

This chapter explores the nature and behaviour of fire, before moving on to the rational investigation and reconstruction of fire scenes for forensic purposes. The following headings are used.

- The Nature of Fire covers the basic science that is required to understand fire in the depth required for sound forensic investigation. It includes the chemistry of fuels, types of flame and classes of fire that may require investigation.

- Types of Evidence Specific to Fire Scenes examines the range of material evidence that can be found in the remains of a fire, and discusses how this evidence may be of use in understanding the sequence of events that took place.

- Locating the Seat of the Fire considers how an experienced fire investigator can make use of a number of techniques to narrow down the place or places in a fire scene where the fire is likely to have started.

- Evidence Gathering Methods looks at the practical aspects of fire scene excavation and the ways in which fire scenes present special challenges to investigators.

- Methods for Ascertaining Whether a Crime Has Been Committed considers the motives for arson and the ways in which it is sometimes possible to distinguish between a fire that has started accidentally and one that is deliberate.

- Health and Safety Considerations briefly reviews the issues that fire investigators must consider before entering a scene and how their response must be modified based upon these assessments.

Suggested further reading

Icove, D.J. and De Haan J.D. (2003) *Forensic Fire Scene Reconstruction*, Prentice Hall.
DeHaan, J.D. (2006) *Kirk's Fire Investigation*, Prentice Hall.
Drysdale, D. (1998) *An Introduction to Fire Dynamics*, John Wiley & Sons.

10

Examination of Recovered Stolen Motor Vehicles

Keith Trueman

10.1 Introduction

Chapter 1 describes crime as divided into 'Major' and 'Volume' categories, for administration purposes. In the main, offences involving motor vehicles fall under the volume category and are referred to as 'Auto Crime' or 'Car Crime'. For the purposes of this chapter the term *Auto Crime* will be used.

The part that auto crime plays in overall criminal activity should not be underestimated. This chapter endeavours to expand on the term 'motor vehicle', describe some of the legal issues governing theft as they relate specifically to motor vehicles and details the processes involved in assessing and recording an auto crime scene.

Every person old enough to own and drive a motor vehicle is affected by the high level of auto related crime. Even if you do not directly become a victim of a theft you will certainly be paying high insurance premiums to help cover those who have. Nearly two million auto related crimes are reported in England and Wales yearly (British Crime Survey) impacting on the everyday life of a large section of the general public understandably causing a great deal of concern.

The police service, nationally, has endeavoured to provide extra resources to tackle this category of crime and, with the advent of DNA and employment of volume crime scene examiners (VSCE) some success has been achieved. Also, motor

Crime Scene Management: Scene Specific Methods   Edited by Raul Sutton and Keith Trueman
© 2009 John Wiley & Sons, Ltd

vehicle manufacturers have improved their security and immobilization systems greatly. This has improved the situation to some degree, but unfortunately, it has also caused a rise in offences of robbery and burglary that have been carried out to obtain the ignition keys to, in particular, expensive or high performance vehicles.

Motor vehicles are not only stolen for their value but also to enable their use in the commission of other offences, the most common being theft and burglary. More serious crimes, such as rape or assault, may be committed inside a vehicle. On occasions, vehicles themselves have been used as the murder weapon or used to deposit a murder victim. The variants are endless, but there is little doubt that the ability of a SOCO or VCSE to deal effectively with an auto crime scene can greatly impact on a whole variety of other crimes.

Then of course there are the 'joy riders'. Offenders who simply steal cars for the fun of it, drive them to excess, causing untold damage, and then abandon them to the mercy of any passing thief who wishes to take the vehicles' component parts. This is not much 'joy' for the owner!

Recovered stolen motor vehicles are crime scenes in their own right. Because offenders, usually, have a good contact with the inside of the vehicle they have an excellent potential to provide evidence. They are compact and relatively straightforward, making pre-printed diagrams specific to vehicle crime simple to produce. They are portable, so they can be driven or picked up wholesale and taken elsewhere if a more thorough examination is required. When a motor vehicle is reported stolen, specific forms are completed and details are entered upon the Police National Computer (PNC). This ensures that all information relevant to the stolen vehicle is kept and accessible to every police officer in the United Kingdom. In crime terms, this puts the theft of motor vehicles into a unique category worthy of special attention.

Before we get onto the subject proper, there are other organizational issues surrounding auto crime that sometimes cause confusion and need to be explained to better understand the whole process. Firstly, there is a huge, and sometimes structured, criminal trade dealing in stolen motor vehicles and their component parts. Sometimes the vehicle is simply dismantled and the component parts are sold. On other occasions, the stolen vehicle is altered, by various means, to the extent that it is not easily recognizable. The vehicle is then given false credentials and sold on. This process has gained the term 'ringing'. Either way, attempts are made to obliterate engine and other vehicle identification marks. Secondly, there is a worrying trend that when a stolen vehicle is abandoned, the thief, in an attempt to destroy evidence, sets fire to it. In both of these situations an important part of the investigation will be the identification of the vehicle. It is here where the confusion sometime lies. Specially trained police or support officers, who are usually employed on a Stolen Vehicle Squad, carry out this task. These officers are called 'Vehicle Examiners' and they are neither SOCO nor VCSE. The other and equally important duty of identifying the offender(s) is carried out by a SOCO or VCSE.

You will already have gathered that the processes involved when dealing with auto crime can be complex. In an attempt to simplify matters, in this chapter the role of the SOCO will be limited to the principles relating to crime scene assessment and recording in straightforward cases where stolen vehicles are recovered. The procedures to recover the different types of evidential material and their collection may be found elsewhere in this book.

Before we look at the process of dealing with the crime scene it may be useful to appreciate the legislation that deals with motor vehicles and auto crime.

10.2 What is a motor vehicle?

For legislative purposes the various types of mechanically propelled motor vehicle intended for use on the road require to be clearly defined. Section 108 of The Road Traffic Act 1988 provides the definitions of the many different weights and passenger capacities of each category of vehicle. Police officers require knowledge of this subject when deciding whether an individual is properly licensed or authorized to drive certain vehicles. However, in crime scene examination terms, such exact detail is not always required. More general terms, that everyone understands, are normally used. When describing a motor vehicle on any documentation it should always start with the make followed by the model. It is this part of the description that may cause some confusion to people who are not totally conversant with current vehicle design. The models listed below may assist.

- Saloon motor car (these can be 2 or 4 door and have a boot compartment).

- Coupe (these have 2 doors, are sporty looking and usually have a hatch type boot lid).

- Convertible (these are 2 door and have either soft or hard tops that can be folded down electrically or removed completely).

- Estate (these have 2 or 4 doors, a large rear compartment with fold down rear seats and large lift up rear door. Designed to carry loads).

- Hatchback (similar to estates these have 2 or 4 doors with a lift up rear door and fold down rear seats but designed more as a car).

- People Carrier or MPV (these can have up to 8 seats some of which may be removed to provide multi purpose use. Usually 5 door, sometimes with side doors that may slide open).

- Four wheel drive or 4×4 (these range from 3 door 2/4 seats to 5 door 11 seat versions. Some have a twin cab with a pick up back).

- Taxis (black cab version most recognizable, but any model of motor car can be used as a taxi when properly licenced).

- Mini-bus (designed to carry a maximum of 16 passengers).

- Buses and coaches (designed to carry more than 16 seated passengers. Single and double deck versions).

- Vans (These vary in size with load capacity. Normally 2 or 3 seats in front cab with the rear section being either open or a separate compartment. Rear doors may be lift up, normal opening or roller shutter. Some vans are curtain sided for easy load access).

- Motor homes (these are basically vans that have been designed and adapted to include facilities to live, cook and sleep).

- Pick-up trucks (These can be single cabs with up to 3 seats or crew cabs with extra seating capacity. The rear section is open and there are flat back, drop side and tipper versions. An enclosed rear section on this chassis is termed as a box or Luton van).

- Lorry (this is a term used to describe a rigid heavy goods carrying vehicle. Like pick-ups they can be flat back, drop sided, curtained, boxed or tipper. Some are constructed for more specific purposes such as cement mixers or transporting bulk liquids or powders).

- Artic (this is the abbreviation of 'articulated lorry and trailer'. Again designed for transporting heavy goods, but in a trailer drawn by a *tractor* or *locomotive* unit).

- Motor cycles and scooters (the former is a general term used to describe any vehicle with two wheels and an engine that the rider sits astride. Although not strictly true in legal terms it is an adequate description for our purposes. The latter describes a smaller machine with leg guards and a more upright natural seating position).

- Moped (this is the generally accepted term for small pedal assisted motor cycles).

- Caravans and trailers (although not motor vehicles in their own right for crime scene examination purposes they are treated the same and will need to be individually described).

Although the list is by no means exhaustive most of the different types of motor vehicles encountered by SOCOs and VCSEs on a day-to-day basis are shown. Another category of motor vehicle, although rarely encountered for examination, is none the less worthy of note. The vehicles in question are given the blanket description of 'Plant'. This term covers the very large machinery such as bulldozers and tractors, etc. that are used in the construction and farming industries. Should an item of plant become the subject of an investigation, then the same principles would apply to it as any other mechanically propelled vehicle.

10.3 The definition of an auto crime

Under terms of section 1 of the Theft Act 1968 a motor vehicle is property and can, therefore, be stolen. However, because of their nature, motor vehicles or more precisely conveyances, can pose a legal dilemma. This caused the inclusion to the Theft Act of a vehicle, or conveyance, specific section. The five main areas of legislation that cover 'Auto Crime' are briefly explained below.

1. Theft of the motor vehicle itself or of property from it. This constitutes an offence contrary to section 1 of the Theft Act 1968.

   Such an offence is normally committed when a motor vehicle or trailer has been left unattended and either it, or property from it, or the trailer is stolen. Obviously, where the vehicle, trailer or both have themselves been completely removed, there may be little or no evidence of the offender left at the scene. This situation can change greatly when the vehicle or trailer have been forcibly entered to obtain the property within.

2. Taking a motor vehicle without the consent of the owner. This constitutes an offence contrary to section 12 of the Theft Act 1968.

   The difference between offences under sections 1 and 12 will depend upon the intention of the offender. To prove an offence of theft, it must be shown that the offender intended to permanently deprive the owner of the property. Where a motor vehicle has been taken, then later found abandoned and restored to the owner, unless an attempt has been made to disguise the true identity of the vehicle, that is the engine, chassis or registration numbers have been altered or its colour has been changed, then a charge of theft under s. 1 cannot be substantiated.

   Offences committed under section 12 are variously known colloquially as:

   1. 'TWOC' (Taken without consent).
   2. 'UTMV' (Unauthorized taking of motor vehicle).
   3. 'TDA' (Take and drive away).

   By whatever title they are known, it will be seen later that vehicles taken and then abandoned are capable of providing information that can lead to the identity of the offender.

3. Interfering with motor vehicles. This constitutes an offence contrary to section 9 of the Criminal Attempts Act 1981.

   When a person attempts to commit an offence under either of the above categories, but for whatever reason is unable to carry out the full offence, then a charge of vehicle interference may be preferred against them. The offence of vehicle interference also includes attempts to the trailer section of a vehicle.

The level of interference or damage caused during the attempt can directly affect likelihood of contact trace material being left behind.

4. Motor vehicles used in other crimes. The type or seriousness of the crime committed may take precedence in any subsequent trial.

As a form of transport, motor vehicles are used, in one way or another, to commit a high percentage of all crime categories. Sometimes the vehicle actually belong to the offender but often motor vehicles, especially high performance cars, are stolen, changed in identity and then used in the commission of serious crime. These will range from burglary and armed robbery to murder. As explained in Chapter 2, 'First Officer Attending', the offence committed would elevate the crime into the major category and attract a higher level of police investigation. However, it should be reiterated that, in both investigative and scientific evidence recovery terms, the standard of any examination must always be aimed at identifying the offender and providing evidence of their involvement in the offence. The category of offence is immaterial and the crime scene examiner must remain impartial.

5. Motor vehicles involved in road traffic collisions (RTCs). A crime committed under this heading, unless involving a murder or an assault, will normally constitute offences under various sections of the Road Traffic Act of 1988.

When a motor vehicle is involved in a collision on a public road it is the responsibility of the driver to stop and provide any interested party with their name, address and the vehicle registration details. If, for whatever reason, the driver decides to drive off and leave the scene without complying with their legal responsibilities, then that person commits an offence. Evidential material, in the form of paint and/or broken vehicle components are frequently recovered from such scenes. An attempt is then made to identify the offending vehicle and connect it, and hopefully its driver, to the scene of the impact. In cases where the collision caused the death of any person, then, in addition to a SOCO being involved to recover contact trace evidence, an officer from the relevant police force Accident Reconstruction Unit may be requested to attend the scene. It will be appreciated that the work carried out by officers of this unit are very specialized and serve a totally different purpose to the work carried out by a SOCO. For that reason the practices undertaken to reconstruct collisions are not included in this book.

Self-assessed questions

10.1   What do the acronyms PNC, RTC and TWOC stand for?

10.2   What do you understand by the term 'ringing' as it relates to auto crime?

10.3   Name and describe six of the different design of motor vehicle.

10.4   What is meant by the abbreviation 'artic'?

10.5   Which act and section legislates for the unauthorized taking of a motor vehicle?

10.4 Auto crime scene examinations

Having described the general circumstances when and why a motor vehicle may be examined by a SOCO or VSCE, the methods used to record a scene and ensure the systematic recovery of all potential evidence will now be explained. The actual recovery of evidential material is dealt with elsewhere in this book. For that reason, this chapter will only deal with the initial assessment and recording of an auto crime scene that must always precede the recovery stage.

Attendance at an 'Auto Crime' scene requires the SOCO or VSCE to take ownership and be fully responsible for any evidential material that is identified and recovered. In doing so correctly, and by considering all aspects of integrity, continuity and elimination, officers can ensure that their work is accepted, not only by their own respective organization, but also by courts of law. Full details of this role and responsibility can be found in Chapter 3.

A successful scientific examination of a motor vehicle can be very productive in terms of providing both hard evidence and intelligence information. Although there are no definite statistics on the subject, it is generally accepted amongst practitioners that pro rata, auto crime scenes generally show a higher success rate, in fingerprint and DNA identification terms, than any other crime category. The reasons for this are simple and can be better understood by considering three things involved in every crime scene: that is 'surfaces, pressure and time'. The principles governing contact trace evidence are detailed in Chapter 3. There, Locard's Principle of Exchange is explained, and it will be seen that for any exchange of material to take place the surfaces involved have to be receptive and the pressure of the contact has to be for a period of time sufficient for the transference to occur.

The metal, glass and plastic surfaces of a motor vehicle are all receptive to latent fingerprints. Each of these materials also has the potential, when broken, to cause an injury that may bleed, so leaving a very useful DNA sample. In addition, the seats, head rests, seat belts and carpets are mostly fabric and have surfaces suitable for the transference of fibres and the retention of bodily fluids. To these surfaces add the time factor. Once stolen, a vehicle can be in the possession of the thief for an extended period of time generally more than adequate for the transference of most materials to take place. The longer a vehicle is at large the more complacent and relaxed the driver and accomplices may become. They will eat, drink and smoke, leaving the packaging material, remnants and residues behind so providing potential fingerprints and DNA evidence. All things considered recovered stolen motor vehicles are crime scenes worthy of a careful and thorough examination.

10.5 Requests to attend an 'auto crime' scene

The initial request for a SOCO or VSCE to attend at any crime scene is fully explained in Chapter 3. However, to reiterate briefly, they can come from one of a number of possible sources, which can be either:

- computer generated;

- radio or mobile telephone messages;

- personal requests.

In addition, for auto crimes the following information will be provided to the scene examiner:

- Make and model of the vehicle.

- Registration number of the vehicle or some other method to identify it, that is chassis or VIN number. Since 1979, legislation laid down by the European Community has meant that every new vehicle has a 17-digit number stamped on its main body shell (chassis) during manufacture. The legislation does not stipulate where this number is located and, depending on the make of vehicle, can be found in a range of places, some quite inaccessible. However, it is also stipulated that the same number is placed in a position easily visible for inspection. Hence the term VIN or Visible Identification Number. The VIN is usually on a plate fixed to the top of the dashboard and visible through the nearside of the windscreen.

- Name, address and telephone number of the registered keeper of the vehicle or, on some occasions, details of the person reporting the loss of the vehicle if it is different from the registered keeper. The telephone number in particular is very important. This provides the examiner with an easy and direct link to someone having knowledge of the condition and contents of the vehicle. This greatly simplifies the task of eliminating any potential evidence, recovered from the vehicle, to a legitimate source. It should always be borne in mind that, on occasions, individuals will report their car stolen in order to cover up their own criminal activity.

- Current location of the vehicle. It may be convenient, sometimes, to examine a recovered stolen motor vehicle in the place where it is found. Generally, when a stolen vehicle is recovered, it will be either restored to the possession of the owner, taken into a police compound or to the garage of a registered independent recovery operator. This procedure is intended to prevent any further criminal offences occurring. On occasions where the owner has recovered the vehicle to a private location, an examination can take place there.

- Witness information. This can greatly assist the following scene examination by providing information about the number of offenders involved in the crime, their descriptions and seating positions.

- Other relevant information. This can include all kinds of data and will change from scene to scene. However, any information regarding the condition of the vehicle and the circumstances of the theft can be very useful and ensure that equipment, necessary to deal with a particular situation, is available.

The astute crime scene examiner will take nothing for granted. Even though certain information is provided as a matter of course it is always best to check some things for oneself. It should be borne in mind that mostly the information is passed on by officers who have not, themselves, attended the crime scene. So it might be prudent to check certain things. For example:

- Is the vehicle locked and secure preventing access for examination? If the answer to this is yes, then another question becomes important.

- Who is in possession of the keys? As previously stated, if at all possible, recovered stolen motor vehicles will be locked in an attempt to stop any further criminal activity. This is a good practice, but it can be very frustrating to carry heavy equipment along an almost inaccessible dirt track to get to an auto crime scene, only to find the car secure, with its keys safely stored at a police station miles away.

- Is the vehicle dry and undercover? A motor vehicle is constructed of materials that nearly all provide excellent surfaces that retain latent fingerprints. However, if the vehicle is outside in wet or frosty weather a fingerprint examination cannot take place until all the surfaces have been dried. It should also be borne in mind that on dry but very cold days, unless a vehicle is in a warm dry location, the body heat of an examiner will cause condensation to form on the interior surfaces of a vehicle. This will also render a fingerprint examination impossible. Making an assessment of a surface before carrying out a fingerprint examination is fully explained in Chapter 5.

So, armed with all the relevant knowledge, it is now time to make a full and comprehensive assessment and examination of the motor vehicle. The main aim of the examination is to provide evidence that will place the offender(s) in the various seats in the car and, most importantly, the driver. To do this effectively, ambient

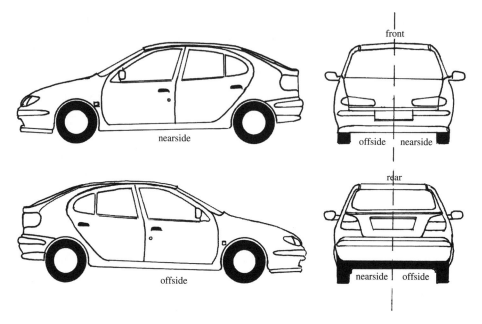

Figure 10.1   Stylized diagram of motor vehicle.

light alone must never be relied upon. A powerful hand lamp should be used so that every dark and inaccessible area can be checked. The examination will take three stages. During the whole process, accurate notes will need to be made starting with the time, date and location the examination is taking place. To assist with the detailed examination a diagram of the motor vehicle can be used. A typical stylized diagram can be seen in Figure 10.1. It should be pointed out that there is no need for the diagram to be of a specific make or model of vehicle. It is perfectly acceptable for a stylized drawing to be used as long as it gives the basic shape of a saloon, hatchback, estate or van, etc. and it has the correct number of doors. It should also be remembered that when describing a vehicle the use of 'left' and 'right' must be avoided because of the confusion this can cause. The terms 'off side' or 'driver's side' and 'nearside' or 'passenger side' are better and more explicit descriptions. It will be taken for granted in the United Kingdom that the vehicle being examined is a standard right hand drive model. Where this is not the case, diagrams and descriptions must be endorsed accordingly.

10.6 The examination process

Stage One is the 'hands off and observe' stage in order to *assess* the vehicle and *reconstruct* the events leading up to the examination. If the vehicle is still in the place where it was abandoned, then consideration must be given to any contact trace material in the surrounding area. For example, if the ground is suitable to retain them, footwear impressions may be evident or items from the vehicle may have been disposed of nearby.

During this first phase of the examination, unless evidence is otherwise likely to be destroyed, nothing should be touched. Things should be noted, either mentally or preferably in writing; everything will eventually be returned to and dealt with in sequence. It may seem obvious but the first consideration should be whether the vehicle you are looking at is the one you have been requested to examine. Very often a recovered stolen motor vehicle may be taken to a specially designated garage. There is, therefore, the potential for a number of similar cars to be together in one place, thus providing an opportunity for mistakes to be made. Having established that it is the correct one, the whole of the outside of the vehicle should be observed and the following points noted:

- Registration number. Check whether false registration plates have been fitted. These may have been fitted with proper fixings or just stuck over the original plates with adhesive tape. False registration plates and the adhesive material used to fix them to a vehicle can be an excellent source of fingerprints, DNA and fibres. It should also be remembered that, if false plates have been fitted, the original plates may also be somewhere in the vehicle. These also have the potential to reveal material transferred by the offender during removal.

- General condition of the bodywork. Look for signs of new damage. Try to establish whether the vehicle could have been involved in a collision, either with another vehicle or a building. Also, look for signs of a recent repair to the bodywork.

- Road Fund Licence. The Road Fund Licences or Tax Discs should be displayed on the front nearside windscreen of the vehicle. A quick examination of it will show whether the registration details correspond to the motor vehicle. The licence itself is liable to theft and fraudulent use so it should be checked for alterations. Any changes are usually quite discernible, so when it shows signs of being tampered with either it or its holder can provide fingerprint evidence.

- Visible Identification Number (VIN). As explained above, vehicles are now manufactured to display the 17-digit chassis, or visible identification number (VIN), through the near side bottom edge of the windscreen. Although this plate is clearly visible, its location makes it impossible to replace without removing the windscreen. Because of this the plate may be covered over to conceal its information. Any interference in this area requires a closer examination.

- Condition of the door and boot locks. Do the locks show signs of being forced? Defeating the locking mechanism requires the use of an implement to manoeuvre the lock linkage. Therefore, unless the implement is a duplicate key, some telltale sign should be apparent. Screwdrivers top the list of instruments commonly used. These need to be used with brute force to effectively break the lock and move the linkage. When a screwdriver has been used, either by insertion into the keyhole or by puncturing the skin of the door, the signs are very clear. The more subtle method of inserting a rod or banding wire between the glass and weather strip, to access the linkage and unlock the door, leaves less obvious damage. Therefore a more careful examination of the rubber weather strip is required to identify relevant damage to it.

• Condition of the doors, boot lid and bonnet. Do they show any sign of being forced open or are they out of alignment? Where an instrument has been used as a lever to force open a door or the boot lid or bonnet, striation marks, (see Chapter 8) will be apparent in the paint or metal of the bodywork. Another method used to gain entry to some vehicles involves using the bare hands to prize the window frame of one of the doors out of its seating with the body of the car. Once a large enough gap has been made an arm can be inserted to unlock the door. Once the offender has effected an entry the window frame is repositioned. However, it is almost impossible to replace the window frame exactly so there will be some misalignment. Also, there will be a noticeable crease in the metal window frame usually at the point where it joins the door. This method requires a great deal of physical contact between the offender and the vehicle so increasing the possibility of material being transferred.

• Exterior surfaces. In addition to any signs of recent damage the exterior glass and reflective surfaces should also be examined for any signs of latent finger-prints. The use of portable artificial light, directed onto a surface obliquely, may be needed to illuminate any latent finger impressions. In addition, check visible, dirty areas of the car for any signs of fingerprints. These may be present around the bonnet, wheel arches or wheel trims especially if the wheels or other components have been stolen from the vehicle.

If, during this stage, anything is observed as being potential evidence then steps may then be taken to prevent its damage or destruction.

Having fully assessed the outer surfaces of the vehicle, if there is no likelihood of causing damage to evidential material, the doors may be opened and an assessment of the interior conducted.

Make a note as to which of the doors are locked. You should also record the position of each window. Even though, as the SOCO, you may not be the first to attend a scene it is still relevant to note which of the doors are locked or unlocked and the position of each window. As with all crime scenes, it may appear at the time to be unimportant but it could, at a later time and with other information, provide useful intelligence to the investigation. It is worth noting that before the examination is completed partly opened windows should be closed to ensure that evidence has not been missed on areas hidden from view.

- Having looked through the car windows to check that no evidence may be disturbed it is best to start by opening all of the doors. Standing outside the vehicle observations can be made that will determine whether the transference of fibres, from the offender(s) to the seat(s) or from the seat(s) to the offender(s), is likely. This will depend on two things:

  - Is the seating material of the type that will shed or retain fibres?
  - Are foreign fibres or hairs apparent on the seat?

  If the answer to either question is yes, then fibre tape lifts of the seat must be considered. Therefore, entry to the vehicle will still be restricted at this stage.

- Whilst still looking into the interior of the vehicle from the open driver's door, other information can be noted, that is:

  - Has the ignition cowling been forcibly removed and has the ignition system been tampered with?
  - What position has the driver's seat been located in? Very far forward or very far back? Even though tenuous, this observation when coupled with witness information relating to the description of a suspect may provide useful intelligence.
  - Is it apparent from the contents of the front centre console ashtray that someone has been smoking in the vehicle?
  - Is there anything else in the driving position that could have been introduced to the car by the offender(s), such as cigarette butts, chewing gum, sweet wrappers and food containers?

  Similar observations can now be made through the open doors of the front and rear passenger compartments, noting all pertinent items and identifying any interior surfaces suitable for further examination.

  Having covered the interior of the vehicle, now open the boot lid/hatchback of motorcars or the rear doors of a van. Again, spend some time just observing and noting the relevance of items in these areas. Places such as these are ideal for concealing stolen property and may be the first indication that the vehicle has been used in other crime.

- At this stage, consideration should also be given to examining the engine compartment. However, reaching the bonnet release catch, which is normally located underneath the steering column or dashboard, may compromise fragile contact trace material on the driver's seat or in the foot well. If this is the case it may be more prudent to delay this examination until some time later. In most cases it is unusual for anything of significance to be found under the bonnet. However, sometimes the engine compartment can provide critical information. Everything found under the bonnet of a motor vehicle tends to get a layer of road dust, oil and dirt uniformly distributed upon it. When something is added or altered it will tend to stand out making it quite easy to identify. For example:

– During assembly motor vehicle manufacturers fix build plates in a variety of conspicuous places in the engine compartment (build plates contain numbers and other information pertinent to the construction and original colour of the vehicle). If any of the original build plates have been removed or replaced this will be readily apparent. An area exposed by the removal of a plate will be made obvious by its sheer cleanliness. Similarly a new false plate and the screws or rivets used to secure it will not blend in with the background surface making it stand out distinctly to an experienced eye.
– Occasionally a vehicle with standard specification may be stolen and then have its performance capability increased to make it faster. This may involve engine components being replaced. Again these components will be new and stand out from the rest of the engine. This process will also show that engine dirt and oil deposits have been disturbed. Of course this disturbance could also indicate that the vehicle has recently been serviced. This, and anything else observed in or on the vehicle may be there legitimately. It must, therefore, be established, as soon as possible, whether the owner can account for its presence. This will save a great deal of wasted time and resources.

The next stage is to derive a *plan* of action and *recover* evidence. This is now the time for getting hands on to record and recover evidential material. Common types of contact trace material will be described in the following text. However, the methods used in recording and recovering them are described fully in Chapters 6 and 8, DNA and Physical Evidence respectively.

Recording the scene, and any evidence in it, by photography is the very first consideration to be made. Photographing a crime scene is not always necessary because diagrams and written notes may suffice. However, if the decision is made to take photographs then this should be done before anything is disturbed. The location and condition of an item may be very significant to a forensic scientist or fingerprint expert and photographs can sometimes assist them in drawing their conclusions. Photographs can also be useful in proving the integrity and continuity of an item. A full explanation of the methods and practices involved in crime scene photography can be found in Chapter 4.

During the time spent observing the whole crime scene, different types of potential evidence will have been identified. At the same time, the need to wear certain items of personal protective equipment (PPE) to prevent the possibility of contamination will also have been considered. For example, if fibre evidence appears to be present then a clean sterile coverall suit must be worn. If DNA evidence, of any type, is apparent then in addition to the coverall suit, a facemask and double gloves need to be added. Where auto glass has been broken, this poses a real health hazard that will require careful handling wearing suitable protective gloves.

If there is no broken glass present, then fibres or hairs that can be seen on the car seats should be recovered first. The most obvious areas where fibres and hairs may adhere will include the driving position and all passenger areas. Unless there is evidence to indicate that other offenders, in addition to the driver, have been in the vehicle there is no need to examine every seat. As previously mentioned, witness information may be available giving information on the number and seating positions of the offenders in the vehicle. This information is, however, very rare. It usually becomes apparent that more than one offender is involved only when extraneous items, such as drinks containers and cigarette ends, are seen distributed untidily around the vehicle. A check with the owner will quickly establish whether such items belong in the vehicle or not.

Once established then each seat position must be dealt with separately. Each seat position can then be divided off into five main areas. These are:

1. the seat;

2. the squab or back of the seat;

3. the headrest;

4. the door panel and armrest adjacent to the seat;

5. the seat belt.

Other areas, such as a centre armrest may also be considered but this will depend on the type of vehicle and materials involved. Obvious hairs and fibres may be removed with tweezers and secured to a clear vinyl sheet with adhesive tape. Once this is done, fibres adhering elsewhere in the five areas described above, should be lifted off each surface using adhesive tape. Systematically, areas are taped with strips of adhesive tape and each area is marked on a diagram. A stylized diagram of a car seat, showing one method to section or zone it into smaller manageable areas, is shown in Figure 10.2 below. The number of adhesive strips used in each section can be governed by the amount of debris being lifted. It is important not to overload each strip. The accuracy of the diagram is important if it is to give assistance to the scientist in working out distribution patterns.

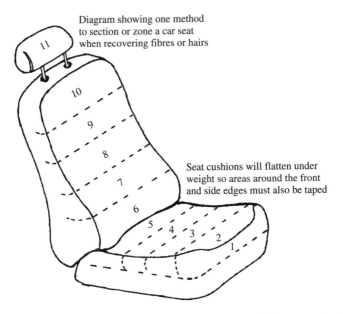

Diagram showing one method to section or zone a car seat when recovering fibres or hairs

Seat cushions will flatten under weight so areas around the front and side edges must also be taped

Figure 10.2   Diagram showing one method to section or zone a car seal when recovering fibres or hairs.

Once the fibre tapings have been taken a closer examination of the vehicle interior can now be made. In addition to the interior rear view mirror and other glass surfaces this will include looking in the following places:

- in the glove box;
- in the door compartments;
- in the ashtrays front and rear;
- in the centre armrest (if fitted);
- behind the sun visors;
- on the top of the sunroof screen (this is best done by looking through the glass sunroof);
- under the front seats;
- under the mats;
- under the back seat (in cars that have a hatchback the rear seat often lifts up and folds forward exposing an area that could be used to conceal evidence);

- in the spare wheel well under the spare wheel;

- in any of the compartments in the boot;

- in any of the compartments under the bonnet;

- in roof storage boxes;

- behind the wheel trims;

- underneath the vehicle itself.

The list is not exhaustive and will vary with each different type of vehicle and the circumstances of the offence. An inspection of these various places is usually done as the examination progresses, but the important thing is that each area must be checked before an examination can be marked as completed. It is crucial that nothing, however trivial it appears at the time, is missed. The worst thing that can happen is that an important piece of potential evidence is found after the vehicle has been returned to its rightful owner.

The other essential consideration to make during the search is one of health and safety. Never put your hands into confined spaces, such as under the dashboard, unless you can see that nothing is there that will cause injury.

Although not prescriptive, experience shows that the different types of evidential material are best recovered in the following order:

1. items likely to bear DNA material;

2. other types of contact trace material;

3. items requiring chemical treatment for fingerprints;

4. areas to be examined for fingerprints using powders.

10.6.1 Items bearing DNA material

The most common items found in recovered stolen motor vehicles that may provide a source of DNA include:

- blood smears (on broken glass or vehicle components);

- cigarette ends;

- chewing gum;

- drinks containers;

- nasal secretions.

Where possible the whole item, upon which the DNA is believed to be, should be recovered and submitted to a Forensic Science Provider (FSP). Where this is not possible due to the location, for example a smear of blood on a steering wheel, then the blood should be swabbed off the surface. The swabs may then be submitted to a FSP.

10.6.2 Other types of contact trace material

Material under this heading can include:

- drugs of abuse and drugs paraphernalia;

- broken glass;

- footwear marks and or impressions;

- soil;

- vegetation;

- building materials;

- paint;

- firearms;

- discharged cartridge cases;

- firearms and explosives discharge residue.

This list is by no means exhaustive and the presence of any item found in an auto crime scene will depend upon the circumstances surrounding the crime. This endorses the need to establish as much information as possible before starting an examination. Details of how to recover, package and store the above material can be found in Chapter 8.

10.6.3 Items to be chemically treated to develop fingerprints

The most common items that can be included in this category include:

- broken plastic vehicle components i.e. ignition cowling;

- false registration plates;

- forged tax disc and holder;

- metal, plastic and waxed drinks containers;

- paper and polystyrene food containers;

- documentation, that is car parking tickets/ parking fines;

- music CD/tape boxes;

- tools and weapons;

- packaging from stolen property.

Like the other trace material shown above this list is not exhaustive. The presence of any item in a recovered stolen motor vehicle will depend upon what else has happened whilst it is in the possession of the offender(s). It will be noticed that some items in this list are also shown in the DNA list. It regularly occurs that an item, such as a drinks container, will provide a good source for both fingerprints and DNA. In these circumstances the neck or rim of the drinks container can be swabbed for DNA-rich material and chemically treated for fingerprints at a later time.

The chemicals and methods used to develop latent fingerprints or enhance visible fingerprints can be found in Chapter 5.

10.6.4 Areas to be examined for fingerprints using powders

This examination at any crime scene is normally left until last. The powders themselves do not have any real adverse effect on other tests, and in some cases they are intentionally used first in a sequential process involving either other chemicals or DNA extraction. However, by leaving what may be described as quite a messy procedure until last it avoids the unnecessary soiling of other evidence.

Common areas to be *considered* when making a fingerprint examination of a motor vehicle, when attempting to identify the driver only, are as follows:

- window of the driver's door, inside and out;

- the metal trim around the driver' door window inside and out;

- the roof just above the driver's door;

- the front offside 'A' post and adjacent windscreen on right hand drive vehicles;

- the front nearside 'A' post and adjacent windscreen on left hand drive vehicles;

- exterior rear view mirrors (if they require manual adjustment);

- interior rear view mirror;

- the metal buckle of the driver's seat belt;

- boot or hatchback lid in areas naturally held when opening or closing;

- bonnet in areas naturally held when opening or closing;

- items with a dry, smooth, clean and non-porous surface that have been handled by the offending driver.

There can be many other surfaces that need to be *considered* but, again, it will depend upon the circumstances and the keen observation of an examiner to determine what else may be worthy of examination. If it is known or suspected that offenders, other than the driver, have been in the vehicle then the above list may be extended to the relevant number of doors and windows and so on.

10.6.5 Review of the examination

Having completed the examination it is always advisable to review what you have done and quickly go over the vehicle again. This can sometimes reveal areas or items that may have been initially overlooked. It is worth reiterating that when the vehicle is returned to its owner, every potential evidential item must have been located and removed.

10.6.6 Elimination process

When any type of potential evidence is recovered from a crime scene it is important that the possibility of it being there legitimately is researched. This may simply involve asking the owner of the vehicle certain questions. The item(s) may then be submitted for further examination, or not, depending on the answer. This can best be explained by considering circumstances where a cigarette end has been recovered from an ashtray for possible DNA examination. It must first be established if the owner, or anyone else having legitimate access to the vehicle smokes. If the answer is no, then the submission can go ahead and any DNA extracted can be entered onto the National DNA Database. If the answer is yes then another question should be asked to establish the brand(s) of cigarette that are smoked by the owner and other people legitimately using the car. If the brands do not correspond then again, the submission can proceed. If, however, the brands were the same then the only way to make a definite elimination would be to take a control DNA sample from any person who may have left the cigarette in the vehicle. This process is, however, very expensive and not likely to be authorized during the investigation of a volume crime.

The elimination process is much easier where fingerprint evidence is concerned. When fingerprints are developed in a recovered stolen motor vehicle or from property in it, anyone having legitimate access will be asked to provide their fingerprints. These are taken on specially provided elimination forms that are destroyed after use. When a fingerprint has been fully eliminated only then will it be searched against the criminal database.

10.7 Conclusion

Having carried out a thorough and successful examination it is equally important that all relevant documentation is fully completed and the evidential items are correctly packaged and stored or expediently submitted for further analysis. Finally, the investigating officer must be fully briefed with the results of the scene examination and any on going work.

Self-assessed questions

10.6   What three factors influence whether latent fingerprints may be left at crime scene?

10.7   What is a VIN number?

10.8   Where is a VIN number normally displayed?

10.9   What terms are used to more accurately describe the left and right sides of a motor vehicle?

10.10   What should be the first stage of an 'auto crime scene' examination?

10.11   Where, on a motor vehicle, would you expect to find a manufacturer's build plate?

10.12   What does the acronym PPE stand for?

10.13   When considering the driving position in a vehicle what are the five areas that would be examined to recover contact trace fibres?

10.14   What are the most common items left or deposited in motor vehicles which may provide DNA material?

10.15   What surfaces are considered suitable for fingerprint examination using powder?

11

Preparing Reports and Statements

Keith Trueman

11.1 Introduction

The procedure of examining a crime scene (see Chapters 2 and 3) is aimed at finding the truth of a particular situation. This may be achieved by gathering all available intelligence, including materials of possible evidential value, which could assist the investigation. When this is done with integrity and impartiality the information and material gathered may subsequently be used to support a criminal prosecution.

It can therefore be argued that from the outset, a crime scene examination is carried out in the knowledge that, at some time in the future, a court could examine every action taken.

For this reason it must always be remembered that, despite the category of crime, there is only one standard of evidence that should be prepared and presented before a court. That standard must be excellent. Any less a criterion, where evidence is concerned, will always leave open questions of its true credibility and value. The completion, to the same high standard, of all ancillary documentation (and there is a large amount) will stand scrutiny and go a long way to prove the integrity of the evidential item(s).

Crime Scene Management: Scene Specific Methods   Edited by Raul Sutton and Keith Trueman
© 2009 John Wiley & Sons, Ltd

Previous chapters have discussed actions that are taken by police officers and SOCO when assessing crime scenes and then recovering, and submitting the various types of potential evidence for examination or analysis. Work is not complete even when every item has been properly collected from the scene. To use an old adage 'the job isn't finished until the paperwork is done'. Not only will the job be unfinished but poorly completed reports and other documentation could mean a wrong analysis is made, thereby negating any preceding good work and rendering any possible evidence inadmissible in court. The importance of compiling good, clear, accurate and unbiased records, reports and statements cannot be over emphasized, as this documentation is essential to the satisfactory conclusion of a case.

The type of documentation that requires completion can be divided into two distinct types, that is those that must be completed at the crime scene and those that are completed subsequently. Further, in depth, descriptions of each type of document and the information they should contain will now be explained.

11.2 Documentation at the crime scene

Having carried out a cursory visual assessment of the crime scene and taken all necessary steps to preserve both the whole scene and individual items within it, the process of scene recording begins. It is best practice, during this process, to make any notes in an official notebook issued for the purpose by individual police services. However, whether a notebook or other document is used, as long as the notes can be proved to be contemporaneous provision is made under The Criminal Justice Act 2003 for witnesses to use documents and to refresh their memory.

Section 139 of the Criminal Justice Act 2003 states:

> A person giving oral evidence in criminal proceedings about any matter may, at any stage in the course of doing so, refresh his/her memory of it from a document made or verified by him/her at an earlier time if—

(a) he/she states in his/her oral evidence that the document records his/her recollection of the matter at that earlier time; and

(b) his/her recollection of the matter is likely to have been significantly better at that time than it is at the time of his/her oral evidence.

For the purposes of s.139 a 'document' means anything in which information of any description is recorded. That description covers every document used to record the crime scene and any evidential material within it.

11.3 Photography

Recording a crime scene using video and still photography is detailed fully in Chapter 4. Suffice it to say here that each set of photographs should be accompanied by a written index. This is an important record and should explain the location and view of each photograph, thus putting the images into context for the viewer.

11.4 Plans, sketches and diagrams

Plans and drawings of a scene are extremely useful, both in their own right and to help orientate a set of photographs. Depending on whether a person is qualified, drawings may be just rough sketches or properly drawn plans. Examples of each type are shown below in Figures 11.1 and 11.2.

   If properly drawn plans are required, for whatever reason, a police officer or qualified draughtsman normally carries out the task.

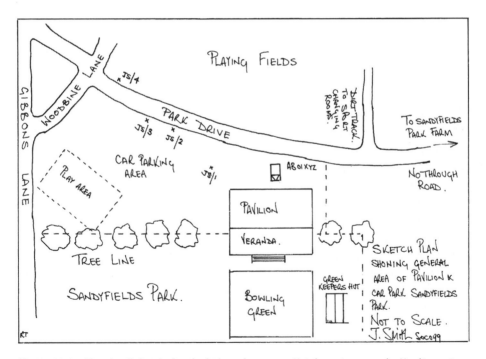

Figure 11.1 Thumbnail sketch plan depicting crime scene. Not drawn to any scale. Used to portray a general area and locate places and item referred to in a statement. Notes: contemporaneous sketch plan of crime scene.

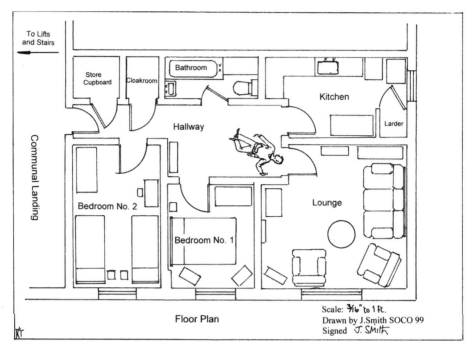

Figure 11.2   Plan of crime scene drawn to scale. Used to complement and orientate an album of photographs. Notes: sketch plan of crime scene.

The importance here, in evidential terms, is that details of the person drawing the plan, together with any scale, must be certificated on the plan itself. This requirement is legislated for in section 41 of the Criminal Justice Act 1948 'Evidence by Certificate of Plan or Drawing' (the certificate is in addition an exhibit label that will also need to be fully completed as described below). Sketch plans will not be to any particular scale and may simply be drawn to assist the memory of a scene examiner when required to remember the location of recovered items.

Diagrams are somewhat different and the most common use of a diagram is to site the position of fingerprints within the scene or upon an item. Such diagrams are normally made on the actual fingerprint lift (see Chapter 5) although there is no reason why they cannot be made on a separate sheet of paper. It is perfectly acceptable for sketches and diagrams to be made for the sole purpose of using them later as an aide memoire. As such they would fit the criteria for a 'document' as described in section 139 above. However, as with every other item of potential evidence, an exhibit label will need to be completed. A typical fingerprint lift with a diagram is shown in Figure 11.3.

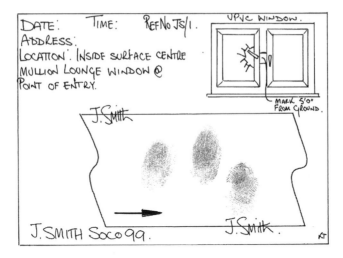

Figure 11.3 Illustration of a powdered and lifted fingerprint mounted onto a vinyl sheet. Diagram drawn to show location of fingerprint needs sufficient information to provide a ready and permanent aide-memoire. Notes: fingerprint lift showing proper labelling procedure.

11.5 The exhibit label

Properly completed exhibit labels are, arguably, the single most important document involved in evidence collection.

The provisions of section 9 of the Criminal Justice Act 1967 allows that, if certain criteria are complied with, the written statement of a witness may be read to the court, thereby allowing evidence to be admitted without the need of calling the actual witness (see Statements of Evidence below). In order that evidential material referred to by the witness may be similarly presented to the court an exhibit label must be completed. Therefore, a fully and clearly completed label must accompany every item of potential evidence that is recovered from a crime scene. The exhibit label shown in Figure 11.4 is typical of those used by police services worldwide. Though the wording and layout of a label will undoubtedly differ slightly between each different service, its purpose is the same. Labels may either be individual documents in their own right that can be attached to an item, or they may be printed onto the many and varied types of packaging material. Whatever the design of a label might be, its overriding purpose is to identify an item and help prove its authenticity, integrity and continuity. For these standards to be met, a label should be completed immediately an item is recognized as being potential evidence.

Because the completion of this document is of extreme importance to an investigation, each section of it is explained in detail below.

Constabulary Exhibit Label	
	Name, Rank and Number (Block Capitals)
Reg.-v-............................	....
	Signed..
Station/Dept..............Op.Name.........	Time...........................Date..............
Exhibits Officer.............................	
I.D.Mark..................Exhib.Ref.......	Name, Rank and Number (Block Capitals)
	....
Description:	Signed..
....	Time...........................Date..............
....	
....	Name, Rank and Number (Block Capitals)
....	....
....	Signed..
	Time...........................Date..............
Where Found/Seized:	
....	Name, Rank and Number (Block Capitals)
....	....
....	Signed..
	Time...........................Date..............
By Whom:	
....	Name, Rank and Number (Block Capitals)
Time.......... Date.....................	....
Crime No.............. Dp No...........	Signed..
	Time...........................Date..............
Lab.Ref:	
	Name, Rank and Number (Block Capitals)
	....
	Signed..
	Time...........................Date..............

Figure 11.4 Courtroom exhibit label. Notes: front and rear aspects of an exhibits label.

Reg.-v-. This heading is unique to the United Kingdom and some Commonwealth Countries. Courts under sovereign rule are designated by and act on behalf of the Crown, and so Reg. is the abbreviated form of Regina (Her Majesty the Queen). v stands for versus. Whoever stands charged before the court has their name entered in the space provided.

Station/Department. This is to identify the police station or department within a police service where the officer recovering the item of evidence is employed. In the event of the item being first seized by a non-police witness, this section is still completed giving the station details of the officer who later receives the material. This information acts as a point of reference, usually to identify the location of the storage facility.

Op. Name. When an investigation commences into a major crime an 'Operation Name' is allocated to the enquiry. This is in order to stop confusion caused by officers using different names or locations to describe the same incident.

Exhibits Officer.   An exhibits officer ensures the integrity, continuity and storage of all material at all times. Not only throughout the investigation but also during any subsequent trial and appeal process. Normally, it is only during a major investigation that a specially trained officer will undertake this role. The officer whose name appears in this section will have knowledge of and access to every single item taken during an investigation. Depending on the scale of the enquiry, information regarding exhibits may be recorded in bound books or on a secure computer system. Whichever is the case the location of a particular item at any one time will be recorded.

ID Mark.   The ID or identification mark is allocated to every item seized during the course of an investigation. The mark will consist of the initials of the finder followed by a consecutive number. For example the first item recovered by John Alan JONES would be referenced as JAJ/1 the second would be JAJ/2 and so on. These identification marks are different to and must not be confused with exhibit numbers.

Exhib.Ref.   Exhibit references are only given by a court and they may be numbers or letters. During the course of a trial, a witness will be called to give evidence. Where that witness refers to an exhibit, it will be handed to him or her and they will be asked to identify it. The witness, referring to the previously allocated Identification Mark (see above), will do this. The prosecuting solicitor or barrister will then ask for the item to be tendered in evidence and the court exhibit reference will be allocated. From then on during the trial that exhibit will be referred to by that means. For example John Alan JONES identifies his first exhibit as JAJ/1 and will prove its integrity and continuity. The court may then accept it as evidence and reference it as Court Exhibit A or Exhibit 1 whichever system is chosen.

Description: The fact that this is by far the biggest single section on the label is for a very good reason. During a trial, the witness will be required to conclusively prove to the court that the item being referred to is indeed the same item that was seized during the investigation. One-word descriptions such as 'knife' will fail to impress the court and could result in the item not being admitted as evidence. Everything has size, colour and texture that will enable a full description to be written. For example, knives are designed for various purposes; they have particular types of different handles with specific blade lengths. Thus 'knife' becomes a 'a black plastic handled carving knife' (overall length 30 cm) with a serrated blade 17 cm in length tapering from 2.5 cm at the handle to a curved point, with the words 'Chefs Demon Sheffield' embossed on the blade. There may be a need to add to that any particular damage or blood staining to give a comprehensive description.

Writing precise and accurate descriptions is a valuable skill that adds to the overall proficiency of all officers engaged in handling evidential items.

Where Found/Seized: The place where it was found also requires a full and clear description, similar to providing a full description of the item. Addresses should include the room and the specific place within the room. For example the knife described above may be recovered from: the cutlery drawer in the ground floor kitchen at 12, East Street, Bridgetown.

Property relating to crime is often recovered from motor vehicles. Any reference to a motor vehicle should always include: its make, model and registration number. Then, importantly, the place within the vehicle where the property was found and the location of the vehicle at the time.

Photographs and plans can assist in describing an item and the place it was found and are often used in court. However, they should be used in support and not as a substitute for good pen descriptions.

By Whom: The full name of the person who first finds or seizes the item should be entered here and should obviously correspond with the initials shown at 'I.D. Mark'. Police officers and support staff also have personal identification numbers that should be included in this section.

Time and Date. These areas are self-explanatory.

Crime No. When an incident is reported to the police and it has been accepted that a criminal offence has been committed than a unique reference or crime number will be allocated to it. Every UK police force has to record such numbers because they are used for statistical purposes both locally and by the Home Office. The configuration of a crime number may vary from force to force but they will identify the area in which the crime was committed by a unique reference number followed by the year (see Chapter 3).

Dp or DP No. Property of whatever kind coming into the possession of a police force must be properly accounted for. There are two main categories of property. Those that are 'found' by members of the public having previously been 'lost' by another individual, and items that are seized by the police during an investigation. Crime scene exhibits fall into the latter category and are entered onto a 'Detained Property' computer system. This enables individual items to be referenced and tracked during their whole time under police control. Thus the DP number and the accountability it provides assists in proving the integrity of an item or exhibit.

Lab. Ref. This refers to the number allocated by any one of the Forensic Science Providers to whom an item may be submitted for examination. This number allows for an item to be tracked through the provider's system and, as with the DP number, assists in issues of integrity.

Continuity. The rest of the label is devoted to proving the continuity of the item. Starting with the person who first finds or seizes the item, details of every individual who subsequently have possession of it should be shown in chronological order. An exception to this need is where the person handling the exhibit purely carries or stores it for another, and has no actual interest in the case. However, in such instances, records of the handling and movement will be accessible elsewhere, that is on a Detained Property Computer System.

As may be gathered from the above text this small and quite insignificant looking document, when fully completed, provides volumes of information and plays an extremely significant part in authenticating evidence.

11.6 Handling the evidence

Having seized an item it then has to be decided what to do with it. There are really only two courses of action that can be taken and these are:

1. Retain the item until other information is available.

2. Submit the item for further comparison or examination.

Retention. Even though nothing is to be done with the item initially, certain documentation must still be completed. This, as previously explained, is in order to maintain the integrity and continuity of the item. Although the requirement of different police forces may vary, this documentation will include:

- detained property registers or computer records; and

- crime scene examination reports.

Detained Property Records. The detained property system is described above. Suffice it to say here whether a written or computerized system is used, the documentation will consist of simple questions and answers. Most importantly, however, the item must be entered onto a system at the earliest opportunity. Failure to do this could require explanation during any future criminal proceedings.

Crime Scene Examination Reports. Although crime scene examination forms are now mainly computer generated the information they contain is fairly standard. To assist in understanding the general format and content a copy of a typical form is reproduced in Figure 3.1.

Crime scene examination reports are completed for a number of reasons. Obviously they assist SOCO to record precise information about the scene and any evidential items taken from there. They are invaluable when making accurate statements of evidence. They can provide vital information to police officers when interviewing persons suspected of committing that particular crime. They double as a submission form where fingerprints are concerned (see below) and they assist in the compilation of crime statistics. As the name suggests this document is used by an individual SOCO to record, against a unique reference number, the time and date they attended a particular scene; the duration of the examination; the type(s) and location(s) of the evidence collected with individual reference numbers (see Chapter 3.9.5) Most of this information is straightforward and involves the simple task of answering pre-determined questions. However, one area requiring some further explanation is in the field headed MO. The 'modus operandi' or 'way of working' is used to describe the method used by the criminal to perpetrate the crime. Like everyone, criminals tend to be creatures of habit. So having successfully used a particular means to commit a crime the offender tends to use the same method repeatedly, even after having been previously convicted of committing offences using the identical method.

By accurately recording this information and launching searches on local police MO databases offenders have been identified and arrested. This underlines the fact that properly detailing an MO can be of great value to an investigation.

The initial scene assessment involves listening to the account given by the injured party whilst making your own observations of the scene. The overall picture is later translated into an MO typically worded along the following lines:

> During the hours of darkness, while I.P. asleep upstairs in bed, person(s) unknown went to the rear of a detached dwelling house. There they reached through an open and insecure ground floor kitchen transom window, released the casement window catch, opened it and climbed into the premises. Tidy search made of ground floor rooms, cash stolen from a handbag and a wallet left in lounge. Egress via front door.

MO descriptions need not contain times, dates, complainant's name or location as this information is recorded elsewhere. A good descriptive MO will only cover aspects of the criminal activity. The above method shows that the criminal is targeting houses at night when the occupier is in bed. The perpetrator selects premises with insecure windows and concentrating on searching only the ground floor to minimize noise that might alert the occupiers. The offender, by only stealing cash, by is less likely to raise suspicions if later stopped and searched by police officers. Using the front door as the exit point would involve just turning a knob on the night latch and provide a relatively quiet and easy escape route into the street.

MO descriptions can also be used to link a series of offences. For example: in the event of a suspect being arrested for burglary, when using a particular method, if computerized records are checked they could assist officers in detecting the other similar crimes.

In addition, once a particular MO has been identified relevant information can be used to alert members of the general public thus, hopefully, preventing similar crimes being committed.

Submission of evidential material: Unlike the crime scene examiners depicted on the television, a police SOCO almost never examines or analyzes the items they recover from a crime scene. That duty falls to experts employed in the many and various specialist agencies. That does not, however, detract from the essential information provided by the SOCO (often the only person with intimate knowledge of the actual scene) when completing submission forms.

Very often the police force employing the SOCO will also employ fingerprint experts who, in addition to identifying an individual from their ridge characteristics, are capable of using chemicals to develop latent fingerprints on difficult surfaces (see Chapter 5). Submission to Force Fingerprint Bureau is relatively easy as the expert generally works from the relevant area on the crime scene examination form.

However, the submission of items for examination by a forensic scientist requires the completion of a completely different form. Again these forms are available via police computer systems. The format for these forms is mainly question and answer, however, there is the opportunity on the form to provide information regarding the circumstances of the offence and what the submitting officer hopes the examination may achieve. It is vital that this information is provided in full to the forensic scientist because in most volume crimes they will not have attended at the scene. Photographs, diagrams and statements from both suspects and witnesses will allow the scientist to fully appreciate the alleged circumstances and, following their examination of the submitted exhibits, make a more accurate hypothesis.

In some cases simple but relevant information can help the scientist greatly. For example when the distribution of a material is important, then knowing the height and whether a suspect is left or right handed can assist in making an overall assessment. Understanding what other people need to know and having the ability to pass on that information, can be the key to successful results.

Self-assessed questions

11.1 Which single document is designed to provide the best proof of continuity of an item?

11.2 Once an item has been seized what two courses of action will be taken with it?

11.3 What is an Identification Mark and how is it configured?

11.4   What are the provisions made by s.139 of the Criminal Justice Act 2003?

11.5   What document should accompany an album of photographs to put the images into context?

11.7 Statements of evidence

A witness statement is normally written down by a police officer at the dictation of the witness. When complete the witness then signs and dates the declaration (see below) and every page of the statement. The officer then endorses those signatures. A variation to this is where the witness is a member of the police service. The SOCO falls into this category and the narrative given below deals, in the main with crime scene examination statements.

Generally a SOCO only prepares statements of evidence when, following the arrest and charging of a suspected person, a case file is being prepared by a police officer. In order to present the case before a court, documentation must be prepared containing evidential material pertinent to the charge or charges. It is at this juncture that the information entered upon all the previously completed documents is referred to and used. A request to make a statement can appear a considerable length of time after the commission of the crime and scene examination. It is at such times that the importance of making and keeping accurate documentation is realized.

11.8 Criminal Justice Act 1967, section 9

Briefly section 9 of the Criminal Justice Act, 1967 allows for written witness statements to be admissible as evidence before a court, to the same extent as oral evidence, if certain conditions are complied with. The main conditions are:

- the statement is signed by the person who made it;

- the statement contains a declaration by that person that it is true to the best of that person's knowledge and belief and that it was made knowing that, if it were tendered in evidence, that person would be liable to prosecution if they wilfully stated in it anything that they knew to be false or did not believe to be true;

- before the hearing, at which the statement is to be tendered in evidence, a copy of the statement is served on each of the other parties to the proceedings;

- none of the other parties or their solicitors, within seven days from the service of the copy statement, serves notice objecting to the statement being tendered in evidence.

Police forces throughout the United Kingdom provide pre-printed statement forms for use by officers. Page one is headed by the name, age and occupation of the witness (addresses are not shown) and the declaration, as outlined above. The main text of the statement follows and can be continued on additional pre-printed continuation sheets.

11.9 Crime scene examination statements

Statements that explain the actions taken by a SOCO at crime scenes need to be truthful, clear and concise when dealing with the scene examination and recovery of potential evidence in chronological order. The statement must be written in ink, proper English grammar should be used and family and place names should be in block capitals. Mistakes should be corrected by a single line being drawn through them so that the original text is clearly visible. Each page should be sequentially numbered and the total number of pages comprising the statement indicated in the caption. Conjecture, slang words and jargon should not be used. If these general principles are adhered to, not only will they assist whoever has to read and understand the statement, they will also add to the apparent professional ability of the witness.

In addition to the general principles, by answering the following six questions, the statement will be kept in context and help to maintain clarity and chronologies. The questions will be obvious and are:

- Who?
- Why?
- When?
- Where?
- What?
- How?

These questions should all be considered and, where relevant, included in the text. For example:

Who?   Explain who you are and give your credentials. The first paragraph of the statement should outline the full qualifications and experience of a SOCO witness. This is because the opinion of a witness is generally inadmissible in court. However exceptions are made when the matter in question presented before the court require specialist interpretation. Witnesses, who by their knowledge and/or experience are able to assist the court with such an issue are classed as experts. For example pathologists, doctors and scientists are given expert status.

The SOCO is not usually classed as an expert per se. However if the evidence is in their field of knowledge and they are sufficiently experienced then the court may accept their opinion. Such an opinion might involve explaining the position or location of a fingerprint as it relates to the commission of an offence and the involvement of the accused.

Why?   The SOCO only attends a crime scene, victim or suspect following a request made by another member of the service. Therefore, the reason why the SOCO has responded to an incident needs to be included in the second paragraph of the statement and can be explained in the following terms ' As the result of a request from Police Constable 1234 Mary JONES at (time) on (day and date) I went etc.' If the request was made using a telephone, computer or written message this will need to be explained and included.

When?   Every statement will contain any number of 'when's'. The first when will be the time and date of arrival at the crime scene. Following that, chronologically through the text, will be the times and dates when evidence was recovered, handed to another person, received from another person or placed into storage. How this fits into the general text of the statement is shown below.

Where?   This normally follows after 'when' and provides details of the location. If the examination involved a motor vehicle then details of that should also be given with the location. Thus the statement might continue to read '. . .at (time) on (day and date) I went to BROWNS GARAGE, 77-79 HIGH STREET, NEWTOWN where I saw a red Peugeot 305 saloon motor car registration number PQ51XYZ'. Further locations where items are subsequently delivered and/or stored will also need to be shown later in the statement.

What?   This question covers a whole range of actions and requires a full explanation of what was done at the scene or with the exhibit. It is when detailing the 'what' that identification or reference numbers need to be included. For example if the above statement was being made by SOCO James SMITH it might continue . . . 'When at BROWNS GARAGE I made a fingerprint examination of the Peugeot 305 saloon motor car registered number PQ51XYZ. Using the aluminium powder and lifting technique I developed a latent fingerprint on the interior rear view mirror. I lifted this fingerprint and placed it onto a clear vinyl sheet. I produce this lifted fingerprint Reference Number JS/1 (Exhibit No.) and I have signed an exhibit label identifying it' (note that because the court issues the exhibit number it remains blank at this stage). Where large numbers of exhibits are involved it is better to list them individually. Including numerous items in the text makes the statement difficult to read and understand. Keep things simple.

How?   The normal process will be that the fingerprint will need to be examined by an expert and so it must now be explained how the fingerprint lift passed from the possession of the SOCO to the expert. The statement will then continue and explain what happened to the exhibit for example 'At (time) on (day and date) I went to Police Headquarters where I handed the fingerprint lift (JS/1) to Fingerprint Officer Mr Andrew GREEN'.

Statements will also be prepared by Police Constable Mary JONES and Fingerprint Officer Andrew GREEN to complete the whole sequence of events. Andrew GREEN will also need to show in his statement the continuity of the exhibit by referring to signing the exhibit label.

11.10 Conclusion

The reputation of being a good and proficient crime scene examiner is not only built on the skill of an individual to identify and recover key evidential material. Officers who are rated as being the best in their field also display the ability to discipline themselves and complete all relevant documentation with the same accuracy and timeliness. By honing both of these talents and using them to complement each other an officer can excel.

Self-assessed questions

11.6   What section of the Criminal Justice Act 1967 allows statements to be tendered as evidence?

11.7   What are the provisos of this section?

11.8   What documents would be used to help compile a statement of evidence?

11.9   What should the first paragraph of a statement made by a SOCO include?

11.10   What are the six questions that should be considered when compiling a statement of evidence?

Appendix
Police Service Rank Structure

Chief Constable	Deputy Chief Constable	Assistant Chief Constable
Chief Superintendent	Superintendent	Chief Inspector
Inspector	Sergeant	Constable

Crime Scene Management: Scene Specific Methods   Edited by Raul Sutton and Keith Trueman
© 2009 John Wiley & Sons, Ltd

Index

Note: Figures and Tables are indicated by *italic page numbers*

Index compiled by Paul Nash